The Transition from Capitalism to Socialism

The Transition from Capitalism to Socialism

John D. Stephens

With a Foreword by
Michael Harrington

University of Illinois Press
Urbana and Chicago

This book is printed on acid-free paper.

Library of Congress Cataloging-in-Publication Data

Stephens, John D., Ph.D.
  The transition from capitalism to socialism.

  Bibliography: p.
  Includes index.
  1. Communism.   2. Socialism.   3. Capitalism.
I. Title.
HX40.S7943   1986   335   86-1329
ISBN 0-252-01332-8 (cloth; previously published
by Macmillan Press Ltd. under ISBN 0-333-23406-5)
ISBN 0-252-01323-9 (paper; previously published
by Macmillan Press Ltd. under ISBN 0-333-23407-3)

To Evi

Contents

Foreword

By Michael Harrington

John Stephens's *The Transition from Capitalism to Socialism* is obviously an important book on a number of counts. It illuminates and analyzes the experience of one of the most creative labor and socialist movements in the world in Sweden; it provides a realistic, class-based analysis of why that movement acted as it did and thus dispels the fantasy that Swedes are somehow genetically or culturally fated to find a "third way." But what is not perhaps so obvious is that Stephens's reading of the Swedish case has profound implications for both the analysis and advocacy of structural political and social change throughout the world.

The Transition from Capitalism to Socialism, in short, is not simply a very useful and informative account of a fascinating particular case, though it is certainly that. It also lives up to the promise of its title, theorizing the problems and possibilities of structural change in advanced capitalist societies in general.

It has long been known that Sweden presents some kind of paradigmatic case. After all, this was the first country that consciously made the transition to a Keynesian—some would say "social democratic"—capitalism. Leon Blum, who understood what he was doing, tried to accomplish something like that during the brief period of the Popular Front in France; and if he introduced reforms which have lasted to this day, he clearly failed in his plan to deal with the Depression. Franklin Roosevelt had the political power which Blum lacked, but he was not at all aware of the profound implications of the strategies which he improvised. How else to explain that his attempt to balance the budget in 1936 led to a new recession within the Depression?

The Swedes were different. The School of Stockholm—above all, Ernst Wigfors—not only achieved a synthesis of Marxian and Keynesian theories of underconsumption, but it also persuaded the Social Democratic party and the unions to what has been called a "precocious Keynesianism" in the 1930s. Stephens outlines this familiar history and then, more to the point, explains it, and subsequent developments in Sweden, on the basis of the political and economic relation of class forces. And, in keeping with the larger theme announced in his title, he relates this analysis of a specific society to the evolution of advanced capitalist class and political structure in general.

The same history is visible in the bitter struggles over the creation of a funded social security system in the 1950s and in the fight over the wage earner funds in the 1970s and 1980s. Indeed, I was struck in reading Stephens's account of the development of the "active labor market policy" in the early 1950s by how radical it was—and how it anticipated the struggle for "comparable worth" in the United States today. The Swedish unions and socialists were not simply dealing with the problem of gender discrimination—although their policy has eliminated much of the male-female wage differential found in the United States—but with an even larger structural issue.

They insisted, as Stephens documents, that there should be no wage differentials of *any* kind based on the dictates of a labor market which decreed that those in more advanced industries should get higher pay than those in the less advanced industries. Rather than accept logic, the "solidaristic wage policy" proposed to change the very nature of the labor market, altering it so that it conformed with the priorities of social policy rather than, as in other Western countries, shifting social priorities to fit the demands of the labor market.

But, and this is perhaps the greatest single value of this excellent book, Stephens does not simply document and analyze a Swedish "exception." In a careful theoretical analysis of cross-national differences, he relates the Swedish case to the political and trade union realities to be found in other societies. There are, to be sure, Swedish historical and cultural differences which play a role in this extraordinary nation. But "Swedish" solutions are possible for other countries, on the condition that they emulate Swedish levels of union organization and political mobilization. And those other economies can be better understood in their own right if they are compared with Sweden.

In the 1930s, we now know, the Swedes were the vanguard of

what turned out to be the Western leftist response to the crisis of the Great Depression. In the 1980s, that history could repeat itself. John Stephens's study is an incredibly compact, brilliantly argued analysis of a Swedish past and present which may well be relevant to the Western—and even American—future. This is, in short, that rarity, a book for both specialists and generalists.

Preface

This is a short book with a long personal history. The central theoretical idea was developed in a seminar I took with R. Stephen Warner in 1971, my first year of graduate work at Yale, and tested in a paper I wrote for a statistics course the same semester. The empirical research on the ideology of Swedish Social Democratic leaders cited in Chapter 6 of this book was carried out in the summer of 1972 as part of a pre-dissertation research project in the Comparative Sociology Program at Yale which was directed by Wendell Bell and funded by the National Institute of Mental Health. The rest of the material on Sweden as well as most of the theoretical ideas on the transition to socialism contained herein were developed in my dissertation, the research for which was funded by the Foreign Area Program of the Social Science Research Council and American Council of Learned Societies, and the National Science Foundation. I would like to thank all those who helped me on that project for their indirect contribution to this book. Juan Linz, Hans Zetterberg, John Low-Beer, Sten Johansson all contributed comments on the final draft of the dissertation which proved useful in writing this manuscript, as did comments by Erik Olin Wright on a revised version of the theoretical chapter of the dissertation. I am deeply indebted to Michael Mann for his encouragement to turn away from the Swedish focus of the dissertation and write a more general comparative book. His comments on the entirety of this manuscript were extremely valuable. I am also very grateful to Andrew Martin, Dietrich Rueschemeyer, Evelyne Huber Stephens, Gøsta Esping-Andersen, John Low-Beer and Walter Korpi for their helpful comments on earlier drafts of this book. No doubt many of these people will disagree with some of the ideas contained in it and I take full responsibility for the opinions and conclusions expressed in the following pages.

1

Marx's Theory of the Transition from Capitalism to Socialism

Karl Marx's analysis of the internal dynamics of capitalist society led him to conclude that this order would be replaced by socialism. Since Marx laid down his pen, academics and political activists alike have hotly debated the accuracy of his predictions and the adequacy of his theory. Though this discussion is by now almost one hundred years old, a few basic lines of argument have been repeatedly advanced by the various antagonists in the debate. Conservatives and liberals have generally argued that various structural developments in capitalist society – such as the growth of the middle class, increasing affluence and the separation of ownership and control – have made Marx's theory, and socialism, irrelevant. Moderates in the right wing of labour and social democratic movements have contended that Marx erred in underestimating the flexibility of capitalism and the independence of the state in capitalist society. In their view, through the extension of universal suffrage and the expansion of the welfare state, the working class in the West has been politically and economically integrated to play a major role in capitalist society. Revolutionaries, on the other hand, have contended that the changes in capitalist society in the past hundred years have been merely cosmetic. The basic exploitative structure of advanced capitalist society is unaffected by the welfare state or affluence. They argue that Marx was largely correct and that his predictions await realisation. Though other theories of the structure of advanced societies have been proposed, virtually all of them share one of two presumptions with the three broad positions mentioned here. Either they claim that capitalism has changed little or they claim that it has changed in a direction entirely unanticipated by Marx owing to the fundamental flaws in his system.

In this book we will advance a distinctly different position from those mentioned. We will argue that capitalist society has been modified in a socialist direction for reasons identified by Marx. It will be our contention that many of the changes in capitalist society support Marx's view rather than contradict it. This is not to argue that Marx's theory can be accepted in its totality. There are flaws and oversights in his system and these problems account for the fact that the transition from capitalism to socialism will be a much more protracted process than Marx anticipated – if, indeed, it occurs at all. In fact, we are not prepared to argue that the transition is the highly probable event that Marx thought it would be. However, we do hope to establish that it is an objective possibility.

Marx contended that once capitalism had created the material conditions for socialism the growth of working-class organisation would be the critical development for the transition to socialism. This contention will be strongly supported in this book. Not only will we argue that the development of working-class organisation is the key to the transition to socialism, we will also show that the two central changes in the structure of capitalist society in the past hundred years – the development of democracy and the development of the welfare state – were largely due to the growing strength of organised labour. These developments are not a product of the flexibility of capitalism or the autonomy of the state nor are they merely products of the new needs of capitalism associated with the development of the monopoly stage of capitalism. They are products of working-class struggle to transform capitalism and as such they represent steps towards socialism. We will document that reforms won by organised labour have resulted in substantial redistribution of the means of consumption where organised labour is strong. Furthermore, we will argue, admittedly with some reservations, that it is possible that socialism can be achieved through reforms gained through an extension of the class struggle in the future.

Marx's central error was his projection of the future development of the class structure; that is, his prediction that an increasingly small bourgeoisie would be faced by an increasingly large proletariat with middle strata progressively falling into the proletariat. While this two-class model can be maintained at a high level of abstraction and has been useful in analysing domination and subordination relations, it cannot adequately explain distribution and class formation. Class formation is a particularly critical point since social action arising out of common class position is of such great importance for the transition to socialism. Had class formation and class consciousness proceeded as Marx predicted, a rapid transition would have been unproblematic. Thus it is essential to theorise adequately the problem of class formation in order to understand why this has not occurred and what implication this has for the future.

Despite Marx's errors, his theory is correct on a sufficient number of crucial points for it to form the point of departure for the development of an updated theory of domination, distribution, class formation and the dynamics of change in capitalist society. One of the great strengths of the Marxist system is its attempt to explain all of these aspects of social inequality with one integrated theory. This is rarely attempted by modern students of stratification, but any adequate theoretical conceptualisation of the change from one system of distribution and domination to another must attempt to do this. Thus we will begin our study with a brief examination of Marx's theory and then go on to develop our own model of stratification in capitalist society and the transition to socialism utilising parts of Marx's theory and rejecting others in order to make the model consistent with changes in the structure of capitalist society that have occurred since Marx's time.

Domination and distribution in the capitalist mode of production

For Marx, the basis of any society is the system of production. The situation of any individual in a society is determined by his relationship to the means of production. Since virtually all power in society flows from ownership of property, the owners of the means of production will have both a monopoly of domination and complete control over the economic surplus. Domination is an element of production relations themselves. It is a part of the owner's right to dispose of his property as he sees fit. Domination both in the productive unit and in the society at large is a product of the historical development of a mode of production. The absolute property rights and market relations characteristic of capitalism were established and extended because of the growing importance of capitalist production and bourgeois political power. Distribution of the means of consumption is determined by production relations (Marx 1875:120; 1857:29).

Distribution in the capitalist mode of production can be understood by examining the basic condition assumed to exist in the abstract model of the capitalist mode of production. The means of production are concentrated in the hands of the few while the mass of people are owners only of their labour power. The form of appropriation of the surplus labour of the producers by the owners is different in capitalism from in other modes of production. The worker in capitalism is not politically or legally tied to the capitalist: he is formally free. The relationship between the two is a commodity relationship: the worker sells his labour power to the capitalist. Capitalist production relations assume a concentration of capital into the hands of the few, the existence of free labour, and a market. Thus, capitalist production relations are both property relations and market relations. In the absence of either property concentration or the market, capitalism cannot exist.

Marx's abstract model of the capitalist mode of production rests on two additional assumptions: the absence of labour organisation and the existence of an excess supply of labour power. Given these two factors and the concentration and short supply of capital, it follows not only from Marx's analysis but also from neo-classical economic theory that workers' wages will be held to subsistence level through competition.

This scheme of distribution and domination does not, as we just pointed out, depend on Marx's analysis of labour value, though it is compatible with it. What the labour theory of value allowed Marx to show was that an appropriation of surplus value did occur in capitalism and consequently that it was an exploitative system. Even if one rejects Marx's analysis of the role of labour value in price determination and capitalist development, his conclusion concerning the appropriation of wealth created by the working population by a small minority of owners cannot be rejected unless one considers such passive activity as dividend collection to be productive activity. We do not.

Production and distribution relations are reinforced by the state, since the action of the state is a reflection of the distribution of power in civil society. 'The executive of the modern state is but a committee for the managing of the common affairs of the whole bourgeoisie' (Marx and Engels 1848: 486). This is not to say there is a one-to-one relation between the state and civil society. As Avineri (1968: 41) points out: 'the political never appears as a mechanistic or automatic reflection of the economic' in Marx's writings. He merely tried to put out that the state was an instrument of particular interests and not the general will as Hegel claimed.

The transition to socialism

Modes of production are abstractions from concrete societies. In some cases, societies may approximate a single mode of production, such as the period of Continental European feudalism before the rise of towns. On the other hand, the social order of late feudalism was characterised by two exploitative modes of production, one based on feudal rent and the other based on wage labour, and two non-exploitative modes of production, petty bourgeois simple commodity production and subsistence farming of free peasantry. A social order can be called feudal, capitalist, etc., according to which mode of production is dominant in the society. In transitional stages of social development, identification of a clearly dominant mode may be difficult.

Most contemporary interpretations of Marx's writings agree that his theory of change was not an inevitable mechanistic theory in which the development of the productive forces was the prime mover. The dialectical nature of the theory retains a role for conscious human action. Indeed, class action is theorised to be one of the main forces of change. This indeterminacy in the process of change is reinforced by the fact that transitions from one social order to another do not follow a regular pattern. For instance, developments in the forces of production and the relations of production and their interrelation exhibit quite different patterns in the transition from antiquity to feudalism than in the transition from feudalism to capitalism. Though definite conclusions about the process of one transition cannot be drawn from another, a brief sketch of the transition to capitalism will prove useful in highlighting some of the important features of the transition to socialism.

The bourgeoisie originated in the municipal movement of the twelfth century in which urban communes freed themselves from the political arrangements of feudalism and created an autonomous sphere of economic activity. This class then monopolised the ownership and development of a new progressive force of production, capital; progressive in the sense that it represented an expansion of human productive capacity. The feudal relations of production, in particular serfdom and barriers to free economic activity, become a fetter to the further development of the productive forces of society since the development of capital depends on the existence of a pool of free labourers and freedom of economic activity. As the bourgeois forces of production develop, so does the social power of the bourgeoisie since power is derived from property holding. At a certain point, the bourgeoisie becomes strong enough to throw off feudal relations of production and political domination. The capitalist era and bourgeois rule are ushered in.

This example of the transition from feudalism to capitalism helps elucidate some aspects of one of the central themes of this work, the question of revolutionary versus evolutionary change. The development of the forces of production is of necessity 'evolutionary'. (We use the term with some hesitation because, for Marx, any transition from one mode of production to another is by definition a 're-volutionary' change, no matter how long it takes.) And since the development of capitalist forces of production presumes at least some development of capitalist relations of production, the de-velopment of the relations of production cannot lag too far behind the development of the forces in this case. Only the political and legal superstructures lend themselves to rapid revolutionary change. Even here revolutionary change is by no means a necessity. In Britain, the bourgeois 'revolution' lasted a minimum of 180 years. According to Marx it began at least as early as institutional-isation of the demands of the communal movement in the settle-ment of 1660. Though a decisive step forward was made in the Glorious Revolution when the political limitations of property were abolished and freedom of inheritance was finally established, the full triumph of the British bourgeoisie did not come until 1846 with the repeal of the Corn Laws. And while the French revolution is considered to be the epitome of a bourgeois revolution, the first political concessions to the bourgeoisie were made well before the revolution and full victory for the bourgeoisie did not come until 1870. This leads us to two related points of theoretical importance for our subsequent discussion of the transition to socialism. First, the transition from one social order to another cannot be achieved by political revolution alone. The forces of production must be developed beforehand. Second, since it cannot be argued that the transition from one social order to another *always* involves a radical break, it follows that there are no purely *theoretical* reasons why the transition from a capitalist social order to a socialist social order cannot be evolutionary.

The transition from capitalism to socialism differs from the transition from feudalism to capitalism in a number of ways. Most crucially, the emergent class, the proletariat, is also the subordinate class in the capitalist system; it owns no new force of production and thus does not exploit another class.[1] It is precisely because of this that Marx thought that capitalism was the last class society in history. Instead of developing a new system of domination based on a new force of production, the proletariat ushers in a classless society by transferring control over the existing productive forces from the capitalist class to the collectivity.

The role which the development of the forces of production played in the transition to capitalism is taken by two interrelated but distinct processes, the socialisation of labour and the organisation of workers. These two developments are interrelated because they share the same antecedents, but they play quite different roles in the transition. By the socialisation of labour, Marx means the development of a fully co-operative and interdependent process of production. Whereas in previous modes of production the producers worked by and large independently of one another, capitalism is based on a complex division of labour and interdependence of the producers at a national and even international level (for example Marx 1894: 266). There is no new force of production but rather an emergent form of work organisation. Fully socialised labour, along with the abolition of scarcity, can be said to be the material base, the material precondition, for socialism. Labour organisation might be called the active side to the development of socialism. It is through organisation that men make socialism. It is also through the organisation of labour that theory is realised, that theory becomes a material force, as Marx would say. The labour movement is the carrier of socialist ideology. For ideology to have any impact it must be connected to a force with some root in material life. This brings us to an extremely important point: unlike previous emergent classes the proletariat derives its power not from ownership but from organisation, from consistent, organised collective action. Organisation appears as a source of power in capitalism for the first time in Marx's theory because capitalism is the first mode of production which puts the subordinate class in a situation in which they can organise. This is one of the internal dynamics of capitalism which lead to its demise. Let us now examine in more detail some of the more important of these dynamics.

Concentration and centralisation of capital

The progressive concentration and centralisation of capital which is associated with the development of capitalism is perhaps the most important internal development of capitalism which paves the way for the transition to socialism. Virtually every other aspect of the internal dynamics of capitalism which aid the transition is related to concentration and centralisation. Concentration refers to the accumulation of capital by individual capitalists. If the number of individual capitals (individuals and corporations or joint-stock companies, as Marx calls them) stays the same while the total amount of social capital increases, then the average individual capital increases: concentration increases but centralisation does not. Centralisation refers to a reduction of the number of capitals: 'In any given branch of industry centralisation would reach its extreme limit if all the individual capitals invested in it were fused into a single capital' (Marx 1867: 763). Both concentration and centralisation increase the average size of productive units. While concentration is important to the transition to socialism, because accumulation is needed to abolish scarcity, it is the centralisation process which is critical to the other aspects of internal dynamics of capitalism which lead to socialism (see Marx 1867: 763). Centralisation is obviously intimately associated with the socialisation of labour since it makes the productive process increasingly interdependent. This in turn means that it intensifies the contradictions of the capitalist system. Centralisation also furthers the process of polarisation of classes and the development of labour organisation. And it intensifies the economic crises of capitalism. These developments are all important tendencies of capitalism which lead to its transcendence.

Centralisation itself is promoted in three ways. In addition to the competitive undercutting of the smaller capitalist by the larger ones, Marx points to the development of the banking and credit system and joint-stock companies (Marx 1867: 626–8; 1894: 438). These developments create the opportunity for the merging of existing capitals, quickening the pace of centralisation. Concentration and centralisation, independent of their effects on the other factors mentioned, are necessary but not sufficient conditions for the transition. They create the material preconditions for the development of socialism, the socialisation of labour and the abolition of scarcity.

Polarisation of classes

In developing the 'active side' of the transition, Marx believed that capitalism had created the 'seeds of its own destruction', a class with nothing to lose but its chains, the industrial proletariat. The proletariat would become the huge majority of the population and with the growth of class consciousness would act to transform the society. The polarisation of the classes into a small owning class and a large working class would be the result of two factors. On the one hand the centralisation of capital would force all but a very few out of the ownership class. On the other hand, mechanisation would replace skilled labour and hold the growth of white-collar employees to a minimum. By the same token mechanisation would keep the ranks of the 'industrial reserve army' filled, thus holding wages to subsistence. As a result, advanced capitalism would be characterised by two highly distinct social classes.

Labour organisation

The material conditions of capitalism create a situation where the subordinate class can become conscious of its situation and organise collective action to change the system (Marx 1848: 496). Not only does capitalism necessitate the development of a class of free labourers, the very conditions of capitalist production, large-scale industry, bring the members of this class into communication with one another making organisation and class consciousness possible. The market makes workers in different enterprises interdependent and thus makes the success of organised action by workers in one enterprise dependent on what other workers do. The development of communications, the centralisation of capital and the polarisation of classes all further the growth of organisation and class consciousness. The improvement of communications associated with the technological advance of capitalism puts workers in different localities in contact with one another. The centralisation of capital furthers the development of nationwide organisation by bringing more and more workers from diverse regions of a country under the domination of fewer and fewer firms. By creating two highly distinctive social classes, the process of polarisation also facilitates the growth of class consciousness and organisation.

As we pointed out earlier, the proletariat derives its power to transform the social order from organisation, not ownership of a new force of production. But like previous emergent classes the proletariat does not wait for a 'final battle' to use this power. Marx points out that even the earliest 'combinations' were able to 'club together in order to keep up the rate of wages' (Marx and Engels 1848: 493). The transition to socialism actually begins at this point. When the workers stage the first successful strike, the social order in question can no longer be said to be a 'purely capitalist' social order.[2] One of the presuppositions of the abstract model of distribution and domination in the capitalist mode of production is no longer present. Namely, there no longer exists a pool of free labourers in competition with one another for a few scarce jobs. The workers, at least some of them, have put an end to competition among themselves and now face the capitalists as a united front. In the process, an element, however small, of socialist principles of distribution has been introduced into capitalist society.

Actually, Marx (1865: 61) was pessimistic about the amount to which the proletariat could affect its condition by economic action alone. On the other hand, he was optimistic about the political effects of unionism. Of course, the combination of workers into unions was a necessary prerequisite to revolutionary action, and this is what he focused on in his earlier writings. But even in the *Manifesto*, he emphasised the possibility of workers' combinations being able to affect legislation in capitalist society, as in the passing of the Ten Hour Bill in Britain. Thus it might be argued that *total* bourgeois domination of the state in Britain lasted less than two years, from the repeal of the Corn Laws to the passing of the Ten Hour Bill (see Marx 1867: 283–5). Even within capitalist society, the worker could affect distribution in his favour by applying political pressure. This occurrence is fully consistent with Marx's general view of the state: a change in the distribution of power in civil society should be reflected in the activity of the state. By the time of the First International, Marx not only placed the supreme emphasis on organising trade unions and workers' parties, but also re-emphasised the possibility of getting some legislative concessions as a short-term strategy (Lichtheim 1961:103). In a sense these 'concessions' should not be viewed as modifications of capitalism at all. They represent moving beyond the capitalist model toward socialism. This is the political side of the beginning of the transition to socialism mentioned previously. Again the organisation of workers has violated one of the premises of the pure capitalist model.

Contradictions of capitalism

The central contradiction in capitalism is between the social character of production and the private form of appropriation. This is a contradiction between the forces and relations of production because the development of the capitalist forces of production furthers the socialisation of labour in the context of a system of private ownership. From an examination of the internal functioning of the capitalist system, Marx attempts to show that this contradiction manifests itself in a number of ways such as the tendency of the rate of profit to fall, overproduction of capital goods in relation to consumer goods, and overproduction in general. These factors all contribute to the periodic crises which are inevitable under capitalism.

The role of crises in Marx's theory of the transition to socialism is the subject of some controversy. Some interpreters argue that Marx maintained that capitalist relations of production would become a fetter on the further development of the forces of production and that crises were a prefiguration of an inevitable breakdown of production (Sweezy 1942: esp. Part III; Kautsky 1971). Giddens (1971: 55) on the other hand, contends that crises 'do not represent a "breakdown" of the capitalist system but on the contrary form the regulating mechanism which enables the system to survive the periodic fluctuations to which capitalism is subject'. Rather, the importance of crises for the transition is that they stimulate further development of class consciousness and increase centralisation by driving smaller inefficient undertakings out of business.[3]

Marx on revolution and reform

Since one of our main concerns in this book is to make a case for the possibility of a gradual parliamentary democratic evolution to socialism, it may be useful to summarise Marx's position on this question. As we pointed out earlier there is no purely theoretical reason why the transition from one social order to another must be 'revolutionary' or 'evolutionary'. To reiterate another earlier point, any transition is in some sense 'revolutionary' for Marx. Posing the question in terms of 'revolution or reform' obscures more than it clarifies. At least two separate questions should be posed, one concerning the rapidity of the transition and the second concerning the role of force versus parliamentary institutions in the process of transition. Certain characteristics of capitalist society in general led Marx to have some definite expectations concerning the rapidity of the transition to socialism. The historical circumstances of various countries led Marx to have differing evaluations of the likelihood of a parliamentary road to socialism in the country in question.

One aspect of the development of socialism clearly must be gradual. The material base of socialism – abundance and fully socialised labour – cannot be created overnight. This is the limit to political revolution. Socialism can only be created through the abolition and transcendence of advanced capitalism, not because history is predetermined but because socialism is nothing more than the negation of capitalism, the realisation of the potentialities created by capitalism but suppressed by its contradictory structure. While Marx conceded that the revolution might break out in less developed sections of Europe, the success of such a revolution would depend on its spreading to the more advanced capitalist nations (Marx and Engels 1882:56).

Once the material conditions of socialism have been created, then a rapid transition is possible since the transition to socialism is not associated with the development of a new force of production but rather with transferring control of an existing productive apparatus from one group to another (Marx 1867:764). Though the material conditions of capitalism create the possibility of a rapid transition to socialism they cannot bring it about. The objective conditions must be complemented by human action, the organised class action of the proletariat. Though early in his life Marx advocated conspiratorial revolutionary activity, by late 1850 he had decidedly rejected the vanguard conception of revolution (Avineri 1968:200). By the time of the first International he put supreme emphasis on the organisation of labour and mass workers' parties. On the question of the role of peaceful means or force in the transition to socialism, Marx made it clear in a speech in London and an interview in the *New York World* in 1871 and in a speech in Amsterdam the following year that the historical conditions and the responses of the governments of the countries in question would determine the response of the socialist movement (McLellan 1973:406). He believed a peaceful transition to socialism was possible in countries such as the United States, Holland and the United Kingdom. On the other hand, he did not rule out violence if it was the only possibility. It should be pointed out here that Marx conceived of the bourgeois state as the limited parliamentary rule of the nineteenth century, in which there were ordinarily property qualifications for voting. In fact, as Avineri points out, throughout his works Marx equates the achievement of universal suffrage with the achievement of socialism because universal suffrage would abolish the distinction between the state and civil society (Avineri 1968:210). Given that the proletariat would be (or in the United Kingdom was, according to Marx) the huge majority of the population, such an equation is not merely a philosophical construct but also a reasonable assumption about the probable course of events. In discussing the Chartists' demand for suffrage, he says:

> Universal Suffrage is the equivalent of political power for the working class of England, where the proletariat forms the large majority of the population, where, in a long, though underground civil war, it has gained a clear consciousness of its position as a class, and where even the rural districts know no longer any peasants, but only landlords, industrial capitalists (farmers) and hired labourers. The carrying of Universal Suffrage in England would, therefore, be a far more socialistic measure than anything which has been honoured with that name on the Continent.
>
> Its inevitable result, here, is *the political supremacy of the working class.* (Marx 1852:200).

Though Marx never is very specific about the time span of the transition, we think that the thrust of his writings is unambiguous. Whether the working class took power by parliamentary or violent means, the accession to power would be followed by a fairly rapid transition to socialism. Kautsky's vision of two decades is probably not terribly inconsistent with what Marx would have thought. The reorganisation of production could not be achieved overnight, but with such a broad social base as Marx envisioned, a working-class government could move rapidly and radically in a number of areas at once. We would guess that Marx might have expected an evolutionary transition to socialism in a country such as England to occur in the following way. The first phase of the active side of the transition begins with the organisation of the first unions. The first successful strike and/or the first political concession to the labour movement mark the beginning of the process of erosion of the capitalists' monopoly of power in the system. Though these early reforms won by organised workers do transform the system to some degree, the 'real fruit of their battle lies, not in the immediate result, but in the ever expanding union of workers' (Marx and Engels 1848: 493). The struggle for universal suffrage is of much greater importance because universal suffrage 'is the equivalent of political power for the working class of England' (Marx 1852: 200; also see Marx and Engels 1848: 504). Because the working class is a huge majority of the population, the achievement of universal suffrage will be followed by the conquest of political power by a workers' party with an extremely broad social base. Then a period of rapid transition begins. However, even in one of his most polemical texts, the *Communist Manifesto*, Marx does not mention nationalisation of industry as a measure that the proletariat should pass immediately after achieving state power. All ten measures that he mentions in the *Manifesto* have as their common denominator the wielding of state power for the attainment of universal goals instead of particular interests (Avineri 1968: 210). Some of the measures – such as the centralisation and establishment of state control of credit, communications and transport and the abolition of inheritance – would pave the way for the subsequent socialisation of industry. Though the transition to a socialist economy could not occur overnight, it seems to us that Marx's time perspective for the transition is much shorter than that of modern social democracy. The broadness of the social base of the proletarian government makes such a rapid transition possible.

2

Contemporary Capitalism and the Transition to Socialism

In our review of Marx's theory of the transition to socialism, we purposely emphasised elements which will be of use for the development of a theory which takes into account capitalist development since his death. In this chapter, a theory of domination and distribution in contemporary capitalism and the transition to socialism will be developed building on two key elements of Marx's theory, while rejecting or elaborating other elements of his theory. The two factors in Marx's theory that will form the basis for our theory are the role of labour organisation and of the centralisation of capital in the dynamics of the transition to socialism.

The weak point in Marx's theory is his view of the development of the class structure of capitalism. The first part of this chapter will be devoted to the task of developing a model of the class structure of pure capitalism. First, a theory of control relations which emphasises factual control of production rather than legal title of ownership will be developed building on the insights of Marx himself and contemporary Marxists. Second, a theory of the distribution of the means of consumption will be elaborated in which possession of skills and education as well as capital are hypothesised to be important stratifying influences. Third, the process of formation of distinct social classes which constitute bases for collective action will be examined. On the second and third aspects, our theory of the class structure of capitalism will depart radically from current Marxist thinking on the subject.

The second part of this chapter will be devoted to analysing the transition to socialism. Marx's four causes of the transition will be reassessed on the basis of our theory of the development of the class structure as well as other changes in capitalism since his death. Then, the process of change from capitalism to socialism, and domination and distribution in transitional social orders will be examined.[1]

The class structure of capitalism: control relations

Many critics of Marx have argued that he failed to distinguish between the legal title to ownership and the actual patterns of control in the economy (Berle and Means 1937; Burnham 1941; Dahrendorf 1959). The modern corporation, they contend, involves a separation of ownership and control in which the real power lies with the manager not the capitalist. This change in the economic structure has made the ownership question and thus socialism irrelevant. Dahrendorf has gone so far as to claim that Marx shared this view of the corporation. But, Dahrendorf contends, given the primacy of ownership in Marx's system, he erred in thinking that the joint-stock company represented a transitional form to socialism, essentially the end of class domination due to the end of the importance of ownership.

In fact, Dahrendorf is incorrect both in his interpretation of Marx and in his analysis of the meaning of the advent of the large corporation. It is inconsistent with Marx's method to assert that legal and juridical categories – such as the legal title to ownership – determine elements of the economic substructure, such as actual patterns of control in the enterprise (for example, see Marx and Engels 1846: 91). Furthermore, a close examination of Marx's discussion of joint-stock companies in the third volume of *Capital* clearly contradicts Dahrendorf's interpretation of Marx's position on the joint-stock company (Marx 1894: 438). Marx's main emphasis is the separation of labour from ownership – not control. Throughout his earlier economic writing a theoretical division between the capitalist as manager and the capitalist as owner was necessary. Here, in the joint-stock company, the division was reality, the expropriation of the surplus value by the non-producing owner was naked. Furthermore, the joint-stock company could far exceed the old capitalist enterprise in size, thus increasing the centralisation of capital and the socialisation of labour. The joint-stock company represents a transitional form not because it makes ownership irrelevant, but because it constitutes complete socialisation of the labour process within capitalist production relations. It is capitalism in its most contradictory form.

Marx did think that the joint-stock company represented a partial separation of ownership and control but with very different results from those hypothesised by proponents of the managerial revolution thesis. The corporation allowed the major stockholders who sit in on the board of directors to gain control of the capital of small stockholders (Marx 1894:389). Credit markets offer similar opportunities for extension of control over capital not legally owned by the capitalist in question (Marx 1894:439). Both credit and the joint-stock company represent increased centralisation of control in the economy without entailing increased concentration of ownership.

By arguing that control is not necessarily coincident with the legal title to ownership in corporate capitalism, we have also made the coincidence of the two concepts in earlier stages of capitalist development problematic. Thus it is incumbent on us to theorise the development of control relations in capitalist society.[2] Unfortunately, most current conceptions of control, both Marxist and non-Marxist, are not too helpful here. They reify control relations. The Marxists see the distribution of control as fixed by the control of capital by major stockholding directors and managers and the necessity for delegation created by the complexity of the division of labour in capitalist society. Non-Marxists tend to see control relations as fixed by the functional requirements of running an enterprise. Furthermore, both schools of thought conceive of only a very limited number of categories of control defined by giving and/or taking orders. Taken to its extreme, theorising about the distribution of control purely in terms of domination and subordination can lead to a dichotomous conception of control relations, as in Dahrendorf's theory. Even in multi-levelled conceptualisations, the chain of command is often considered to be an adequate approximation to the actual control relations in the enterprise. What is overlooked is that the number and scope of orders that subordinates must obey can vary considerably across societies and within societies at any point in time and through time. In slave systems, for example, the slave must obey virtually any order that a master gives, including those concerning such highly personal matters as sexual activity. In capitalist societies, the concept of job control indicates a condition where subordinate employees manage to restrict the number of orders they must obey. The degree of job control can vary considerably according to the existence and strength of labour organisation in the enterprise, among other factors.

Swedish Social Democratic economists, such as Östen Undén, Ernst Wigforss and Gunnar Myrdal, have made an important contribution to the conceptualisation of control relations. They stress that ownership is not only a divisible concept, it can be thought of as a set of different ownership functions or decision-making rights (Adler-Karlson 1967). These decision-making rights, or control rights as we shall call them, theoretically can be distributed in a number of ways between the legal owners of capital, the state, the workers, financial intermediaries, etc. The task here is to explain the causes of the distribution of control rights in pure capitalism. Admittedly, our explanation will be tentative, but it is important to attempt to theorise this aspect of class relations in order to understand changes in control relations that occur with the development of labour organisation. First, we will make the simplifying assumption that all managerial work is carried out by the capitalist owner. Then we will examine the changes in control relations created by the separation of legal ownership from management and the development of bureaucratic structure to carry out managerial work.

In order to understand control relations in capitalist society it will be useful to develop a model of a pure type of capitalist production along the lines of the abstraction developed by Marx. The system has the following characteristics:

1. Capital is concentrated in the hands of a minority;
2. The mass of people have only their labour power to sell (actually rent: if they sold it they would be slaves for life rather than for a limited period of time each day);
3. Labour power is in excess supply and workers are not organised;
4. The capitalist buys the productive force offered by the labourer (labour power) rather than the other way around;
5. Property rights are virtually absolute – that is, every individual has the legal right (though perhaps not the *de facto* ability) to do what he or she wants with his or her productive force.

Ultimately, the fifth point comes down to the fact that the person has the right to enter or withdraw his or her productive force without reference to the wishes of others. The proletariat is legally free to withdraw its labour unlike serfs or slaves, whose masters exercise partial or complete ownership rights over their subordinates' labour power. The compulsion to work at prevailing wages and working conditions is economic, not legal. Under these conditions, all control in the enterprise will be concentrated in the capitalist's hands though he may, of course, delegate it to others. The worker is forced to give up control of his or her labour power in return for his or her subsistence.

Conditions 4 and 5 point to the existence of a market and certain legal property relations. The market itself requires a complex set of legal conditions to operate: definitions of contractual rights and responsibilities, etc. The existence of the market and absolute property rights, two key elements of capitalist production relations, can only be understood by examining their historical development which can only very briefly be sketched here. As Marx points out, capitalist social relations developed when the urban communes freed themselves from the political arrangements of feudalism. The development of capitalist productive forces (machines, etc.) made capitalist production increasingly important *vis-à-vis* feudal production. With their increased economic strength, the political influence of the bourgeoisie increased, and this in turn was used further to reduce limitations on free economic activity: to extend the market and shake the mercantilist and/or feudalist limitations and obligations on property. Thus, historically, we can say that free market relations expanded because of the power of the bourgeoisie, rather than that the bourgeoisie became powerful because the market expanded. Of course, the latter must also be true or else the bourgeoisie would not have promoted the market. This same argument concerning the historical relation of the market to bourgeois power can be applied to the absolute nature of ownership of labour power as well as of the physical means of production. Capitalist production requires a fluid labour force, thus it is advantageous not to exercise property rights over labour power.

However, control in the enterprise is not completely determined by the property rights and market structure of capitalism. Two further elements must be added: the relative scarcity of capital (points 1, 2 and 3 above) and the buyer/seller relationship (point 4). In capitalist society, the capitalist rents the labour power of the worker; the worker gives up control of his or her productive forces for a specified period of time in return for a wage. But the buyer/seller relation does not completely determine the control relationship: relative scarcity conditions the outcome. This can be demonstrated by reference to situations where the owners of the physical means of production rent their productive force to the owners of labour power, as in land tenancy. The tenant farmer rents the means of production of another, but he does not necessarily gain control of it. In fact, the landholder will normally retain the highest order decision-making rights (see p. 24 below) such as investment decisions and distribution of profits. But from this point on, control can vary somewhat due to the relative scarcity relationship between labour and landholder. Where labour has no other alternative and the landholder does, the control exercised by the landlord can extend to choice of products (crops) to be produced and to overall planning of working schedules (for example, time of planting and harvesting, etc.). This example demonstrates at the same time that the buyer/seller relationship is important independent of scarcity. The tenant farmer almost always will control the distribution of work tasks, work methods, choice of tools, etc., whereas the industrial worker does not.

It is important to recognise the historical interaction between the development of property rights, the buyer/seller relationship, the market and supply relations on the market. Given the huge factories of the present, it is hard to imagine the capitalist in any other position than that of the buyer and indeed the very physical characteristics of the forces of production help explain why the buyer relationship between land and labour and capital and labour is different. And it is the physical characteristics of factory production that make detailed control of the labour process by the capitalist possible.[3] But capitalist production was not also always factory production: early capitalism was characterised by the putting out system or cottage industry rather than factory production. In an effort to gain greater control over the work process the capitalists forced direct producers out of their homes and into the factories. Of course, this process would have been impossible had the producers had any alternative. Thus the relative oversupply of labour contributed to the development of the factory system.[4] The relative supply of labour and capital also helps to explain why the bourgeoisie was so enthusiastic about expanding the market in the first place. Conversely, the excess supply of labour power was ensured in part by the capitalists' political power.

Why does the capitalist want control over the entire labour process? Marxists and non-Marxists give apparently different answers to this question which in the end are actually quite similar. The Marxists argue that the accumulation process is hindered when labourers control the pace of work, the length of the working day, etc., because this makes it difficult to raise the rate of exploitation. Non-Marxists maintain that rational cost accounting characteristic of capitalism requires predictability which is enhanced by control over the labour process. Both arguments contain some truth and they come to the same conclusion: control over the labour process increases profits. Control is sufficiently important in this respect that capitalists faced with an organised work force ordinarily attempt to pay higher wages rather than give up control in the enterprise.

It is not entirely correct to say that all control lies with the capitalist. Even in the absence of the need for the delegation of authority, employees with skills to sell may be in a position to demand some control if market conditions are favourable. Since the supply of skilled labourers is relatively less than that of unskilled labourers, the former may receive more monetary remuneration but will still give up control over work during work time. However, even under the worst condition, skilled labour, especially white-collar labour, will manage to gain some minimal control over the conditions of their employment beyond monetary remuneration. Typically, they will receive some guarantee of conditions of employment and discharge, description of rights and duties, etc. As one moves up the hierarchy, the number and scope of these rights (security of employment, opportunities for promotion, etc.) increase. But even at fairly high levels the employee's control is limited to defensive, or negative, control – mere job control. He has no rights to change the distribution and allocation of work, planning of the development of business, etc., but only the right to resist changes which alter something that has been specifically guaranteed in his contract.

Recent Marxist works have made some important contributions to the analysis of the impact of the separation of ownership and management and the bureaucratisation of managerial work on control relations in the enterprise and on class formation (Poulantzas 1975; Wright 1976; Carchedi 1975a, 1975b). Elaborating on Marx's analysis of the consequences of the centralisation of capital for control relations, Poulantzas has argued that class identification must be made on the basis of 'real economic ownership'; that is, the actual patterns of control of property, rather than formal legal ownership. The development of the corporation involves a partial separation of the legal and real ownership: thus small stockholders cannot be considered part of the bourgeoisie while top managers, along with large stockholding directors, can be considered part of the bourgeoisie since they exercise real economic ownership. Poulantzas also argues that the processes of concentration and centralisation have created a disjunction between real economic ownership, control over investments and resource allocation, and possession: the control over the immediate labour process. Supervisors who participate in possession but not real economic ownership must be excluded from both the bourgeoisie and the proletariat. They form part of a middle stratum, the 'new petty bourgeoisie'.

Carchedi (1975a) takes Poulantzas' analysis a step further. He argues that capitalism is characterised both by a technical division of labour which derives from the development of the forces of production – from technological advance – and by a social division of labour, a division based on one's relations to production. As exemplified by the development of the modern corporation, centralisation and concentration have resulted in a differentiation of the role of the individual capitalist, separating out the labour role from the purely managerial role. With advances in differentiation associated with the development of the forces of production as well as concentration and centralisation of capital, both the role of the capitalist and the role of the labourer become increasingly internally differentiated.

In Carchedi's terminology, an agent's (individual's) position in the social division of labour depends in part on whether he or she performs the global function of capital (that is, the role of the capitalist), the function of the collective worker (that is, the role of the labourer), or both. The capitalist class or the bourgeoisie is defined, as in Poulantzas and Wright, by real economic ownership and performs only the global function of capital. The proletariat performs only the function of the collective worker. The new middle class performs the global function of capital or both the global function of capital and the function of the collective worker, but does not participate in real economic ownership. Thus, Carchedi pushes Poulantzas' analysis a step further maintaining that there is internal differentiation in the new middle class based on the relative weight of the function in the division of labour associated with a position.

There are some ambiguities in Carchedi's analysis of the determination of class by the exercise of control of production. The global function of capital is performed by a bureaucracy. However, one's position in the bureaucracy (and thus the degree of control one has) is not determined by the relative weight of the function in the social division of labour. The foreman, for instance, performs only the global function of capital. It is for this reason that Carchedi must introduce real economic ownership as a criterion for membership in the bourgeoisie. Otherwise foremen would be members of the bourgeoisie.[5]

Wright's approach not only indicates a solution to this problem but also is more parsimonious. Wright defines class entirely in terms of control relations. Real economic ownership, it should be remembered, is control over investment and resource allocation. The concentration and centralisation processes generate a further differentiation of possession into control over the means of production and control of labour power. The same processes create the need for further differentiation within these three basic categories of control. This latter differentiation occurs along clearly hierarchical lines. In the case of control of means of production, the highest levels control the entire apparatus of production, while the next level down controls only one segment of the production process, and so on. Though it is not stated, Wright implies that the three types of control also form a hierarchy with control of investment and resource allocation being the most important and control of the labour process the least important. Perhaps because this seems almost obvious intuitively, Wright offers no rationale for this ordering.

In his work on workers' control, Karlsson (1973) has developed a model with yet finer distinctions among the types of control (or decision-making powers in the enterprise) and he has provided a clear rationale for ordering them in hierarchical order. The higher up in the order a decision is, the more importance it has for committing the resources of the firm, particularly in the long-range future. A single decision higher up in the hierarchy will involve a greater cost than one lower down. Positions invested with a greater number of decisions at higher levels exercise greater control. Figure 2.1 depicts a slightly modified version of Karlsson's model (E. H. Stephens 1977). The highest level is equivalent to control of investment and resource allocation in Wright's definition. The next two are roughly the same as control of the means of production and the last three are similar to control over labour power.

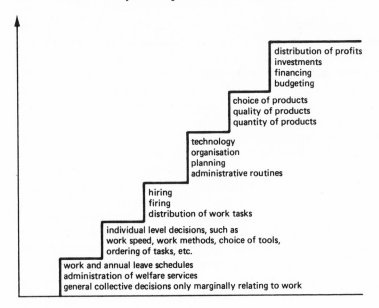

FIGURE 2.1

To summarise our argument to this point: property rights are a set of rights associated with the ownership of a given piece of property. Two basic types of property rights are income rights (see p. 50) and control rights. Control rights of capital – our concern here – are determined by a historically and politically established set of market and property relations as well as by the buyer/seller relationship, the physical characteristics of the productive forces, and the relative supply of labour, capital and educated labour. In the pure type of capitalism, almost all control rights in the enterprise will belong to the capitalist. The processes of concentration and centralisation of capital increase the technical complexity of the work of management creating the need to delegate control in varying degrees to various levels of a bureaucratic apparatus. The development of the corporation, which is also associated with concentration and centralisation, creates a partial division between legal ownership and control. The individual's position in control relations depends on the consequences of decisions invested in the position that he or she holds for the enterprise's present and future resource commitments.

Those individuals exercising control over overall investment, profits, financing and budgeting can be termed the real economic owners.

The exercise of control is coincident with the performance of the global functions of capital only in pure capitalism. Once workers begin to organise, they may begin to exercise some control over the shop floor organisation of work, but may not be performing the global function of capital. Nor can the work of contemporary Swedish safety stewards, who have the right to veto plans for expansion which do not meet safety standards, be considered a performance of the function of capital despite the fact that such work involves control of some aspects of the higher level decisions in the hierarchy of control. To be performing the global function of capital the individual must make decisions in accordance with criteria established by capital's need for profit and accumulation. This will be the case if the control invested in the position an individual holds is a product of delegation from real economic ownership, but not if it is the result of organised working-class power.

The concept of property as a set of decision-making rights is of considerable importance for a gradualist conception of the transition to socialism. It is possible – indeed, it has been the practice of Swedish Social Democracy – to socialise certain control rights of capital but not others. Government control of the location of industry and local trade union control over aspects of working conditions are typical ownership rights that have been socialised. This method of socialisation does have several advantages. First, it does not involve a government budget outlay. Second, it enforces a universal set of rules on industries rather than demanding that only nationalised firms act in terms of the social good. The concept of divisibility of property rights is particularly important in analysing the transition to socialism because the emergent class owns no new force of production. In earlier transitional periods, a mixed mode of production was easy to recognise because it entailed the coexistence of two distinct forces of production. In the transitional period to socialism, on the other hand, one must examine the actual patterns of control of the single type of productive force in order to discover at what stage of transition a given society is.

Based on this discussion of control relations, we can now place the concept of socialism meaningfully in the context of modern society. As noted earlier, the abolition of the distinction between the state and civil society can be seen as the movement from a condition where decisions are made in accordance with particular interests to a condition where they will be made in the general interest. They will be made by the collectivity through universal *vote* suffrage. Democratic control of production, then, is socialism. The transition to socialism can be conceived of as shifts of control of property from owners to democratically elected bodies in the workplace as well as the state. Though shifts in control might be rapid, a gradual transition might occur as a result of the growth of labour organisation and, thus, a gradual shift in the distribution of power in civil society. This will cause gradual shifts in the control of property and changes in the distribution of the means of consumption.[6]

The class structure of capitalism: consumption relations

Clearly, the growth of the importance of skills and education as a factor of production and the growth of a class of propertyless non-manual workers accompanying that development is counter to what Marx predicted. As Low-Beer (1978: 5–6) points out, it is an oversimplification to say that Marx completely fails to anticipate the growth of the middle class. In Volume III of *Capital* he does remark that the absolute number if not the relative proportion of office workers will grow. However, he goes on to note in the same passage that the growth of white-collar workers will be extremely small compared to the growth of blue-collar workers. In the few passages he does devote to analysing the middle class as a social group, Marx distinguishes two groups, the senior officers of capitalism (engineers, managers and management representatives) and its junior officers (foremen, *in charge of workers* supervisors, superintendents) (Crozier 1965: 21–2). Marx pointed to the ambiguous position of the latter, themselves an exploited group, at the same time charged with carrying on the exploitation of others. But he thought that an intensification of exploitation would be achieved through rationalisation, simplifying and devaluing their tasks, and keeping the number of white-collar jobs at a minimum. Marx thought that this same process of rationalisation of method would also lead to a decline in the importance of skilled labour. These predictions were shared by many economists of the period, bourgeois and socialist.

The prediction of class polarisation is the only important element of Marx's theory of the transformation of capitalism to socialism which must be rejected. Two of the primary tasks to be accomplished in this work are the development of a theory of distribution and class formation to replace that element of Marx's theory and the examination of the implications of the changes in the class structure subsequent to Marx for the development of socialism. The rest of this section in the chapter will be devoted to the former task.

In developing a theory of the distribution of the means of consumption and class formation, we will depart radically from current Marxist thinking on classes and class determination. In particular, we will argue that the relative scarcity of skilled or educated labour is an important determinant of income distribution and that class formation is dependent on ownership of skills as well as control of production. Perhaps more outrageous from a Marxist point of view will be our contention that skilled labour (the term must be broadly conceived to include all forms of education) can exploit others without purchasing another's labour power.

Essentially what we are preparing to argue is that under pure capitalist production the distribution of the means of consumption is market determined (remembering, of course, that the market itself is politically and historically determined). However, the market determination of income has two dimensions. Only part of the income differentials between skilled and unskilled labour are due to the relatively scarce supply of the former. The rest of the income of some skilled labour is attributable to the market position of the firm the worker is employed in. Carchedi's (1975a: 54–9) analysis of the incomes of the new middle class is helpful here. He divides the income of this group into two parts, revenue which is attributable to performing the global function of capital and wage which is equal to the cost of the reproduction of labour power and the skill in question. The size of the revenue component can be determined by the importance of the global function of capital the individual carries out. Thus it can be predicted by the degree of control he or she exercises according to the hierarchy developed earlier and by the market position of the firm he or she works for.

According to Marx's theory, the wage component is determined by the cost of reproduction. For unskilled labour, this is socially determined subsistence. For the skilled labourer, this is subsistence plus the cost of production of the skill. A moment's reflection should convince the reader that this factor cannot account for very large variations in remuneration of skilled versus unskilled labour. In fact, holding effort and talent constant (residual and relatively unimportant factors in Marxist theory anyway), lifetime income of skilled and unskilled labour should be exactly the same. In the United States at present, for example, most individuals complete secondary school and are supported by their parents to that point; so secondary education can be considered our baseline. Those receiving jobs requiring further education should receive their subsistence for the present plus the cost of their subsistence during the extra years of education, that is, the cost of the production of their skill. If the public did not foot the bill, the students' payment for the teachers' labour time and the schools' capital must also be paid. In either case it is obvious that *lifetime* income should not vary with skill. Now let us consider the reality of the situation. A subsistence wage in the United States is about $6000 and this is in fact approximately what unskilled, unorganised workers get. A lifetime subsistence is around $280,000. Compare this to the lifetime salary of a professor of art at a small elite four-year college – at least $650,000. Our art professor cannot possibly be deriving this from performing the global functions of capital. Or consider the doctor employed by a public hospital – lifetime income: at least $1,500,000. The only way to explain these discrepancies within the Marxist paradigm without reference to relative scarcity is to admit that they are a product of differences in intensity of labour input due to the greater efforts and innate talents of the professor or doctor.[7] It is our argument that these differences are due to the relative scarcity of the skill in question and that this factor is an important determinant of income distribution.

By the same process of comparison, the fact that performing the global function of capital has an impact on the individual's income can be seen. Compare the education required to become a top executive and university professor and then compare their relative income levels (excluding of course income from legal ownership of stock, etc.). Or compare the relative remuneration levels of management and top level staff in capitalist societies with persons in the same position in market socialist systems such as Yugoslavia (Flaes 1972:140). The income of the capitalist manager is higher in relative terms in both cases because he performs the global function of capital.

The part of the income of skilled labour which is not attributable to performance of the global function of capital or the reproduction of labour power (including the time put into producing the skill) can be termed the salary component of income. Unlike revenue, salary is not derived from buying[8] the labour power of others. Rather it is derived from selling a productive force, (skill.) But contrary to current Marxist thinking we would argue that, like revenue, salary is exploitative. (At least it is if salary more than makes up for the difference between the wage component and the value produced by the worker.) Thus, the exploitation contained in the salary component occurs in the circulation process, not in the production process. Who then is exploited? In the competitive model of capitalism, this will depend on the buyer/seller relationship. If the capitalist is the buyer then it comes out of the surplus value produced by the workers. Obviously, this also lowers revenue, but ultimately it is the worker who produces the value and thus it is she or he who is exploited. If the buyer is a consumer then it is the consumer who is exploited. Of course, this too reduces revenue since it increases the reproduction costs of labour power.

Since all income derived from selling a skill at greater than its reproduction cost is salary, it is apparent that the income of some petty bourgeois capitalists, such as doctors in a private practice, also contains a salary component. In the case of the doctor with one or two employees, the salary component is dominant. He certainly makes more money from overcharging his patients than he does from exploiting his nurse and secretary.

Though the idea that exploitation can occur in the process of circulation may sound heretical to some Marxists, it is of great importance for the explanation of relations between nations as well as class relations within nations. Differential market power is one of the main mechanisms through which rich nations exploit poor ones.

The examples offered above were helpful in making the distinction between wage, revenue and salary, and in elaborating a theory of income distribution. But they do not prove that the theory offered holds empirically. Some recent work on income determination sheds some light on this problem. Wright and Perrone (1977) show that Marxist class categories, operationalised as closely as possible in accordance with Wright's (1976) definition, explain variation in income independent of education and age. Education, which is the best operationalisation of skill level provided, explains substantial variation independent of Marxist class categories.[9] The standardised regression coefficients are ·28 for education, ·22 for age, ·27 for employer class membership, and −·11 for working-class membership. The four variables together explain 25 per cent of the variation in income. Robinson and Kelly (1977) build on Wright and Perrone's work by refining the measurement of control. Though they give a quite different interpretation to the variable, their operationalisation of authority in the enterprise is a rough approximation of our gradations of performance of the global functions of capital excluding those who have real economic owner-ship. Robinson and Kelly find that this refinement improves the model developed by Wright and Perrone.

To recapitulate briefly our theory of domination and distribution in pure capitalism as defined by the five characteristics listed previously:

1. Control is determined by the buyer/seller relation, the physical characteristics of capitalist productive forces, and the relative scarcity of capital in a historically/politically determined set of market and property relations. In corporate capitalism, control will be held by those who perform the global functions of capital. Very skilled labour may hold some job control.
2. Income distribution will be determined by supply and demand relationships within the market. Those individuals performing the global functions of capital will receive revenue in addition to wage and salary income, skilled workers will receive salary and wage income while unskilled workers will receive only wages, their subsistence.

It is probably not necessary to emphasise that a departure from the basic conditions of pure capitalism, such as a decline in unemploy-ment or the development of labour organisation, will result in at least some change in income distribution. But that such develop-ments can also change control relations is often overlooked. It is important to note that, even with the development of labour organisation, capitalists have attempted (for the most part success-fully) to restrict the scope of bargaining to wage and hour issues. But to assume that capital must for some theoretical reason retain all control is to reify the distribution of power in capitalist society, which makes the study of transitional stages particularly difficult.

Along this same line the importance of the market to capitalist class relations should be emphasised. Market relations are an essential part of capitalist production relations. Of course, production relations are not reducible to market relations because the market itself is a product of the historical development of capitalist property and political power. But capitalist production is commodity production, production for sale on the market, and the interrelationship of people in capitalist production is a commodity relationship. Thus the worker has a relationship not only to his or her boss but also a relationship to every other boss and every other worker in the system, a relationship which is mediated by the market. As Mann (1977) points out, this is a specific characteristic of capitalism. In precapitalist modes of production, production was localised, independent of production elsewhere, so class relations were also localised. It is the interdependence of capitalist production that makes the nationwide organisation of workers possible; even necessary, if it is to succeed. Furthermore, this interdependence is crucial in explaining some apparent discrepancies in our theory of income distribution. Individuals with similar productive capacities to sell will tend to have more similar incomes than one would predict by their immediate position in production. The revenue income of top-level managers affects the income of business school professors, whose salary income will exceed their colleagues' in the art department. The income of the medical professor will be favourably affected by the market conditions of his fellow doctors. The ununionised worker will be favourably affected by the higher pay of his or her unionised fellow worker, especially if labour is in short supply.

Given that we have argued that the income of both skill and capital is determined in the market and involves some sort of exploitation, it is incumbent upon us to address the question of whether capital and skill are just two different 'market capacities' not fundamentally different from one another, as Giddens (1973) has claimed. Capital is different from skills in several ways. First, the market was the historical and political creation of capital, and the terms of market bargaining – labour laws, contract law, laws governing union activity, etc. – are determined by capital in pure capitalism. While some professions, like the medical profession and legal profession, have achieved a certain degree of legal closure, this hardly compares with the political power exercised by capitalists.

Second, because of their nature as something not detachable from the owner, skills have properties which separate them from capital. They are not as easy to pass on to the holders' offspring as capital is. They are not subject to the centralisation tendency: there is a limited amount of skills that one can accumulate. And since skilled labour in advanced capitalism is in a seller not a buyer role, it takes orders rather than issues them when it is employed (that is, rather than in independent practice). This differing position of skilled labour in the distribution of the means of consumption and the distribution of control is quite important for shifts in class alliances in the political developments in capitalist society, as we shall see.

Given the controversy about the labour theory of value, some readers may feel uncomfortable with our analysis of exploitation in terms of labour value. It should be pointed out again that our analysis of income determination differs from that of neo-classical economics or Weberian sociology only in the case of revenue income, where the evidence shows our analysis to be superior. Furthermore, most Marxists would not argue that supply and demand are of no importance and most would explicitly deny that the price of a commodity will equal its labour value once the conditions of competitive capitalism have been violated, as in monopoly capitalism (for example, Sweezy 1942). What is usually lacking from the neo-classical or Weberian analysis is any explicit notion of exploitation. But this is more of a comment on theorists in these traditions than the nature of the theories themselves. In fact, Giddens (1973: 131–2) has developed a notion of exploitation tailored to fit his version of Weber's market model. He defines '"exploitation" as any *socially conditioned form of asymmetrical production of life chances.* "Life chances" here may be taken to mean the chances an individual has of sharing in the socially created economic or cultural goods which typically exist in any given society.' According to Giddens, his concept has in common with Marx's treatment of alienation 'the premise that exploitation implies a separation between the social *creation* of human faculties on one hand, and the social denial of access on the other'. Since possession of capital and marketable skills gives one differential access to 'economic and cultural goods' in pure capitalist society, any inequalities in the distribution of these productive resources will result in exploitation. Giddens' definition of exploitation will result in the identification of the same individuals as exploiters and exploited and of the same degree as our analysis using labour value did. In both cases any deviation from complete equality not due to innate differences in humans is a sign of exploitation.[10] Any 'socially conditioned' difference in access to the acquisition of skill or capital ('socially created human faculties') will lead to exploitation in a market society.

The class structure of capitalism: class formation

As we pointed out, because Marx predicted polarisation of classes as a consequence of capitalist development, the process of formation of easily distinguishable social classes which would be bases for organisation and political action posed no special problem for him. The future class system would be characterised by an homogeneous impoverished mass of propertyless workers and an equally homogeneous elite of wealthy property owners. The tremendous gap in living standards would help to ensure that the two groups would form concrete and isolated social groups within which class consciousness could develop.

The differentiation of the role of capital from a single entrepreneur to a hierarchical structure, and the growth of the strata of salaried employees, makes problematic the process of formation of distinct social groups out of which collective action arises. Recent Marxist works on the new middle class have not addressed this problem in an adequate way. Besides denying any importance to the influence of skill level, they theorise at such a high level of abstraction that they end up ignoring some divisions in the class structure which have been repeatedly found to be important for the development of collective action. The manual/non-manual line, for instance, is of no importance whatsoever at the highest levels of abstraction since lower non-manual workers and manual workers are both propertyless (control-less) employees. Yet this division in the class structure is, or at least was, the most important dividing line in the collective political and social action of groups in capitalist society. The central problem is that the structure of positions, not the interrelationship of individuals or families, is the object of analysis at this level of abstraction. The objective interest of an individual is determined not only by his or her current location in the class structure but also by the location of one's spouse and the objective chances for movement to another position (that is, the normal career pattern; for example, individuals in positions with no mobility chances show a higher propensity to resort to collective action). Furthermore, social action to maintain or change the structure of inequality can never be understood independently of individuals' concern for the situation of their offspring.

This is not to deny the validity of Marxist class categories at this higher level of abstraction. The classes we identify below might be termed class fragments or sectional interests within classes in Marxist sociology. Furthermore, the central axis of all class struggles whether over control or distribution is defined by the ownership of capital. The long-run development of society is defined by private control of capital and the struggle against it. But the shifting alliances in this struggle cannot be analysed without reference to the process of class formation at a more concrete level.

Non-Marxist sociology has generally been guilty of the opposite error. The classes are identified in an entirely atheoretical, empiricist fashion. Typically the only justification for breaking up the 'status structure' into distinct groups is that such distinctions appear to correspond to social and political behaviour or consciousness. Anthony Giddens (1973; also see Parkin 1974) is an exception in this respect. Building on Weber's work, he introduces the concept of 'structuration' to distinguish a few clearly defined classes. Since our model of classes faces a similar dilemma as the Weberian model, it might be useful to outline this dilemma briefly before proceeding to the solution proposed by Weber and developed by Giddens. Weber equates class situation with market situation. Individuals' ownership of property, skill and labour power determines his or her income and thus class. The problem is that this logically results in the identification of a class for every minute variation in the degree of capital or marketable skill owned.

Our theory of class results in a similar problem of class identification. While the real economic owners are placed at the top of the class system for theoretical reasons rather than for empirical reasons as in the market model, the divisions between classes cannot be determined by reference to the theory of domination and distribution. As in the Weberian model, there are no clear breaks in the distribution of the means of consumption. As in the Weberian model, there are qualitative differences in the type of productive capacity (capital, skill and labour), but the quantitative differences among those holding the first two are sufficiently great that a three-class model based on type of productive capacity alone cannot be defended. Our treatment of control relations does not allow us to make clear distinctions either. The only qualitative break is between those performing the global functions of capital and those not. The theoretical importance of this distinction is vitiated by the fact that those at the bottom of the hierarchy may actually spend almost all of their time performing the functions of the collective worker rather than the global functions of capital. And among those performing the global functions of capital any breaking point would be arbitrary from a theoretical point of view. Furthermore, once labour organises, control will not be monopolised by those serving the global functions of capital.

Weber proposes a solution to this problem in his second essay on classes. In order to translate the infinity of market situations designated by his definition of class into a few identifiable *social classes*, he argues that the enclosure of mobility is the variable which one might use to define the boundaries of a social class. 'A "social class" makes up the totality of those class situations within which individual and generational mobility is easy and typical' (Weber 1922: 302). Based on this definition, Weber contends that modern capitalism is characterised by four classes: the working class, the petty bourgeoisie, propertyless non-manual employees and large property holders. Since property can be inherited without difficulty, the propertied classes can easily reproduce themselves within and across generations. The division between manual and non-manual work is not ensured by the possession of skills since skilled workers, like non-manual workers, do have something more than their labour power to sell on the market. Rather, the manual–non-manual line is a strong barrier to mobility. It is not 'easy and typical' for skilled workers to move into non-manual jobs. Nor is intergenerational mobility across this line typical due to the social mechanisms conditioning educational achievement, such as the intellectual environment in the home, access to education, etc.

The problems posed by our analysis of control and consumption relations can also be solved by looking for significant mobility blocks in the class structure. This implies that we must be concerned with characteristics of individuals and families, not positions. What is most critical is the type of productive capacity possessed by an individual and the consequences it has for one's career development and that of one's offspring. For instance, those individuals exercising the global functions of capital without legally owning any capital at all cannot automatically pass their position on to their offspring. Of course they can use the revenue from their position to give their children educational advantages. Or they can use the revenue to accumulate capital, in which case they can become capitalists.

Weber's four-class model is a useful starting point. Empirical research has shown that the manual/non-manual line is a strong mobility barrier, so Weber's contention on this matter can be accepted. The definition of the capitalist class is somewhat more problematic. At first glance, it appears that the use of mobility closure as a criterion for class identification would exclude top managers from the capitalist class. In fact, there is no great empirical problem here. Virtually all managers in a position that involves exercising real economic ownership are substantial property holders. For instance, in the United States in 1962, the top executives of the 94 largest firms owned an average of $650,000 of stock in their own firm alone. Forty per cent of their income came from dividends on this stock and to this must be added their increase in net worth due to stock appreciation (Pryor 1973: 121). The practice of offering stock options ensures that most top level managers will also have large property holdings. This not only contributes to the intergenerational continuity of the capitalist class, it also minimises the purported effects of the separation of ownership and control on the behaviour of corporations. The direct financial benefits of firm performance to managers in terms of revenue income, dividends, stock options and stock appreciation is quite substantial.

Thus a distinct capitalist class and a manual working class can be identified in capitalist society on the basis of mobility closure. Weber's designation of the petty bourgeoisie as a single class should probably be modified. It is not 'easy and typical' to move from farming to urban petty bourgeois occupations, so farmers and the urban petty bourgeoisie form separate classes.[11] Between the capitalist class and the manual working class in capitalist production proper lies a group which can hardly be said to have homogeneous situations in the market place. It includes everything from clerks and secretaries to doctors and middle-level managers. It is not surprising that the heterogeneity of the middle class has been a central theme in the literature on this group (see Low-Beer 1978:1–23; Crozier 1965:21–41). This stratum is differentiated not only in terms of income, but also in terms of control. The authority structure in the enterprise cuts across the middle class. Some clerical and sales workers have no supervisory role at all. Furthermore, even the workers in this category who do some supervisory work spend most of their time performing the function of the collective worker and not the global function of capital. The importance of this point is that it can be argued that these lower non-manual employees increasingly form a distinct class below middle-level managers and experts outside of the chain of command, such as lawyers, doctors, technicians or engineers. This would give us four rather than three classes in capitalist production proper. The precise number of classes in a given society is an empirical problem that must be examined from case to case and through time in each case.

The most accurate characterisation of the class divisions in the new middle class is that it was one class up to the Second World War – depending on the country in question – and that it is now two classes. At least, it is in the technologically more advanced countries with universal secondary education, such as the United States and Sweden. In an incredibly insightful passage, C. Wright Mills (1951:297) foresaw that this would happen. As a consequence of the simplification of tasks in clerical and sales jobs and the universalisation of secondary education, Mills predicted that the mobility barrier between clerical and sales workers, and managers and professionals would become stronger while the barrier between lower non-manuals and manual workers would weaken. The evidence on social mobility and political behaviour for both Sweden (J. D. Stephens 1976) and the United States (Hamilton 1972) indicates that Mills was correct. In view of this change, the terminology used to designate these middle strata must vary according to the time period and the country under discussion. Here middle class will be used to designate the situation in which the propertyless non-manuals can be thought of as a single class. Upper middle class will be used to designate the managerial and professional class when it appears to be a class distinct from clerical and sales workers, the non-manual working class.[12]

The suggested division in the middle class is a clear case where the possession of certain productive capacities overrides position in the authority structure or performance of the global functions of capital in class determination. The experts and middle-level managers share similar productive capacities, with the background of at least a college education in the United States or a gymnasium education in Europe. This education is their job qualification, and their ability to pass their social position on to their children depends on passing on this education. The differences between managers and experts in the present occupation are unlikely to affect the educational advantages of their offspring, thus there is no intergenerational closure between managers and experts. Having a common interest in the restriction of supply of highly educated labour, the maintenance of income differences based on education and low marginal taxation, the political actions of managers and experts are also likely to be similar.

Giddens points to ethnicity as one factor accounting for cross-national variation in class formation.

> Where ethnic differences serve as a 'disqualifying' market capacity, such that those in the category in question are heavily concentrated among the lower paid occupations, or are chronically unemployed or semi-employed, we may speak of the existence of an *underclass*. (Giddens 1973: 112)

By influencing patterns of social mobility and social interaction, ethnic division may serve to reduce or increase the degree of closure of economic strata (that is, groups with similar productive capacities). Giddens has pointed to the case of a division within the working class and closure around it created by ethnic divisions. Ethnic divisions may also cut across class lines and reduce closure of economic strata.

The transition to socialism: underlying causes

On the basis of our analysis of the class structure of pure capitalism, Marx's theory on the underlying causes of the transition to socialism can now be re-examined. One causal factor, polarisation of classes, has already been discussed at length and we have found Marx's projections to be faulty. Of the other three causes, we will accept his argument in two cases (labour organisation and concentration and centralisation) and question it in the other (the contradictions of capitalism).

Concentration and centralisation

Capitalism has created the material base for socialism in the advanced capitalist democracies. Concentration, the accumulation of capital, has created sufficient affluence that socialisation would not mean just generalisation of poverty. Centralisation has proceeded to the point where the entire Western economy is dominated by huge oligopolistic corporations. Advanced capitalism is now based on fully socialised labour: it is a complex of highly interdependent concerns, national and even international in scope, based on co-operative labour. Given this degree of centralisation, the socialisation of the principal means of production would be simple from a purely technical standpoint.[13] This can be seen in the nationalisation of monopolies in transport and communications all over Western Europe.

The centralisation of capital has important consequences for distribution and domination which differentiate oligopoly capitalism from pure competitive capitalism. The decline in competition and the growth of oligopoly allows capitalists to do something roughtly parallel to what workers do when they form unions. Both situations enable a group of people with similar productive capacities to act in unison in their common interest rather than to pursue competitively their individual interest to the detriment of the collectivity. Oligopoly allows a few producers to co-ordinate their actions, to fix prices, etc., without any formal organisation since there are so few actors in the situation (for example, four in the case of the US automobile industry). In principle, the same could be achieved with huge numbers of capitalists producing the same item if they formed some sort of organisation which would make decisions for the collectivity. But this is more difficult and, in fact, illegal in some countries. Because the development of oligopoly, and thus price fixing, allows capitalists to charge a higher price than they would under competitive conditions, it allows them to exploit the consumer as well as the workers in their own concern. Thus oligopoly capital exploits people through circulation as well as production.

Perhaps more important, at least for the analysis of the transition to socialism, with the advent of oligopoly capitalism the capitalist class manages partially to free itself at the national level from the 'anarchy of the free market' and gain control over the development of the whole social order. This control is quite distinct from control (domination) in the enterprise. This ability to control social development was furthered by the development and application of Keynesian economics. Consequently, the crises associated with earlier stages can be moderated. Obviously, these changes in distribution and domination characteristic of pure capitalism caused by the development of oligopoly do not entail a movement towards socialism since no democratisation of the control of capital has occurred.

Aside from creating the material base for socialism, concentration and centralisation have an important indirect effect on the development of socialism. They promote labour organisation.

Organisation and class consciousness

Following Marx, we see the pure type of competitive capitalism as beginning to erode in the very process of coming into existence. It is actually a construct developed for analytical purposes. When workers organise and stage their first successful strike, the system is no longer a purely capitalist one. As the organisation of labour increases, the distribution of power in civil society changes. As a consequence the distribution of the means of consumption and the distribution of control changes. On this point, we will accept Marx though we want to emphasise the probability of more gradual change and even the possibility of stagnation. Indeed, it has been asserted that just such a stagnation in labour organising has resulted due to the development of the class structure subsequent to Marx and the lack of growth of class consciousness among all propertyless employees.

One reason why it was necessary to discuss class formation in such detail is that it allows us to lay the foundations for the development of a theory of class consciousness. A major omission in Marx's theory of the transformation from capitalism to socialism is that he did not have a well-developed theory of class consciousness. Given his view of the development of the class structure, this was not problematic. While it is not at all clear that Marx ever believed that the average worker would develop a complex ideology concerning the class nature of capitalism and its abolition in the transition to socialism, he clearly thought that the overwhelming majority of workers would come to recognise that their interest was opposed to that of capital, that they would support movements to alter the system, and that, in most societies, these would be revolutionary movements. In fact, there is considerable variation in the degree to which workers in different societies support even reformist movements or join trade unions. As we shall see, Marx's suggestions are helpful in explaining some of this variability. Before moving on to Marx's contribution, the connection of mobility closure to class consciousness should be examined.

Class conscious behaviour (for example, voting for parties of the left and trade union membership) is greater when only economic factors affect closure of economic strata. Ethnicity and religion often create groupings which cut across economic strata, thus creating mobility and interaction across economic strata while inhibiting interaction within an economic stratum.

In addition to their indirect effect via social closure, non-economic social divisions affect class conscious behaviour directly. This is clearest in situations in which linguistic, religious and/or ethnic divisions coincide with region as in the case of Belgium or Switzerland before the recent inflow of foreign workers. In such situations, even if these non-economic social cleavages have little influence on the degree of closure of an economic stratum, they still may influence the individual's group identification.

In our conception, social class is not necessarily reflected in the subjective consciousness of individuals. The model of the formation of a subjective social class, a class 'for itself' in Marx's terminology, has three elements. First, the group of individuals must share similar productive capacities. Second, the degree of social closure then defines whether the group can be considered a social class or not. Finally, the development of class consciousness may or may not occur according to other factors, such as those we just mentioned. As we see it, social class formation is a necessary but not a sufficient condition for the development of a class for itself.

Both Marx and Engels recognised that ethnic diversity and religiosity were barriers to the development of class consciousness, but they assumed that the forces of capitalist development would break down these barriers in the long run. Though they erred on the question of polarisation, they did point to some factors which have proved to be important in the growth of labour organisation. Everywhere capitalism has created the seed of its own destruction, its negation – the labour movement. Because it brings members of the oppressed class together in communication with one another and makes them economically interdependent, the development of labour movements is an inherent feature of capitalism. For this reason, nowhere is capitalism found in its pure form. It is always at some transitional stage.

On the surface of it, it would seem that Marx's observations on the development of labour organisation would offer little in the way of explanation of variations among advanced capitalist democracies since all of the variables he suggests are associated with the level of capitalist development. He links the development of organisation to urbanisation, technological developments in capitalism and the centralisation and concentration of capital. In the *Manifesto*, he and Engels point out that these processes improve communication among workers. Technological developments in the area of transport and communications make nationwide organisation simpler. Concentration is associated with the growth of plant size which also increases communications among workers. Since large work units and good transportation and communications are characteristics of all industrial democracies, it appears these factors can not account for the variation in labour organisation across countries. If anything, countries with larger work units seem to have weaker labour movements (see Chapter 4). In Chapter 32 of *Capital*, Marx also links organisation to centralisation. He argues that centralisation of capital, that is, the constant reduction in the number of firms dominating the economy, furthers the socialisation of labour. This, in turn, causes workers to be 'disciplined, united, organized by the mechanism of the capitalist process of production itself'. Unfortunately, Marx does not make explicit just how the socialisation of labour is linked to the organisation of labour. What is important to note here is that an increase in the centralisation of capital does not necessarily involve an increase in the average size of work units. If firm A buys up firm B, an increase in centralisation but not in average plant size results.

Ingham's (1974) work on strikes is instructive here. Ingham does not address himself to the problem of the level of labour organisation but he does provide us with an argument that supplies the missing link in Marx's theory. Ingham shows that the 'character of the industrial infrastructure' strongly influences the strike level. The 'character of the industrial infrastructure' is the term Ingham uses to denote the degrees of centralisation, of technical complexity of production and of product specialisation. Combining the argument of the two theorists with some of our own observations, we would argue the following:

1. The size of the population of an industrial nation is the main determinant of the size of the domestic market and, consequently, the degree of industrial centralisation in a country. The smaller the country is, the greater the centralisation will be. The degree of centralisation is the main determinant of the level of labour organisation.
2. Late[14] and rapid industrialisation causes countries, particularly small ones, to have less technically and organisationally complex industrial infrastructures. This aids unionisation.
3. Late industrialisation in small countries leads to greater product specialisation. Greater product specialisation also facilitates unionisation.

The degree of industrial centralisation is inversely related to the size of the population of a country for the following reasons. Small societies had to base industrialisation on export industries because the domestic market is too small. Sharp competition in export industries forced out the smaller companies which could not contend with the fluctuations of the world market. Furthermore, economies of scale imply that there is a limit to how small any firm can be and still be competitive. A firm of this smallest possible size will employ far more people proportionately in a small country than in a large country. For these same reasons, size of population is related to product specialisation. Late industrialisation is associated with product specialisation because highly specialised products assume the presence of an export market. Early industrialisers like England had to produce a highly differentiated range of products aimed at the domestic market.

So small countries, particularly if they industrialise late, are characterised by high product specialisation and great centralisation. Thus the economy is dominated by a small number of non-competing employers. Conversely, the labour movement must organise a much larger proportion of the labour force in such a country. Labour organisations must be of at least a certain size to further their members' interests effectively. First, labour must organise all firms operating in the same market. For example, if only Ford were organised it would be difficult for the UAW (United Automobile Workers) to push up the wages at Ford without seriously damaging Ford's competitive situation and thus reducing employment in the firm. The construction industry in the United States, on the other hand, operates on a much more localised market. In this case, it is possible for unions to be effective at that level. Small countries characterised by high degrees of capital centralisation have fewer purely local or regional industries. Second, the labour movement must organise most or all firms in a conglomerate. If only a few are organised, the employers can use the profits of the other firms as a 'strike fund' in order to weather an industrial conflict. So, in an economy characterised by a small number of non-competing oligopolistic employers, the labour movement must organise a greater proportion of the labour force to reach the minimum size in order to be effective. In Marxist terms, the centralisation of capital increases the socialisation of labour; it makes all workers dependent on one another and thus makes the success of labour organisation in one workplace partly dependent on its success in other workplaces.

Sweden is a good example of this sort of highly centralised economy. The fifty largest private companies employ 21 per cent of all employees in the private sector. The 100 largest account for 46 per cent of total private industrial output. Furthermore, fifteen families together with two corporations have a majority control in 200 large industrial concerns which employ almost 50 per cent of all employees in private industry. The Wallenberg family alone owns a major interest in seventy corporations which employ 20 per cent of all workers in private industry. This indicates that control in the private sector is extremely concentrated in Sweden.

If the Swedish case is indicative of a general pattern, the effect of centralisation and product specialisation on the level of labour organisation is furthered by the organisation of employers. Ingham points out that employer organisation and solidarity is greatly facilitated by an economy characterised by a small number of non-competing firms. For example, Swedish employers developed a highly centralised and aggressive federation (SAF) in the first decade of this century in order to fight the emergent labour movement. The federation supported firms involved in industrial conflicts economically and encouraged lockouts and other aggressive tactics *vis-à-vis* the unions. As a response, LO, the trade union confederation, was forced to centralise in order to avoid being crushed and, subsequently, to organise virtually the whole economy in order to be effective. This high degree of centralisation of power in the hands of the trade union central organisation and the employers' organisation facilitated the subsequent development of centralised nationwide bargaining. This centralisation of bargaining has had some important side effects for the development of Swedish socialism. First, bargaining takes on the character of conflict between classes rather than between one employer and one union. Second, because the national bargain is of such great importance for the government's management of the economy and vice versa, the government has become a *de facto* third partner in the bargaining process. Thus collective bargaining retains a political character and politics retain a class character. This has prevented the Swedish movement from ever sliding toward economism.

Late and rapid industrialisers tend to skip the workshop stage of production and proceed directly to industrial mass production. Workshop production is associated with high differentiation of skills and, as a result, the development of craft unions. Craft unionism is based on the tactic of limiting labour supply in a particular trade rather than organisation of all workers in an industry. Thus the strength of craft unionism is inversely related to the level of labour organisation. This organisational complexity created by the technical complexity of workshop production often survives the workshop stage and continues to impede the organisation of labour. This may be the reason for the lower level of organisation of Danish labour as compared to Norwegian or Swedish labour.

The model of class formation developed earlier is an abstraction referring to the initial formation of classes in pure capitalism. The development of labour organisation feeds back on class formation, strengthening class consciousness and solidarity. The character of labour organisation once it develops in a country (that is, the strength of craft unions, the degree of organisational centralisation) also has an important effect on class formation and class consciousness. Organisation on a craft basis tends to fragment classes. Craft unions create intragenerationally closed strata which often pursue their own sectional interests rather than broader class interests, through collective action. Labour aristocracies are only a special case of this type of class fragmentation. In ethnically divided societies such as the United States, craft closure often reinforces ethnic closure to create highly fragmented social classes, further hindering the development of class consciousness.

Professional associations are nothing more than craft unions for educated labour. They pursue the same sort of limitation of supply which craft unions attempt, albeit more successfully. In particular, professions have achieved legal closure to a degree undreamed of by skilled craft workers. The growth of legal closure of professions is associated with the development of the class structure over the past century (Mills 1951: 139). This development reinforces the growing division between the upper middle class and the non-manual working class. It also fragments the upper middle class to a degree unparalleled in any other class.

To some degree, the sectional view taken by craft unions is a manifestation of a general tendency for less centralised trade unions to take a less than class-wide view in political and trade union action. The beneficial effects of bargaining centralisation previously mentioned are just one aspect of this tendency of centralised unions to promote class solidarity. In Chapter 5, we will elaborate on this point in our comparison of the British and Swedish cases. Suffice it to say here that we are prepared to take the rather unfashionable position that, on balance, the advantages of a highly centralised labour movement for the struggle for socialism outweigh the dangers of oligarchy that centralisation entails.

The contradictions of capitalism

Marx thought that the contradictory nature of capitalist production would contribute to the system's demise. While we can accept the idea that the social and co-operative character of production is 'contradicted' by the private form of appropriation, it is not at all clear that this contradiction must come to an end, partly because two of the expressions of this contradiction – crises and the falling rate of profit – do not seem to occur as predicted. Profit does not fall as Marx predicted because he underestimated the degree to which increases in labour productivity caused by introduction of machinery would offset the changing composition of capital caused by the same factor. Crises have been moderated by the development of some macroeconomic planning. Though it can be argued that some of the factors moderating the crises of capitalism – such as the increased consumption of the masses – were introduced by the labour movement, and thus represent a transitional element in the system, there is no reason why the system cannot stagnate at this more stable transitional stage. In the last analysis, one cannot be sure that capitalist relations of production will ever become a fetter on the further development of the forces of production to the extent that growth permanently stagnates. Even if that were to happen, the political repercussions would not necessarily be favourable to the left. Reaction is at least as likely as progress.

On the other hand, one might argue that the contradictory character of capitalism creates a tension which aids the transition to socialism, albeit on a more ideological plane. Virtually all of the ideological principles, or, better said, justifications of capitalism can only be realised in socialism. The 'invisible hand' of the capitalist market supposedly assures the greatest good for the greatest number, but profit, not need, is the driving force of the system. The ideological proponents of capitalism claim that it is a meritocratic system. The inheritance of property is obviously contradictory to this principle. Only slightly less obvious, but equally contradictory, are the previously mentioned inequalities of social condition which give advantages in the acquisition of skills and education to those on the top. And, finally, the bourgeois principle of political equality can only be realised when people have equal resources at their disposal. None of these 'contradictions' can bring an end to capitalism by their own force. But they are important ideological weapons for the socialist movement with which capitalism can be shown to be inadequate on its own terms.

The role of the state

In accounting for the absence of a socialist revolution to date in advanced capitalist societies, many authors argue that the state has played a mediating role in the class struggle. They contend that Marx erred in arguing that the state was solely an instrument of the bourgeoisie. For instance, Goldthorpe and Lockwood (1969:4) argue that 'the State has played an important and relatively independent role in limiting the power attaching to property and in giving common civil, political and social rights to all members of the national community regardless of economic position'. But if in fact the state has conceded the type of political and social rights mentioned as a result of organised working-class pressure, this is by no means proof of the 'independent role of the State'. It may simply be a reflection of the altered distribution of power within civil society caused by the increasing organisation of the working class.

We do not want to argue that the party political composition of the state makes no difference in its policy output. In fact, we will argue that it is necessary that a socialist party hold the reins of state power for an extended period of time if the transformation from capitalism to socialism is to be made. However, no government in a democracy can ignore the distribution of power in civil society in the process of policy-making. This involves concessions to organised labour on the part of conservative governments as well as concessions to capital on the part of leftist governments.[15] We will return to this point on several occasions.

One point where Marx's ideas about the state in capitalism must be revised is the assumption that the bourgeoisie would be unable or unwilling to make active use of the state. Not only has the state been used in a Keynesian fashion to smooth out economic cycles, it has also been used by capitalists to co-ordinate various aspects of economic life, such as reduction of competition (see Galbraith 1973). This has made capitalism a much more stable economic system than Marx imagined. This growth of the active use of the state has paralleled the growth of oligopoly and can be seen as another manifestation of collective action of the capitalists as a class. Harrington (1972) correctly argues that this type of social order, 'corporate collectivism' as he calls it (that is, oligopoly control in the economy and active state management of the economy in the collective interests of capital), is the only viable future alternative to socialism.

The transition to socialism: processes

Changes in the distribution of productive capacities

Given the importance of the concentration of capital into a few hands for the distribution of control – both in the enterprise and at the societal level – and for the distribution of income, it is not surprising that in the first decades of this century most socialist movements advocated simply shifting all private capital to collective ownership. However, no movement ever gained the political support to do this rapidly, and the socialisation that was done tended to be in areas of natural monopolies and unprofitable enterprises. The weakness of the labour movement, which was mainly due to the growth of the new middle class and the persistence of a significant rural petty bourgeoisie, was responsible for this lack of political support.

Western European social democratic governments have tried to change supply and demand of productive capacities in several ways. First, they have consistently attempted to increase demand for labour by keeping unemployment as low as possible. Hibbs (1977) has recently shown that social democratic tenure is associated with lower rates of unemployment and that low unemployment does, in fact, result in equalisation of incomes. Leftist governments have also broadened access to higher education in order to increase social mobility and increase the supply of educated labour. It is unclear whether or not this has had any effect on the distribution of income. One limitation on this strategy, which is not recognised by neo-classical economics, is that changes in the supply of educated labour do not affect the revenue component of income.

The restrictions in labour supply achieved by professional associations and some craft unions have also affected the distribution of productive capacities to the advantage of certain groups. Obviously, this does not always (or even usually) result in equalisation.

Industrial unionisation

We have argued and will show empirically that the growth of industrial unions has had a very important equalising effect. Industrial unions differ from craft unions and professional organisations in that they do not attempt to monopolise accreditation for occupations, but rather attempt to improve their members' position through collective withdrawal of labour. In other words, they do not attempt to change the distribution of productive capacities; rather, they try to modify the operation of the competitive labour market through collective action. On the other hand, the income and control workers acquire through organisation *is* achieved in the economic sphere rather than through legislation. For this reason we will call the income and control that an individual acquires as the result of bargaining between capital (oligopoly and competitive), skilled labour and labour power (organised and unorganised) *economically determined income* and *economically determined control.*

There is ample empirical evidence – Hibbs's (1977) and our own – to show that changes in market power brought about by low levels of unemployment and labour organisation have resulted in redistribution of income in favour of the working class. We would also argue that low unemployment and unionisation have resulted in modest gains in (economically determined) control on the part of the workers.

In most cases, the control in the enterprise gained by the workers has been defensive control. This is, for example, the case when the contract agreed upon by labour and capital contains (1) a clause giving capital the right to direct and allocate work as it sees fit unless specifically forbidden to do so in the contract and (2) a provision that labour cannot resort to industrial actions (strikes, etc.) for the duration of the contract. This is the situation in the United States and it was the situation in Sweden until 1977. The British and Italian labour movements on the other hand have developed some measure of offensive control in the enterprise through organisation and bargaining in the market.[16]

In the early 1970s, Volvo introduced some experiments in limited increases in workers' control. These experiments included modifications of the assembly line and introduction of self-controlling work groups. Most trade unionists and leftists viewed these modifications of work organisation as an attempt by Volvo and other capitalists to co-opt the movement for increased workers' control. While this view is largely correct, it does overlook one point: it was the increased cost of labour power that induced Volvo to make these changes. Because of the extremely low unemployment level in Sweden, labour turnover at Volvo was very high. By changing work organisation and granting the workers some small measure of control over their work, Volvo was able to reduce labour turnover and thus increase efficiency. Swedish workers were able to affect work organisation by exit from an undesirable situation. When unemployment is high, on the other hand, workers cannot afford to quit their jobs due to dissatisfaction with working conditions because they may not be able to find alternative work. While the gains in control won through this method may be small, they are of some theoretical importance since they demonstrate the link between domination in the firm and the relative supply of various productive capacities.

The ability of organised labour to gain some control over the development of the social order *independent of its influence* on the state has been extremely small. Labour has managed to gain only very limited defensive control over some of the planning activity of oligopoly capital.

Socialisation of income and control rights

Most reforms of social democratic movements have not been aimed at changing the distribution of productive capacities through socialisation or manipulation of the supply of various productive capacities. Rather, through the use of state power, social democratic governments have progressively socialised the rights to economically determined income and control. For the sake of linguistic simplicity, we will refer to this as socialisation of income rights and control rights.

In the market, the distribution of income and control are connected; they can even be traded for one another. In the case of state action, they only have this intimate connection if property is socialised, but not if income rights or control rights are socialised separately. However, in the long run, the distribution of both control and income are a reflection of the distribution of power in civil society operating through the economy or the state. To repeat, the distribution of power in civil society is determined by the level of labour organisation, the degree of capital centralisation and, to some extent, the relative scarcity of productive capacities.

Typically, leftist governments have socialised income rights associated with various productive capacities by means of progressive taxation and provision of free and/or subsidised goods and services. Other examples are the minimum wage and equal pay for equal work. This strategy has been more successful in the case of inequalities due to skill than inequalities due to legal ownership of capital because of ability of the latter, particularly in oligopoly capitalism, to shift the incidence of taxation to the workers or the consumer given favourable market conditions.[17] But it should be noted that taxation on the revenue income of managers, which is, in fact, capital income, is more difficult to shift to other groups.

Second, social democratic governments have also socialised

rights to control over social developments. This usually involves the shift of a decision-making right from capital to the government. Examples of this are investment planning, manpower planning, pollution control, product standards, plant location, land use, and more recently energy policy.

Third, social democratic governments may (but typically have not tended to) socialise control rights in the enterprise. This usually involves shifting a decision-making right from the firm to the workers in the firm. The recent changes in Swedish labour law are a notable case in point (see Chapter 6). These changes are good examples of the various ways in which control can be socialised. In some cases, the new laws specify that a decision-making right is to be entirely in the hands of the worker, for example, safety stewards now have the right to stop work when they feel the workers' health or safety is being endangered. In other cases, the new laws specify what may or may not be included in a legal contract between capital and labour; that is, they forcefully expand or constrict what may be bargained about. Very important in this respect is that the new labour laws make it illegal for a Swedish labour contract to contain the two provisions mentioned previously. Thus Swedish employers must enter into negotiation on any changes in work organisation *and* management of the enterprise which affect the workers in any way. Furthermore, the workers retain the right to strike on any issue not specifically covered in the contract.

Capitalists have reacted in the same way in the political arena as they have in the market. They have attempted, usually successfully, to limit socialisation to income rights. Economism is that situation where trade union economic demands are limited to issues of wages and hours and working-class political efforts are limited to socialisation of income rights.

Many writers on the welfare state claim that all reformist labour movements have been forced into a situation where all reforms are characterised by economism. This precludes any possibility of a reformist transition to socialism. Citing examples from the larger capitalist democracies (France, Italy, Germany, the United States, the United Kingdom), authors such as Gorz (1964) also argue that shifts of control from individual capitalists to the state do not involve democratisation of control. They correctly point out that this often results in a shift of decision-making to a collectivity of capitalists, as in the case of US regulatory boards. While this argument is often true for the countries examined, it does not follow that this is necessarily always the case. But this is the subject of our next chapter. Before moving on to the question of reform or revolution, let us examine the social base of the socialist transition.

The objective interests of different classes in capitalism

In this section, we want to identify the basic sources from which we can expect support for, or opposition to, the modification of capitalism in a socialist direction, based on various groups' objective interests.[18] In the second half of this work, we will look at how – if at all – these interests are translated into concrete social and political movements in that direction. Since the possession of education has a much more significant effect on the distribution of the means of consumption than it does on the distribution of control, it is necessary to examine the issue of control relations separately from the issue of the distribution of consumption. The class alignments in political struggles in capitalist society will depend on whether the reform in question is aimed at changing the distribution of consumption (consumption politics) or the distribution of control (production politics). The use of the term 'production politics' rather than 'socialist politics' has a definite purpose. Any struggle against capitalism would be covered by the latter term and this would include any struggle over the rate of capital accumulation, the level of profit or the distribution of revenue income. Since, at any time, the distribution of income is a zero sum situation, virtually all struggles over distribution are struggles against capital. Only in the case of maintenance of salary income *vis-à-vis* wage income is the struggle not directed against capital. Since any taxation of personal income will affect revenue income and usually dividend income, struggles over the level and distribution of the tax burden are necessarily struggles against capital.

With this said, it is important to emphasise that the transition to socialism cannot be achieved through consumption politics alone. It is impossible to tax capital at confiscatory levels without having very substantial control of capital, particularly capital flight and the level of investment.

Production politics divide society along the lines of control relations. Capitalists and those performing the global functions of capital have an objective interest in the system. Control-less employees have an interest in socialism, while the petty bourgeoisie is in a neutral position. The class alignments on production politics pit the working class or classes against the capitalist class. The upper middle class or the middle class are in an ambiguous position with the managerial fragments pro-capitalist and the rest objectively neutral. The petty bourgeois classes are in a similar neutral position. Since the development of capitalism is associated with the decline in the petty bourgeoisie and the development and growth of the non-manual working class, the proportion of the population with an objective interest in production politics tends to grow.

Consumption politics divide society along quite different lines. The upper middle class or the middle class join the capitalist class on the *status quo* side. The non-manual working class is in an ambiguous position with the top and bottom income strata having different interests. The petty bourgeoisie may have an interest in equalisation. This is certainly true if one defines the group strictly, that is, property owners with no employees other than family members. Thus, when a large peasant class (along with a sizeable urban petty bourgeoisie) exists, as is often the case at early stages of capitalist development, consumption politics may ally the working class and the petty bourgeoisie, particularly the rural elements.

In addition to consumption and production politics, a third type of political reform can be distinguished – mobility politics. Mobility politics involve struggles to increase social mobility. Mobility politics and consumption politics are almost indistinguishable because the *degree of social mobility is highly dependent on the degree of social inequality*. Perfect mobility cannot be achieved without a considerable reduction in social inequality. The influence of inequality on mobility operates in a number of ways. Most obvious is the inheritance of property, but of increasing importance is the 'inheritance' of education. That is, in the United States, for instance, the offspring of a well-educated person is likely to live in a neighbourhood where schools are better, his peers are supportive of the value of higher education, etc. In Sweden, on the other hand, where there has been considerable class desegregation in living patterns and equalisation of school quality, these class differences are reduced, although home milieu is, of course, still important. In general, we may say that the greater the difference in life experiences between classes, the less likely it is that a person from a lower group will acquire the necessary attributes to move to a higher one.

In modern capitalism, the most important of these attributes are property and education but such factors as 'connections', dialect, or even manner of acting are still by no means irrelevant. Given the strong link between the degree of inequality and the degree of mobility, it seems clear that the alliance structure on mobility politics is similar to that on consumption politics. The reason it is useful to distinguish mobility politics is that the *manifest* focus of labour movement politics has often been mobility politics, particularly the expansion of higher education.

Figure 2.2 summarises the process of the transition to socialism according to our theory. Not only is the strength of labour organisation the key to the struggle for socialism, it is also the main causal factor in the equalisation of income and control that has occurred to date.

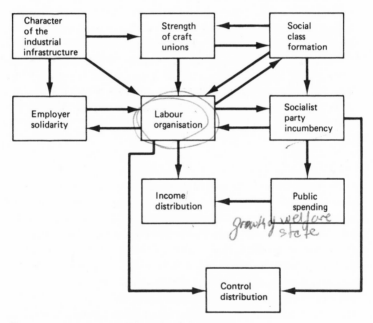

The upper arrows represent the initial causality; the lower arrows represent the feedback relationship after the process has begun

FIGURE 2.2 *The process of the transition to socialism*

3

Revolution and Reform

In this chapter, both the historic controversy over the revolutionary and reformist paths to socialism and more recent theories of the development of the welfare state will be reviewed and examined in the light of the theory laid out in the previous chapter. We will begin with the debate which ensued in the generation after Marx's death carried on by four leading theorists writing in the Marxist tradition: Karl Kautsky, Edward Bernstein, Rosa Luxemburg and V. I. Lenin. This debate involved not only the question of revolution and reform but also a number of other problems related to the transition from capitalism to socialism, such as the pace of change, the need for violence, the problem of dictatorship, the form of party organisation, the development of class consciousness and the changes in the class structure.

The early debate

As we saw, Marx believed that the possibility of a peaceful parliamentary road to socialism would be determined by the historical traditions and the flexibility of the ruling class of the country in question. Though most of Marx's followers would probably have agreed with him on this question, in point of fact virtually all of them tended to generalise from the conditions in their own countries and call for a strategy for other countries which was entirely inappropriate given the social and historical situation of the other country. This is particularly true of the Bolsheviks in the period immediately after the First World War.

Soon after Marx's death, the socialist movements of Western Europe entered into a period of rapid growth. After the lapse of the anti-socialist laws, the German party's advances were especially impressive and it came to be regarded as the vanguard of the international socialist movement. Under the leadership of August Bebel and Wilhelm Liebknecht, the German party's ideological orientation had become thoroughly Marxist. During Bismarck's repression of the socialists, Liebknecht had been extremely pessimistic about the parliamentary road to power. But after the lapse of those laws and the subsequent electoral advances, Liebknecht's and most other party leaders' attitudes changed (Cole 1956:253–4). The spectacular advances of the German Social Democrats also impressed Engels. He subsequently became more and more convinced that most countries would experience a peaceful parliamentary transition to socialism. The superiority of modern weaponry at the disposal of the police made Engels think that violent revolution was becoming increasingly difficult.

Karl Kautsky was the leading theoretician of German Social Democracy in this period, and it is in his writings that the conception of the transition to socialism which dominated the German movement can be found (Kautsky 1902, 1909, 1971). Kautsky's Marxism was very deterministic and orthodox. He accepted and repeatedly reiterated Marx's predictions of progressive centralisation of capital and polarisation of classes and repeated crises. Kautsky believed that these conditions together with continued organising and propagandising would lead to an eventual Social Democratic majority in the German Reichstag despite the distribution of seats which favoured the rural areas. Although the government was not responsible to the Reichstag, Kautsky felt, or at least hoped, that the Kaiser and his ministers would find it impossible to govern against parliament and thus be forced to give in to the Social Democrats' demand for extensive parliamentary reform, the result of which would place the party in power. Unconstitutional action was not ruled out, of course, if the government resisted. But this would only be resorted to after the Socialists had achieved a clear majority of the electorate. Once in power, the working class would move swiftly to institute socialism; first institutionalising all elements of democratic government, abolishing inheritance and passing a graduated income and wealth tax; then nationalising industries beginning with the monopoly sectors. Kautsky's time perspective for this transition was one or two decades. Like Marx's, Kautsky's parliamentary road to socialism is a revolutionary one in the sense that there is a clear break with capitalism and a rapid transition to socialism. Kautsky did think that reforms brought about some changes in the capitalist system but, again like Marx, he felt that their main value was in furthering the organisation of the working class. Socialism would not be achieved through the accumulation of reforms.

The more Marxist-oriented 'reformist' socialists such as the Social Democratic Parties in Austria and Scandinavia and the ILP in the United Kingdom shared Kautsky's perspective. Their main differences lay in the character of the parliamentary institutions in their respective countries. In the United Kingdom, the struggle was for universal suffrage. In Austria and Scandinavia the struggle was for both universal suffrage and government responsibility to parliament. In all cases, it was assumed that the ultimate outcome of democratic government would be the accession of the working class to political power.

This was the orthodoxy that Edward Bernstein (1909) attacked – or more accurately, attempted to revise – in the late 1890s. Bernstein objected that the Marxist predictions concerning the development of the social structure of capitalism were not being borne out. Centralisation was not occurring at the pace predicted and not at all in some sectors. Because of this, the spread of stock ownership and the increasing number of managers and supervisors, the predicted polarisation of classes had not happened and probably would not happen in the future. Bernstein also denied that economic crisis was inevitable and thus the future demise of capitalism in a catastrophe could not be assumed. Furthermore, the industrial proletariat strictly defined was not a majority of the population at that time and might never be one given the persistence of the middle class. Finally, the workers were not becoming increasingly impoverished but, on the contrary, their lot was actually improving. At each point, Bernstein buttressed his argument with statistics from various countries in Western Europe and the United States. For these reasons, Bernstein concluded that the transition to socialism would be gradual of necessity. Not only would the Social Democrats have to moderate their programme to appeal to the middle strata, but they would run into tremendous administrative difficulties if they attempted to socialise so many businesses all at once. Thus even in power the party would only be able to effect a gradual transition.

In his reply to Bernstein, Kautsky reaffirmed the Marxist orthodoxy on the development of capitalism, though he did admit that Marx had erred in expecting the developments to occur so rapidly.

It is often assumed that subsequent events proved Bernstein correct and Kautsky incorrect. In fact, the truth lies somewhere in between. Bernstein's argument on the development of the class structure depended primarily on his contention that the old middle classes – small businessmen and farmers – were not disappearing. He contended that the number of small farmers was actually increasing. In fact, in most advanced capitalist societies, both small businessmen and farmers have become a very small proportion of the labour force and the electorate.[1] Though Kautsky's time perspective was wrong, he was correct in asserting that the economy would be characterised by oligopolistic domination in most sectors. Even agriculture has become increasingly dominated by concerns with capital investment far beyond the means of all but the wealthiest farmers. In the United States, for example, the capital investment needed to make only an adequate living on a farm is well over $100,000. This centralisation is not at all offset by the spread of stock-ownership as Bernstein asserted. Only 8 per cent of Americans owned stock in the 1950s and only a small proportion of these can be considered middle class on the basis of the income they get from stock-ownership alone. Furthermore, as Kautsky correctly pointed out, it is centralisation of capital, not concentration of wealth, which is crucial to the transition, since it is centralisation that furthers the socialisation of labour. Bernstein actually lays very little emphasis on the expansion of propertyless non-manual employees that was to have by far the most important effects on the subsequent evolution of the class structure. On the other hand, despite his errors, the spirit of Bernstein's argument was correct: the middle class was not being crushed out of existence and this had (and has) profound implications for the speed of transition to socialism.

Had Bernstein's 'revisions' of Marxism been limited to projections on the development of the class structure, his theory would be very close to ours. But Bernstein went on to strip Marx's theory of one of its essential elements – the role of class struggle in changing the social order. He began by asserting that economic factors were playing less and less a role in determining social development in 'modern' society (as he calls it), and conscious human action a greater and greater role. It would be going too far to say that Bernstein adopted an 'organic' model of society but it is definitely true that he played down the role of *class* action, as opposed to the action of individual men, in his theory of the evolution to socialism. He went so far as to argue that 'the rights of the propertied minority have ceased to be a serious obstacle to social progress' (Bernstein 1909:218). To say this in Wilhelmine Germany was all the more outrageously untrue. It is Bernstein's de-emphasis of class struggle in the process of change that makes him, along with the Fabians, the ideological forerunner of post-Second World War social democracy. Kautsky, on the other hand, retains the central role of class struggle and working-class organisation in the transition to socialism. Though he would reject the label 'reformist', Kautsky is properly classified as a reformist Marxist since he championed a peaceful, parliamentary road to socialism built up on working-class power.

Rosa Luxemburg joined Kautsky in his attack on Bernstein's revisionism. But she parted from Kautsky on the question of the possibility of a parliamentary road to socialism. She believed that it was a great mistake to assume that the Junker military bureaucratic élite would give up its control of the German Government if the Social Democrats won a majority in the Reichstag. In that event the old regime would probably outlaw the party again. Consequently, she argued that the party should immediately begin to prepare for revolution by undertaking propaganda in the army and getting ready for illegal action. Luxemburg favoured a mass-based democratic but disciplined party which would lead a mass (or general) strike as a prelude to revolution. She believed that class consciousness was developed through political activity and thus it was of the utmost importance to involve as many people as possible in the socialist movement's activity. She did not deny the need for leadership but emphasised that the pace of revolutionary activity would be governed by the development of the masses themselves. Only through a thoroughly democratic organisation could the party remain sensitive to the consciousness of the working class while working to develop that consciousness. Though Luxemburg felt it was a mistake, a reification, to equate an elected assembly with the people's will, particularly in periods of crisis when class consciousness could explode, she was strongly opposed to dictatorship of any sort in the post-revolutionary period. She was very critical of the Bolsheviks on this account, saying that 'Freedom only for the supporters of the government . . . is no freedom at all' (Luxemburg 1961:69). Like most revolutionaries, she attributed considerable importance to a crisis in the capitalist system in bringing on the revolutionary situation (Luxemburg 1961). However, she believed that the capitalists could, indeed had, delayed the crisis through colonial expansion, which gave the capitalists new markets for goods. But this imperialist expansion was likely to lead to war between the great powers as a result of the clash over attempts to acquire and exploit foreign territories. The crumbling of capitalist regimes under the pressure of war would provide the crisis needed for socialist revolution. In summary, Rosa Luxemburg envisioned the transition to socialism as a revolution sparked by an economic or political crisis which would lead to a general strike of the class-conscious masses of the working class under the leadership of a mass-based democratic party.

Lenin's vision of the revolution was quite different. He believed that the revolution must be carried out by a disciplined centralised revolutionary party made up of a small group of dedicated revolutionaries. The central authority was to be absolute. Once a decision had been made by the party congress or, between congresses, by the central committee of the party, all members were to carry out the decision. The powers of the executive extended to appointment of the officers of the section. Lenin's insistence on the necessity of the vanguard role of the party was reinforced by his conviction that, left to itself, the proletariat would only develop 'trade union consciousness', that is, 'it may realize the necessity for combining in unions, for fighting against employers and for striving to compel the government to pass the necessary labor legislation, etc.', but, left alone, it would never see the need for a revolutionary transformation of society (Lenin 1966: 74). It was the duty of the party to bring socialist ideology, which he regarded as absolutely 'scientific' and not a matter of opinion, to the working-class movement. The party, marked out for leadership by possession of this ideology, would lead the working class to revolution. Lenin also attributed great importance to the occurrence of economic crisis as a prelude to revolutionary outbreak. The revolution would be followed by a period of the dictatorship of the proletariat in which the party, as the representative of the working class, would forcibly eliminate all remaining 'bourgeois' opposition to the revolution.

In attempting to assess who was correct in this debate on reform and revolution, the form of party organisation, and the other issues mentioned, it is important to keep in mind the settings in which these theorists were working. Lenin was attempting to bring about change in autocratic Russia, where revolutionary action was the only alternative. Rosa Luxemburg was active in the German, Russian and Polish social democratic parties and her theory was influenced by conditions in all three places. Kautsky and Bernstein, both Germans, faced a situation where organisation and political activity was legal though access to political power was extremely limited.

William Lafferty's (1971) work on the Norwegian labour movement is instructive on the question of the determinants of the political strategy adopted by social movements. His work is concerned with the reasons behind the radicalisation of the Norwegian Social Democratic Party and its entry into the Third International in the early 1920s.

To explain what caused the changes in the Norwegian situation, Lafferty makes use of a model linking together the timing and pace of economic development and Rokkan's typology of thresholds for the expression of protest and the representation of interests in a society. The thresholds are legitimation (recognition of rights of petition, criticism, opposition, etc.), incorporation (political citizenship), representation (the electoral system; is the movement's strength in parliament proportional to its strength in the electorate?), and majority power (check against majority rule, for example in a presidential system). What Lafferty showed was that, with single-member districts in Norway and the fact that, after the introduction of universal suffrage, the liberals had no basis for alliance with the Social Democrats, the latter were very underrepresented in parliament in relation to their strength in the electorate. Since the movement could not use the established political institutions to advance their demands, they began to regard bourgeois democracy as a sham and turned to a syndicalist strategy and joined the Third International. However, apparently as a result of changes in the system of political representation, the movement returned to a more moderate course and dropped out of the Third International.[2] What this example suggests is that the basic choices in political strategy are determined by the openness or closure of the political system. If all protest is illegal, then only conspiratorial revolutionary movements are possible. If protest is legal, but the movement is denied political representation and has little chance of getting it, a mass revolutionary movement is likely. Thus both the question of revolutionary or reformist strategies and the form of party organisation are heavily conditioned by the political situation in a given country. This includes not only the formal properties of the system mentioned above but also the attitudes of other social classes, parties and movements toward the labour movement. For instance, the exclusion of the French and Italian Communist Parties from any share in political power at the national level since the late 1940s has certainly played a role in maintaining their revolutionary rhetoric despite their increasingly reformist strategy in practice.

We are not arguing that there is a one-to-one relationship between the degree of openness of a political system on the one hand, and party structure and political strategy on the other. Other factors, such as the historical inheritance of a party, are very important. For instance, the highly centralised structure of the German Social Democratic Party, necessitated by the conditions of repression under Bismarck's anti-socialist laws, was maintained after the lapse of those laws. However, even the Bolshevik party opened up and became more democratic during the brief period of freedom that existed during the 1905 revolution (Cole 1956: 250, 462–3). Keeping in mind the importance of the openness of the political system, let us return to our four theorists and examine their theories in respect to both the situation they faced and the democratic conditions prevailing for a brief period after the First World War, and for the entire period after the Second World War.

There is hardly any question that a revolutionary strategy was the only possibility in Tsarist Russia. This was not a point of contention with the Mensheviks, Social Revolutionaries or even many bourgeois democrats at the time. It is also probably correct that Lenin's form of party organisation was the most effective in such a situation, though to claim that the February Revolution would not have occurred without the Bolsheviks would definitely be stretching the facts. The real question about Lenin's strategy concerns the transition to socialism, which supposedly began with the October Revolution. The material conditions for socialism – the absence of scarcity and fully socialised labour – were not present in Russia in 1917. Both Lenin and Trotsky recognised this, but they, following Marx, hoped that the Russian Revolution would set off a revolution in the West. When this did not happen, it had serious consequences for the possibilities of socialism in Russia. Since the working class was a small minority of the population and peasants with their petty bourgeois ideals were the large majority, the development of socialism was unlikely under conditions of universal suffrage even if Lenin had wanted it, which he did not. However, this in itself did not cause the tragedy that befell Russia. Nor was the Allied invasion decisive. A true dictatorship of the proletariat, a state based on the enfranchisement of dependent workers only, as suggested by Plekhanov (Cole 1956: 433), could have been set up. The fact that it was not is directly related to the elitist authoritarianism inherent in Lenin's thought: the highly centralised party structure, the assumption of the limited consciousness of the masses, and the absolute certainty of possession of the scientific truth. All this led to a dictatorship by the party and not the proletariat. This was by no means a Stalinist perversion; the suppression of all opposing parties with roots in the working class and all opposing tendencies in the trade unions began under Lenin's leadership.

Is a Leninist strategy a viable one for advanced capitalist democracies? Two questions must be addressed here. First, is it likely that a Leninist party could lead a successful revolution? Second, would that revolution result in democratic socialism? To answer these questions, let us look at Lenin's and Trotsky's critique of 'bourgeois democracy'. They claim that socialism can never be achieved through purely parliamentary methods. This, despite the fact that both still cling to the Marxist orthodoxy concerning the development of the class structure: the working class was or would be the large majority of the population. Yet, based on their analysis of consciousness development and the nature of the state, both theorists argue that the working class would be unable to use parliamentary institutions to achieve socialism. Neither theorist presents a very convincing case why this is so. In their defence, it can be said that neither lived to see the capitalist world as the stable democratic order which it became only after the Second World War. Lenin died in 1924 in a period of turmoil in Europe, and if anything the conditions had worsened with the rise of fascism and the advent of the depression before Trotsky's death in 1939. But their attitudes toward bourgeois democracy are worth considering, if only because they form the basis for more recent Leninist critiques. Trotsky emphasised, in the period immediately following the First World War, that because the peasants were under the ideological domination of the bourgeoisie, the working class could not achieve a majority in parliament at that time. But what about when the working class became a majority? Part of the answer lies, we think, in Lenin's view of class consciousness and the role of leadership. Because he put so little faith in the spontaneous development of class consciousness and so much in the ability of leaders to inculcate the working class with the proper ideas, Lenin naturally blamed the leaders of the working-class movement for the lack of class-conscious action. Lenin may be correct on the question of trade union consciousness, but he clearly exaggerates the extent to which the leadership could influence, and thus was responsible for, the level of consciousness in the working class. Furthermore, even if one were to accept his analysis, there is no reason why new leadership could not encourage the development of 'reformist' class consciousness and thus bring the working-class party to victory at the polls.

Lenin argued that the numerous petty restrictions of bourgeois democracy, such as residence qualifications for voting and obstacles to the right of assembly, served *de facto* to exclude the poor from politics. While, as the US case shows, there is something to be said for his point, it is simply not true that this is an inevitable condition in capitalist society. In Sweden, for example, trade union electoral mobilisation on behalf of the Social Democrats has resulted in the elimination of class differentials in voting turn-outs.

Whereas Lenin and Trotsky never provide an adequate explanation of why a majority cannot be won, they are on much more solid ground when they argue that even if the socialists did get a majority for a socialist programme, they would not be able to put it through. Here we come to the very core of Lenin's argument against a parliamentary road to socialism. The proletariat cannot, he says in *The State and Revolution* (1966: 354–63), use the bourgeois state for its own ends; it must smash the state. The old bureaucratic apparatus cannot be used to institute socialism. Why? Lenin (1934: esp. 21–2) clarifies this in his reply to Kautsky's attack on the concept of the dictatorship of the proletariat in which Kautsky points out that Marx believed that a democratic transition from capitalism to socialism was possible in England and America. That was true in the 1870s, says Lenin, because of the absence of militarism and bureaucracy in those countries. But by 1918 this was no longer true. Everywhere the stage of monopoly imperialist capitalism had developed a bureaucratic militaristic state. In the last analysis, the military and the bureaucracy – with its bourgeois office-holders backed by the interests of monopoly capital – would thwart the socialist majority and even go so far as to suspend democracy in order to maintain class rule. Trotsky (1961) later argued that the fascist seizure of power was one manifestation of this. The recent case of Chile indicates that there is some substance to this argument. However, in the case of a very gradual transition to socialism, which we have argued is most likely in advanced capitalist democracies, it might be possible to change the character of the bureaucracy along with other institutions in society.

Let us now return to our original questions concerning a Leninist strategy. We have spent some time discussing Lenin's view of bourgeois democracy because it relates to our second question, the probable result of a Leninist revolution in the West. If anything, a Leninist type revolution is even more likely to result in an anti-democratic perversion of socialism in an advanced democracy than in an authoritarian state. It would be a *coup* against the wishes of the majority of the population. It does not really matter if it is so-called 'false consciousness' that keeps the people from seeing the necessity and desirability of socialism: a dictatorship of the minority would still be necessary. The situation would be further aggravated by the inevitable economic crisis due to capital flight, investment strikes and the resistance of high-level managers and technicians that would follow such a revolution. This would result in a further narrowing of the government's support.

Fortunately, a revolution led by a Leninist party organisation in an advanced capitalist democracy is unlikely. This type of party organisation is inappropriate in a democracy, as was previously pointed out. Any party adopting strict Leninist principles of party organisation is doomed to social isolation. Given that such a party's *coup* would be against majority opinion, it is unlikely that the ruling groups, the police and the army would not unite against the *coup* once it had occurred. History shows that serious divisions in the ruling class and neutralisation of the army are necessary conditions for the successful seizure of power.

If a revolution ever does occur in a Western democracy, it is more likely to follow the path laid out by Rosa Luxemburg. A mass-based democratic party might, under the correct conditions, be able to carry out a revolution. A possible scenario might be the following: the labour movement develops a high degree of labour organisation and through educational work promotes a very high level of class consciousness among its members. But it remains isolated from political power, either because of intransigence of the centre–left parties or because the rural sector is still significant. Under these conditions, the revolutionary ideology remains a part of the party programme and is held by a very substantial minority of the population. Then the system enters into a severe crisis. In modern society, a crisis brought on by war is out of the question. A limited foreign war such as the Vietnamese war would probably be insufficient and a war between the great powers would be a prelude to the destruction of humanity, not the socialist revolution. The economic crises accompanied by massive agitation by the labour movement and a general strike would lead to an 'explosion' of consciousness among social groups hitherto touched by, but not deeply penetrated by, the labour movement. A revolutionary majority is created. At this point, the army becomes the primary obstacle. To neutralise the army as well as some of the moderate elements of the opposition, it seems to us that some sort of legitimation of the socialist accession to power would have to occur, probably through a special parliamentary election or a plebiscite. This would bring the socialists to power. Since creating a bureaucracy *de nouveau* is impossible, the government would face the problem of securing the compliance of bureaucratic officials. More serious would be the economic crisis. If the crisis was not the occasion for the government's coming to power, a crisis would certainly be created by the capitalists at this point. To avoid defeat (or the development of dictatorship), the government would have to return to the people for support in four to seven years after their accession to power, depending on the political traditions of the country in question. By this time, they would either have to have improved the economic situation or to depend on the absence of any erosion of the consciousness created in the 'explosion' in the face of the continued economic difficulties. Such a scenario is only imaginable in Italy and possibly in France. The possibility of this type of situation hinges on a severe crisis, the occurrence of the explosion of consciousness and its maintenance, and the neutralisation of the army.

What we have tried to do here is to adapt Rosa Luxemburg's ideas to a modern situation. In her time, the conditions were quite different. She was correct in her contention that Kautsky and the German Social Democrats were mistaken in thinking that the Junker militaristic government would give in without a fight once the Social Democrats had attained a majority. That they later showed that they preferred the Nazis and the Third Reich over the Social Democrats and Weimar is strong evidence in favour of this argument. The end of the Wilhelmine government did come in a revolution which was set off by an imperialist war, just as Luxemburg had predicted. But it was not a socialist revolution. In November 1918, a socialist revolution in Germany was a definite possibility had the majority socialists been willing to lead it or simply support it, which they never would have done. However, it is incorrect to assume that the German leadership betrayed the masses, who were ready for revolution. As Harrington (1972:193) points out, 'every time the working class was consulted during this period – in the Congress of Councils, in the elections, in the relative membership strength of the parties appealing to socialist consciousness – they gave their support to the conservative wing of the movement'. What the German Social Democratic leaders can be faulted for was that, in a clearly revolutionary situation, they did not lead the masses: they followed them. The real crime of the leadership, we now know, was that they did not even carry out a complete bourgeois revolution. If they had destroyed the Junker control of the military and the bureaucracy, especially in the legal system, instead of allying with it, and if they had carried out land reforms in the East Elbian countryside, the Nazi's seizure of power might have been avoided.

While Kautsky was incorrect in his assumption that the working class could have achieved universal suffrage through peaceful means in Germany, his analysis did hold for many other European countries, such as the Scandinavian countries. But it did not have the results he expected, that is, a great socialist majority and consequently a rapid transition to socialism. All over Europe, the consequences of universal suffrage were the same for the socialists: they were a minority, often a very large minority, but still a minority. And it became increasingly apparent that the socialists would never get the huge majority that the pre-war Marxists, such as Kautsky, had hoped for. Because of the evolution of the class structure, a rapid parliamentary transition to socialism was now out of the question. The problem for those advocating a parliamentary road to socialism was whether piecemeal reforms could lead to socialism, and if so, how. Bernstein and the Fabians had already given their answer. Kautsky and his followers had to make some reassessment. Before the First World War, they had objected to the idea that piecemeal reform could lead to socialism because many reforms, particularly nationalisation, would strengthen the state. But the advent of democracy had changed things. Legislative reforms, they argued, were now the means of transition to socialism. The orthodox socialists favoured nationalisation, with compensation to the old owners paid for by a progressive income tax. But policy was not the problem. The problem was political support.

The contemporary controversy

Some of the important points of controversy in the early debate on reform and revolution have been decided by history. First, the development of the class structure was closer to Bernstein's projections than to Kautsky's. Propertyless non-manual workers are a large and growing proportion of the electorate everywhere. The living standards of workers have risen in absolute terms during most of the post-war era. Second, the struggle for democracy in the advanced capitalist societies has been won. The contemporary debate turns largely around the question of whether or not these democratic institutions can be used to achieve socialism. One of the main points of contention concerns the meaning of the development of the welfare state. What has caused the development of the welfare state? Has it changed capitalism by redistributing income and wealth? Can socialism be achieved by the same methods used in the development of the welfare state?

One would suppose that reformist Social Democrats, even those who had largely given up their socialist vision, would agree with the opinion we expressed in the last chapter, that is, that the growth of the welfare state was a product of the struggle of the labour movement to transform capitalism. This is indeed what we found in our interviews with Swedish socialist leaders. But Bernstein and the Fabians – and not Kautsky and the Austro-Marxists – are the intellectual fathers of most of modern reformism, particularly as it is expressed in the theory and practice of the UK Labour Party and the German Social Democratic Party. They forget that they had to fight for those reforms and conclude that the reforms developed completely within the capitalist system rather than representing a step towards transforming it.

C. A. R. Crosland's *The Future of Socialism* (1967) is typical of this point of view. In Crosland's view, the welfare state has resulted in very substantial redistribution of income and thus represents a substantial change in capitalism. But he goes further than this to claim that property ownership now plays such a minor role in determining economic control and political power that modern society cannot properly be called capitalist in the traditional sense. Though the growth of trade unionism has played some role in this change, it is definitely a secondary factor. Technological and economic developments inherent in modern industry are primarily responsible for the shift of power away from property. Of central importance is the separation of ownership and control and the growth of corporate size and complexity, which have resulted in a shift of power to the managers, technicians and bureaucrats. The manager is salaried and thus is not dependent on profit. He can and does make decisions based on concerns other than profit, such as public opinion. Because of this independence, management has been influenced by a general process of enlightenment, a broad constant shift leftward in the 'moral consensus of opinion' which Crosland sees present in modern society. It is this leftward move in public opinion which was responsible for the development of the welfare state. To be sure, party politics played a role in this reform process. But the parties represent a struggle between progressive and *status quo* ideals, not a struggle between classes. The state reflects the moral consensus of opinion rather than the distribution of power in civil society.

Crosland argues that ownership is increasingly irrelevant. In his opinion, control relations in the enterprise are a product of complex and large-scale factory organisation, not of the form of ownership. Some changes in control relations are possible but they can only be achieved through enlightened management and enlightened union-ism, not through changes in the ownership structure. And because of the managerial revolution and the development of government economic controls such as fiscal policy and monetary policy, the property-holding class no longer is able to control the direction of social development. Finally, the influence of property ownership on the distribution of income, though still substantial, is declining. Thus Crosland draws the conclusion that achieving socialism is primarily a matter of changing the distribution of income along with some dispersion of stock ownership. He caps his argument for 'distributive socialism' with the contention that the tendency of capitalism to produce for profit rather than need is a product of the unequal distribution of income: 'if purchasing power is distributed more equally, it becomes more profitable to produce necessities and less profitable to produce luxuries' (Crosland 1967:56). Consequently, consumption and mobility politics entirely dominate Crosland's programme of reform. Socialisation of income rights, promotion of high levels of employment, and expansion of educational opportunities: this is Crosland's path to socialism.

Crosland can be faulted on several points which follow from our theoretical discussion in the last chapter. First, his view of the cause of the development of the welfare state is completely inadequate. It was the growing strength of labour organisation that caused the shift leftward in public opinion that brought the Labour Party to power and thus was responsible for the passage of the welfare state reforms of the late 1940s. Consequently, the state is not an independent force but, in fact, is highly dependent on the distribution of power in civil society. Crosland, like most right-wing Social Democrats, reifies 'public opinion'. It is public opinion that limits the progress to socialism, they say. But if our model is correct, public opinion is nothing but a reflection of class consciousness, which in turn is a product of definite social forces, one of which is the level of labour organisation. Furthermore, people can affect this process; there is a dialectical relation between communal action and labour organisation. 'Public opinion' should not be accepted as a given.

Crosland's second error is his assumption that ownership does not matter much any more. We addressed this question at length in the last chapter, so we will refer the reader back to our discussion there and only mention a few specific points here. First, Crosland's view that control relations in the enterprise are a product of technology and have little to do with ownership is based on his observation that control relations were no different in nationalised UK enterprises than in private ones. This fact does not prove anything. The state enterprises were run by the same criteria – profitability and efficiency – that the private ones were. As long as the management is judged solely on these criteria, and not on its relationship with and accountability to the workers, it is obvious that control relations will be the same. Second, Keynesian policy, taxation, state control of credit, investment incentives and similar policies are not sufficient tools to give the state, even under socialist tenure, full control over social development. These tools, important though they are, leave untouched broad areas of corporate decision-making which have profound effects on society. Plant location, product choice, advertising, investment and pricing are only a few examples of decisions that must be directly socialised in order to attain social control of them. And any of these tools must be combined with substantial curtailment of corporate secrecy to be effective. This brings us to our third criticism of Crosland. It is difficult to tax corporate income rights effectively, because the company accounts can often be manipulated. Or the taxes can be passed on to the consumer or worker. Or capital growth rather than profit can be opted for, and so on. Crosland's other suggestion to change the distributive effects of capital ownership – changing the distribution of capital – is equally difficult to implement, for reasons pointed out in the last chapter. His only realistic proposal is to increase collective ownership through the use of pension funds. Finally, because of these problems, we find his argument that private enterprise will produce for social needs given a more equal income distribution hard to swallow.

Some academics have gone a step further than Crosland in their analysis of the growth of the welfare state. They maintain that not only is class struggle irrelevant for the development of the welfare state but so is political struggle. Incumbency makes no difference. Wilensky (1975:xiii) for instance, argues that 'economic growth and its demographic and bureaucratic outcomes are the root cause' of the growth of the welfare state. He contends that the political ideology of the government makes very little difference for welfare state expenditure. Wilensky bases his conclusions on an extensive analysis of cross-national data. If correct, his finding would obviously seriously weaken our argument that the welfare state is a product of labour organisation and political rule by labour parties and thus represents a first step toward socialism.

A similar challenge to our contention comes from the academics who have studied income distribution. There is some disagreement among these writers as to what the actual trends in income distribution are and what effects economic growth and affluence have. Pareto and his followers (Pareto 1971; Kuznets 1966; Jackman 1975) contend that there is a long-term trend towards equality, which is a product of the changes in market forces caused by growth and the level of affluence. Others argue that, in fact, in the post-war period, there has been little change in income distribution, thus economic growth does not have any equalising effect (Titmuss 1963; Roberti 1974; Kolko 1962). Both of these schools agree that politics and trade union organisation have little effect on income distribution *before* taxes. Generally, these academic studies, both on income distribution and the welfare state, do not deny that taxation and public spending can result in a redistribution of income.

The contention that the welfare state has no redistributive effect does have adherents, many of whom base their critiques of post-war social democracy and reformist socialism in general on this contention. Frank Parkin's (1971) work is a typical example of this line of reasoning. Parkin bases his case on three propositions. First, the political composition of governments has no effect on income distribution before taxes are levied. Second, the expansion of the public sector is also unrelated to political incumbency. Finally, the welfare state does not involve a redistribution between classes anyway. It simply transfers income from the young to the old, the single to the married, the healthy to the sick, etc., all within the same class. This is so because various regressive indirect taxes neutralise the effect of the progressive income tax, and many social services, such as education, actually benefit higher classes disproportionately. Thus, the welfare state represents no real change in capitalism and may even have positive effects for the dominant class, since it may prevent demands for more radical change from arising.

Why has social democracy had so little effect on distribution and welfare spending in Parkin's view? He argues that the party leadership shifted its ideological emphasis from redistribution to meritocracy. This shift was not due to an embourgeoisement of the party's base, the working class. If the working class has become more conservative, it is because of the shift in leadership ideology, and not vice versa. Furthermore, the need to appeal to middle-class voters was only a secondary reason for deradicalisation. Drawing on Michels, Parkin argued that the party and trade union bureaucrats developed a vested interest in the system. This interest was only increased when the parties took a share in governmental power and came under pressure to act 'responsibly', that is to say, conservatively.

We will address the arguments of Parkin, as well as those of Wilensky and the other authors mentioned, on the welfare state and distribution in the next chapter, since they rest on empirical data and their errors are methodological. A few comments on Parkin's view of the shift in Social Democratic ideology are in order here. Contrary to what Parkin says, the important shift in ideology was not from equalisation to meritocracy, but from socialisation of production to redistribution of income (or equalisation). The expansion of higher education did become a more important part of the Social Democrats' programmes, but in most cases it was an addition, not a replacement, for the programmes designed to redistribute income. Moreover, the shift that did occur was prompted by the leadership's assessment of what reforms were possible. The bureaucratisation of the party was only secondarily responsible for their cautious assessment. It is true that the working class was not becoming more bourgeois, as some claimed. But by 1950, it was obvious to all party leaders that the industrial working class was not a majority of the population (except perhaps in Britain) and that it would never become one. Up to that year, labour parties had been able to form majority governments in only five countries.[3] Faced with a constantly increasing middle class, the leadership of all parties realised that they would have to get substantial middle-class support to gain an electoral majority. It was a question of maintaining a radical stance and remaining a minority or moderating their programme in order to win a majority and to get some changes through. Their assessment of current public opinion was, in most cases, correct.[4] Their errors were to take it as a given in the long run and to represent their moderated programme as all they had wanted in the first place.

Contemporary revolutionary socialists base their arguments for the necessity of revolutionary change on an assessment of the achievements of the welfare state and social democracy quite similar to Parkin's. The cornerstone of their analysis is their view of the state in capitalist society. The state serves the interests of the capitalist class. Thus, almost all state activity, including welfare state type programmes, function to maintain the capitalist social order. Virtually all contemporary Marxists begin their analysis of the state with this assumption (Gold *et al.* 1975: 31). The Marxist discussion of the state has focused on two questions. The first is the question of how the state serves capital. That is, what are the functions of the state for the maintenance of the capitalist order? The second question concerns policy-making process. What is the mechanism which ensures that all state policy will be in the capitalists' interest? This is particularly problematic given that most contemporary capitalist societies are formally democratic.

Generally, Marxist writers have argued that the state serves two broad functions for capital – accumulation and legitimation (O'Connor 1973; also see Offe 1972b, 1973a, 1973b, 1975; Altvater 1972; and Holloway and Picciotto 1977). In O'Connor's (1973: 6) parsimonious description, 'the state must try to maintain or create conditions in which profitable capital accumulation is possible. However, the state must also try to maintain or create the conditions of social harmony.' The conditions for accumulation include the maintenance of social peace and macro-economic stability, as well as state expenditure for capital assets which, for some reason or another, individual capitalists cannot or will not provide. Often these are collective goods which cannot easily be denied to other capitalists once they are created. Examples of this type of collective good are education and highways. The legitimation function is served through state expenditure on welfare state services, such as unemployment insurance, health care or pensions. Some authors argue that many of these welfare expenditures (for example, health care) also serve to facilitate accumulation since they lower the reproduction cost of labour power. Given that they argue that the state is the servant of capital, it is not surprising that almost all Marxists maintain that welfare state expenditure is not redistributive (e.g. Offe, 1972a: 481).

The mechanism through which a capitalist state policy is produced is a subject of controversy among Marxists. Authors such as Miliband (1969) argue that the capitalist class controls the state directly and consciously. The state is merely an instrument of the capitalist class. Critics of the 'instrumentalist' perspective have pointed out that it cannot account for the frequent instances in which state policy has been carried out despite the opposition of the business community, though in the long run the policies were in the interest of capital (Gold *et al.* 1975: 35). Furthermore, the instrumentalist perspective is unable adequately to explain how policy is produced that is in the long-term collective class interest of capital but not in the short-term interest of individual capitalists (Offe 1972b, 1973b). These two factors are also a problem for Marxists influenced by Gramsci or the Frankfurt school, who focus on the manipulation of consciousness as the primary mechanism which ensures that the democratic state serves the interests of capital.

In fact, 'the relative autonomy of the state' from the direct conscious manipulation of the capitalist class is an unsolved problem in the Marxist controversy over the state. Some writers avoid the problem by leaving the mechanism which ensures that the state performs its functions untheorised (e.g. Poulantzas 1973). To our knowledge, only Offe (1973b) has attempted to theorise the process by which the state produces policies in the interest of capital while maintaining a relative degree of autonomy from the subjective wishes of the capitalist class. Conceding that policy is shaped partly by structural constraints (for example, the threat of capital flight) and conscious instrumentation, he argues that there are constraints on state policy internal to the capitalist state itself which select pro-capitalist policies from possible alternatives. His analysis is provocative but difficult to apply to concrete situations, as he himself admits.

Having established the impossibility of reformism in their analysis of the state, the revolutionary theorists then go on to establish the possibility of revolution in their analysis of the causes of the lack of revolutionary class consciousness among the masses. Like Lenin (and Parkin for that matter), the revolutionaries attribute decisive influence to the leaders of the trade union and socialist movement in the development of working-class consciousness. If the working class is not revolutionary, it is because their present leaders have misled them; they have sold them out. Reasons given for this 'sell-out' vary, but usually include bureaucratisation of the movement, the development of middle-class life-styles on the part of its leaders and direct financial benefits gained by the party and trade union bureaucrats from the capitalist system. Given the right leadership, a revolution is possible.

The advocates of socialist revolution are divided into two camps according to their theories of party organisation like their classical predecessors. We have already argued that the Leninist version of revolution is unrealistic in modern conditions and likely to result in an anti-democratic perversion of socialism if it ever did happen. So here we will focus on the advocates of some sort of mass-based revolution. In their eagerness to deny the possibility of a reformist path to socialism, they go beyond the simple empirical proposition that all reforms to date have achieved nothing. They tend to argue that, by its very nature, the transition from one mode of production to another must involve a radical break. This is most obvious in their view of the state. They assume that the 'capitalist state' always acts in the interest of capital, no matter how well organised and class conscious the working class is. The very term, 'capitalist state', indicates that they have answered in advance the question of *whether* the state reproduces the interests of capital. The question is *how*.

Current Marxist theories of the state can be criticised on a number of points. The assertion that all state expenditure is functional for capitalism cannot be supported empirically. The tremendous variation in expenditure among capitalist societies cannot be accounted for by the varying functional needs of capital in various countries. Why does Swedish or Danish capital require that almost half of income be channelled through the state sector while Swiss and American capital only require one quarter. Furthermore, the empirical assertion that public expenditure is not redistributive is simply incorrect. In many cases it is very redistributive and it is very rarely not redistributive at all (see Chapter 5).

This is not to argue that all public sector spending is a product of the growing strength of labour organisation. Some of it is a product of the functional needs of capitalist society. Highway construction, certain minimal levels of educational spending, and perhaps some social security spending may be an absolute necessity for social survival. It might be argued that public spending in countries like the United States and Switzerland approach this functional minimum. But even here one must ask whether there is a functional alternative that is yet more pro-capitalist than the one in existence. For instance, the destruction of the extended family throws the responsibility for the care of the aged on the state in all industrial societies. And advanced industrial societies require an educated population. Some public expenditure on pensions and education is a functional necessity in industrial society. Thus on the one hand, such expenditure certainly cannot be used as an indicator that class struggle has transformed society. On the other hand, such expenditure can be financed in a number of ways and, if it is not financed in the most regressive possible way, one cannot say the policy is unambiguously capitalist (rather than 'industrial'). Or take the argument that national health insurance is functional for capitalism. This cannot be supported since there is a functional alternative that is more pro-capitalist, namely, compulsory private insurance, which both fulfils the functional need and preserves a sphere of activity for private business.

All of these problems in Marxist theory can be solved by our view of the relationship of the state to the distribution of power in civil society.[5] Furthermore, many instances of the 'relative autonomy of the state' from the opinions of the business community can be accounted for by the fact that the policy in question was initiated as a result of organised working-class pressure.[6] Thus, they are not instances of the relative autonomy of the state from power relations in civil society at all.

By criticising recent Marxist theories of the state for inadequate theorisation of the mechanism of class rule, we have begged the question for our own theory. How is it that the balance of power in civil society is translated into state policy? Capitalist democracies are historically unique societies in their combination of two characteristics. They are based on the belief among the masses that they (the masses) are sovereign. And the masses do, in fact, elect the incumbents in the state apparatus. Thus, domination in capitalist democracies rests on the subjective consent of the masses to a much greater degree than it does in traditional authoritarian or socialist authoritarian societies, which lack one or both of these characteristics. Consequently, the cornerstone of bourgeois domination is the control of 'public opinion' through control of the media and all other institutions, both public and private, as well as through the sheer weight of tradition. Antonio Gramsci (1971: esp. 210–77) can be credited with the most original and important contribution to the analysis of domination in capitalist democracies in his theorising of this phenomenon, which he called hegemony.[7] To challenge the hegemony of the bourgeoisie, the socialist movement must develop its own hegemonic presence in society through union and party organisation. Though some of the socialist movements' methods of opinion influencing will mirror bourgeois methods (for example, the establishment of a socialist press), it must rely primarily on building up a network of personal contacts through the extension of formal organisations. By far the most important form of organisation is labour organisation. Trade unions represent people in the heart of the capitalist mode of production, that is, in their role as individuals dependent on the sale of their labour power. Trade unions perform the double function in negating the pure type of capitalism by ending competition between workers and by confronting capital. And finally, since trade unions represent people in their economic role, they have a financial base that is unparalleled in any other form of popular organisation.

Gramsci's concept of hegemony allows one to link the changing distribution of power in civil society to the policy output of the state. The build-up of labour organisation, and the consequent increase in the hegemony of the socialist movement in civil society, changes the degree of class consciousness or, in the terms of mainstream sociology, the modal opinion in society. In a democratic society this will have an effect on the policy output of the state.

It should be clear from this discussion that the effect of labour organisation on state policy depends partly on the utilisation of the resources of the labour movement by its leaders. Their ideology and strategy will influence the degree to which labour organisation is translated into further working-class mobilisation, the degree and character of political consciousness of mobilised workers, etc. So it would be incorrect to discount completely the effect of leadership on working-class consciousness. But this effect has usually been in a leftist direction. That is, contact with the labour movement usually serves to pull workers out of the hegemonic domination of bourgeois society into the counter-hegemony of the labour movement. The leadership may be faulted for conservative estimates of the potentiality of change toward socialism and thus for not further radicalising the rank and file. But it is rare that the contact with the labour movement has conservatising effects on its members.[8]

Public opinion or consciousness is not the only constraint on state policy. The Marxists correctly emphasise that there are structural constraints on reform in capitalist society. Any government, left or right, must ensure the basic condition for capital accumulation. They must provide a 'good investment climate'. The threat of investment slowdowns and capital flight constantly hangs over any government embarking on a new policy of reform. Leftist governments are particularly dependent on economic growth in their attempts to expand the public sector. It is true that labour organisation places a similar structural constraint on the policy of rightist governments, as the miners' strike during the Heath government shows. While it is important to recognise this and the fact that investment strikes and capital flight are not without costs to the capitalists, the balance of influence created by these structural constraints is heavily weighted in the direction of capital even when labour is very well organised.

Revolutionaries often emphasise the resistance of incumbent bureaucrats and the military as a major barrier in using the capitalist state as an instrument of transition to socialism. For sudden changes, this is certainly true. But even for a gradualist transition, the opposition of upper-level civil servants who come predominantly from conservative backgrounds can be a constraint on policy-making, though this factor is of much less importance than structural and consciousness constraints. The military is of even less importance in day-to-day reformist policy-making.

Public opinion is not automatically reflected in the incumbents in state office. People vote for parties competing in a constitutionally structured electoral system. The relative strength of socialist and bourgeois parties is largely a result of the level of class consciousness, which, in turn, is intimately connected with the strength of organised labour. Thus party electoral strength mediates the relationship of the distribution of power in civil society to state policy formation, but makes no systematic independent contribution in and of itself. However, party electoral strength is not automatically translated into parliamentary seats and consequently into government power. The constitutional representation system often creates deviations from proportional representation. These deviations almost always hurt the left for systematic reasons. First, socialist parties have not usually been in the position to write constitutions in their own favour. At best, they have participated with other forces in reaching a compromise. The rightward biases in constitutions include such things as purposefully gerry-mandered districts, federal systems in which underpopulated (usually rural) districts are over-represented, and single-member districts which bias results against class-based as opposed to geographically-based parties. Second, rural to urban migration often results in the over-representation of rural districts, which hurts the left. In some cases, these biases in the electoral system can be very substantial.

The distribution of power in civil society sets limits on what any government can do by its determination of the consciousness and structural constraints on policy. Within this frame, the incumbent government has a certain amount of autonomy in policy-making. This is not the 'relative autonomy' referred to in Marxist discussion. As was pointed out, part of that sort of relative autonomy can be explained by the fact that the policies in question were passed as a result of working-class pressure. But not all cases of relatively autonomous state action can be explained by this factor. As Offe forcefully argues, a coherent capitalist class policy cannot be arrived at by simply summing up the special interests of individual capitals. In other words, corporate collectivism could never develop. Here, political parties and the executive's and cabinet's relation to the legislature play an important role. Governments formed by disciplined parties with a solid parliamentary base are more likely to produce coherent long-term policy due to their relatively greater insulation from special interest group pressure (see Chapter 5).

We have described the expansion of state activity as being either corporate collectivist or democratic socialist in character, depending on the country in question. In reality, all state intervention will have both aspects (though in varying degrees) given the constraints on policy-making previously outlined.

Our discussion of class consciousness is also germane to that aspect of the theory of transition proposed by revolutionary socialists. They exaggerate the power of the leadership in determining the consciousness of the working class. Their basic image is of a revolutionary consciousness just under the surface, ready to explode during a crisis and under the correct leadership. Mann (1973) argues, convincingly we think, that such 'explosions of consciousness' only take a revolutionary character where the working-class traditions have always had a strong revolutionary component, as in France and Italy. These revolutionary traditions are not something that the leadership invented but, rather, are the result of the social and political configurations of the country in question at the time of working-class mobilisation. Mann contends that the explosions of consciousness that occur during strikes in countries with reformist labour movements tend to be directed to reformist ends. Thus the question of revolution or reform is heavily conditioned by the historical inheritance of a country.

Finally, since the revolutionaries not only reject reformism but often even consider it counter-revolutionary, they end up in a state of political paralysis, particularly when they pin their hopes on some inevitable crisis of the system. In a sense, they 'sell out' the workers' immediate interest for the hope of an eventual revolution. The final irony of their strategy is that a crisis in modern society followed by revolutionary activity is more likely to result in a rightist counter-*coup* given the right-wing leanings of the military and the police in most capitalist democracies.

One of the most original and realistic theoreticians of the revolutionary left is Andre Gorz (1964). Gorz manages to stake out a middle ground avoiding the immobility of revolutionism while rejecting traditional social democratic reformism.[9] He argues that waiting for the crisis, the day of the revolution, will only lead to a dimming of class consciousness and revolutionary spirit. The socialist movement must work for immediate reforms. But it also must avoid the errors of past reformism. Reforms in the past, such as the welfare state, increased wages, etc., have done nothing to change capitalism in terms of redistribution and certainly not in terms of control. These reforms Gorz calls 'reformist' reforms, which he differentiates from 'revolutionary' or 'structural' reforms. Exactly what separates reformist and revolutionary reforms is not altogether clear, but a structural reform will have the following characteristics according to Gorz (1964: 7–9):

1. It is 'conceived not in terms of what is possible within the framework of a given system and administration, but in view of what should be made possible in terms of human needs and demands'.
2. It assumes 'a modification of the relations of power . . . that the workers will take over power or assert a force (that is to say, a non-institutionalized force) strong enough to establish, maintain and expand those tendencies within the system which serve to weaken capitalism and shake it to its joints'.
3. It is 'controlled by those who demanded it' and '*always* requires the creation of new centers of democratic power'.
4. It 'always requires a *decentralization* of the decision-making power, *a restriction on the powers of State or Capital, an extension of popular power*' thus it creates a sphere of 'autonomous power'.
5. It must be clearly linked to the achievement of socialism and not presented as an end in itself.

Gorz strongly criticises traditional reformism for not linking the immediate reforms to the socialist objective and presenting a compromise (and compromise is sometimes necessary, according to Gorz) as a complete victory rather than the partial achievement that it is. Gorz's position has been interpreted as a critique of economism and an advocacy of workers' control. To a certain extent this is correct, but he goes further than this. In Gorz's view, economist demands, demands for welfare state services and wages, can be made effective if coupled with control of the workers or the people over the implementation of the demands. It is only without this increased control that such demands achieve nothing.

The key to Gorz's strategy is the trade unions. Gorz rejects the existing political parties as too bureaucratised and compromised into the system. Only under rare circumstances such as a revolutionary mass mobilisation will the state be an instrument of change. The hostility to bureaucracy and centralisation is a central theme in Gorz's work. It leads him to reject not only political parties and the state as possible tools of change, but also to reject any centralisation of power in the labour movement. The local union and the shop steward directly elected by workers and subject to immediate recall by them should be the main actors in the socialist movement. And it is at this level that the new powers won by the working class should be invested. As unions and parties become centralised and bureaucratised, as they gain some modicum of power within the 'capitalist state', they begin to repress any demands from the workers which might challenge the system. They discipline and police the workers rather than arouse them. In Gorz's view, the party and union bureaucrats are largely responsible for repression of class consciousness. He agrees with other revolutionary theorists who see class consciousness just under the surface, ready to explode. Gorz (1973) emphasises the strike as an important occasion for such an explosion and the subsequent development of autonomous centres of workers' power controlled through direct democracy. Parliamentary action is always a reflection of 'public opinion', of repressed consciousness and thus cannot be a tool in the transition to socialism.

It should be clear by now that Gorz's theory is revolutionary, not gradualist, despite the role he assigns to reform in the process. These reforms are designed to bring the system to a crisis, not (necessarily) an economic crisis, but a political crisis, a crisis of legitimacy. By presenting a prefiguration of socialist society, structural reforms which expand workers' control and services to meet needs will reveal the inadequacies of capitalism and thus raise the general level of consciousness, preparing the way for a rapid transition to socialism. The achievement of socialism will be accomplished outside of parliamentary institutions and will ultimately result in overthrow of the capitalist state.

Gorz's most important contribution is his discussion of the relation of immediate reforms to the achievement of socialism. One of social democracy's great weaknesses is that it has tended to present reforms only as ends and has tended to exaggerate the degree to which a given reform transforms the system. Gorz is correct to emphasise the necessity of presenting reforms as intermediate demands *and* as a prefiguration of socialism. One of the great problems in building socialism is that it is difficult for most people to imagine a totally different society as a realistic practical alternative. Aside from its immediate desirable effects on society, a reform can make that alternative more realistic if the reform is presented as a prefiguration of socialism. In this respect, the struggle for workers' control is particularly important because workers' control gives people personal experience in exercising democratic control over the economic order. Furthermore, since it expands the power base of the working class, it not only entails immediate benefits but, unlike economist gains, it also strengthens the bargaining position of the movement in the next confrontation with the opposition.

However, it is not the case that all previous reforms of Social Democratic governments and trade unions are 'reformist' reforms in the sense that they did nothing to change the system and they dampened further opposition to the system. Gorz is probably correct in maintaining that socialisation of income rights in the absence of socialisation of control rights will have little effect. At the very least, control of financial information on corporations and individuals must be socialised to make taxation effective. But social democratic governments have done this and some reforms have had redistributive effects. Furthermore, even 'reforms' which have no redistributive effect, or even a negative one, are not necessarily co-optative in the sense that they prevent the working class from raising further demands. In fact, reforms more often have the opposite effect. A successful demand is likely to lead to more demands. Victory, not defeat, is radicalising. And as Gorz himself points out, the satiation of workers' immediate financial needs may well lead them to make demands for change in their impoverished work life. The disjunction between work life and leisure may make the former all the more intolerable. Only a few reforms, such as profit sharing, are co-optative by their very nature. The context in which reform is developed is at least as important as the structure of the reform. Reform introduced by conservative governments (Bismarckian or Tory socialism), particularly in the absence of working-class agitation, are likely to be co-optative. We propose the following distinctions as an alternative to Gorz's: a reform which results in the equalisation of control or income is a socialist reform because it moves society closer to socialism. A reform which does not alter distribution is a liberal reform. One which increases inequality can be termed a reactionary reform. The co-optation dimension cuts across this dimension. Only co-optative or reactionary reforms should be opposed by the socialist movement. All socialist reforms and mobilising reforms should be promoted.

Since the distributive effect of a reform is given by the structure of the reform itself, the effect will be the same in all capitalist societies. Most empirical research on the effect of reforms has focused on their distributive aspect. Very little systematic effort has been devoted to the study of the mobilising effect of reforms despite the importance of this dimension for socialist strategy. The research that has been done reveals that the matter is considerably more complicated than one might think. E. H. Stephens (1977) has shown that virtually the same reform, the institution of workers' advisory councils, had the opposite effect in Sweden, where it led to further demands for workers' control, than it did in France, where it met with working-class apathy. She attributes this difference to the strength of labour and the attitudes of working-class leaders towards the reform. She also shows that the industrial reforms of the Velasco government in Peru, which were explicitly designed to co-opt the working class, actually resulted in a massive mobilisation of the working class. In a comparative analysis of Sweden and Denmark, Esping-Andersen (1978) shows that the counter-mobilisation, or backlash, of the working class against the Danish Social Democratic Party can be linked to the contradictory nature of their policies and their failure to complement welfare policies with control over capital. Wilensky (1976) contends that less visible taxes (that is indirect taxes) generate less opposition to public spending. It can also be argued that universal social benefits create greater support for the welfare state than do means-tested benefits. These last two examples demonstrate the necessity of studying the effect of policies for the support of the left since, if the arguments are correct, the left may face a trade-off between distribution and mobilisation in some cases. If there is any one theme to these studies, it is that the mobilising, co-optative, or counter-mobilising effect of reforms has almost always been an unintended consequence of reforms. This raises considerable doubt about the contention that all past welfare statist reforms were conscious and successful attempts at co-optation.

To return to Gorz's theory, one of the reasons why Gorz rejects all past reforms is that he views the state inevitably as an instrument of capital. Thus any shifts of control to the state cannot further the cause of socialism. We would level the same criticism at Gorz on this point that we have at the other revolutionaries. Gorz's analysis of the state is related to his view of parties, trade union bureaucracy and class consciousness. Mann's criticism of the 'explosion' theory of class consciousness applies quite well to Gorz. While this theory may have some validity for France and Italy, it is not universally applicable. The primary reason for the lack of socialist consciousness (reformist or revolutionary) in the working class is not the leadership's effort to suppress it. The leadership is often to the left of the membership and almost always to the left of the electorate. The failure of the socialist movement to develop a hegemony in civil society is the cause of the absence of socialist class consciousness. The class-conscious socialist proletarian mass of past times is a great myth. Militant *socialist* workers have probably never been a majority of the working class outside of France and Italy and nowhere have socialists been a majority of the population. The class consciousness of workers in the past has usually been inferred from the radicalism of movement activists, who are almost always the most leftist elements of the population. Gorz himself raised the 'new working class' to the position of a vanguard in the revolution partly on the basis of their militancy which he believed indicated a high level of class consciousness.[10]

Gorz's mistaken view on class consciousness leads him to a position on party organisation and union structure which makes his proposal for the transition to socialism unworkable. Direct democracy is to be maintained and delegation of power avoided at all costs. This is a completely unrealistic way to carry out a revolution. In the power vacuum that would result from the fall of the old regime, a unified mass movement with a coherent programme planned in advance would have to step in to exercise power. Without this, the revolution would deteriorate into anarchy. In all fairness to Gorz, it should be pointed out that his most extreme opposition to party and union bureaucracy came in the wake of the collapse of the May 1968 rebellion in France, where the French Communists might be rightfully accused of impeding the progress of revolution. With some concessions in the direction of the 'neo-Luxemburgist' model we suggested earlier, his proposal for revolution might be workable (for example, see Poulantzas 1978).

But if a revolutionary situation never developed, which is likely, Gorz's strategy would actually be counter-productive to the advance toward socialism. A gradual transition to socialism can never be achieved through a syndicalist strategy. Even gains made through trade union struggle must be backed up and institutionalised through legal changes effected by the state. Furthermore, a labour movement as decentralised as Gorz favours would be impotent, especially when faced by a highly centralised and solidaristic capitalist opposition. In fact, as we will show, a high degree of centralisation in the labour movement is associated with greater labour organisation, more solidarity among workers, higher levels of class consciousness, and consequently greater advances toward socialism.

Of course, Gorz (1964: esp. 98–9) contends that such a gradualist strategy is impossible. This contention is partly based on his image of the explosion of class consciousness in a crisis situation as the tipping point, the radical break between capitalism and socialism. Perhaps more important, Gorz and most revolutionaries argue that at some point in the reform process the capitalists would draw the line. When the core of their power is threatened, they will resort first to investment strikes and capital flight to wreck the economy and bring down the government and, if necessary, they would not hesitate to use force. Again the Chilean case indicates that this argument cannot be dismissed. Gorz also seems to think a true mixture of the capitalist and socialist modes of production would be an inherently unstable system and would have to give way to one system or the other. But in the final analysis, we think Gorz resorts to the reification of capitalism and the capitalist state that is so common among contemporary Marxists.

In this chapter, we have argued that the question of reform or revolution and related problems, such as party organisation, are heavily conditioned by the social and historical situation of a given movement. Both reformist and revolutionary paths to socialism are possibilities, though a revolutionary transition to socialism is very unlikely outside of France and Italy. But in a sense, the whole debate on which strategy to choose is a sterile one, because the immediate task of the socialist movement is exactly the same whatever one's assessment is of what the capitalists will do in the eleventh hour or at the point of crisis. In advanced democracies, the socialist movement must be a mass movement based on organised labour with the immediate goals of instituting mobilising socialist reforms which are presented as a prefiguration of the future society. In the long run, the movement must try to organise as much of the population as possible and develop a hegemonic presence in the life of the society. Trade union and parliamentary activity are equally important for the movement.

4

Labour Organisation and the Welfare State: a Cross-national Analysis

We have claimed that the growth of the welfare state is a product of the growing strength of labour in civil society and that it represents a step toward socialism. This claim is the key to our contention that a parliamentary road to socialism is a possibility and, indeed, is under way. If our opponents are correct in their assertions that reforms have achieved nothing or that the socialist movement is not responsible for the growth of the welfare state, then our theory falls. On the other hand, if we can present empirical evidence to show that labour organisation is responsible for the growth of the welfare state and a redistribution of income and control, then our position will be considerably strengthened. We now turn to that task.

The empirical evidence on which our hypotheses concerning the role of the socialist movement in developing the welfare state and increasing equality rests will be presented in this chapter and the next. To avoid the narrowness of previous studies, two approaches for verification of our hypothesis will be used, a cross-sectional data analysis and a historical comparison of a few selected countries. We begin with the former.

Sample and measurement

The sample for the cross-national analysis is seventeen developed Western capitalist democracies. The only capitalist countries that have had continuous democratic government since the Second World War not included are several European countries with populations of less than one million, and Japan. This sample is obviously the most appropriate one to test our theory on the relationship of labour organisation to the development of the welfare state and the possibility of a democratic transition to socialism in the developed capitalist world. It has the further advantage that the variables measured are much more strictly comparable than in the case of studies that lump together democratic and authoritarian developed and underdeveloped societies. In fact, one of the main flaws of previous research of this type has been measurement error, particularly on political variables, due to the fact that such social phenomena as labour unions or government ideology play an entirely different role in underdeveloped and/or authoritarian regimes than they do in developed democracies.

The exclusion of Japan from the sample does require some comment. Stein Rokkan (1973) argues that the most fruitful way to analyse macro-social and political phenomena is through the construction of historically specific models for a limited number of geo-cultural areas such as Western Europe, Latin America or Sub-Saharan Africa. Within these area/history-specific configurations, explanatory models can be developed using a few comparable variables, dimensions and historical events. All developed capitalist democracies except Japan share a Western European cultural and historical heritage. In earlier analyses, we found that Japan was consistently a deviant case in terms of the causes and patterning of voting behaviour, labour movement ideology, level of labour organisation, and party configuration, to name a few points.[1] Thus we have chosen to exclude Japan and make no claim to universal validity for the relationships established here. This does not reduce the significance of the findings here for the development of socialism elsewhere. Because of the economic dominance of the western capitalist world, any important social development there has world historical significance.

The appropriate measure for the level of labour organisation depends on the focus of the analysis. If one wishes to get an idea of the vitality of the labour movement or its strength *vis-à-vis* the employers, then a measure of membership density, such as the percentage of non-agricultural employees organised, is the best measure. Our interest here is primarily in measuring the distribution of power in civil society or the hegemony of the socialist movement in society. In this case, the percentage of the labour force organised is more appropriate. Data on trade union organisation in 1930 and 1970 expressed with both percentaging bases was collected. Since it seems possible that the unity and the ideology of the labour movement might influence socialist hegemony, measures for these two variables were developed. Each movement was coded on the basis of whether the largest trade union confederation was social democratic, Communist, Catholic or 'independent'. If the second largest confederation with a distinct ideological orientation had more than 10 per cent of the total organised workers, the movement in question was coded as a divided movement. Separate white-collar confederations were not considered to indicate an ideological split in the movement.

In order to examine the role of the state in the development towards socialism, a measure of political rule by socialist parties was developed. A score of one was given for each year of rule by socialist parties (social democratic and/or Communist) from 1945 to 1970. For coalition governments including socialist parties, the number of parliamentary seats held by socialists was divided by the total number of seats held by the governing parties. These fractions were then totalled for the twenty-five year period. Another index of leftism was constructed by averaging the percentage of votes cast for socialist parties for elections between 1945 and 1970. We predicted that this index would explain less variation in welfare state development since it measured political sympathies rather than effective political power.

Data were collected for a number of other variables which we hypothesised to be intervening or antecedent variables or which were claimed by others to be related to welfare spending or income distribution. Measures of ethnic and linguistic diversity and the Catholic proportion of the population were taken from Taylor and Hudson (1972). These measures are generally for the mid-1960s. Various US government and UN publications were the sources for 1970 data on GDP, GDP per capita, age of the social security system, percentage of the labour force engaged in agriculture, population, and percentage of the population over sixty-five years of age. Each country was coded according to whether or not the form of government was federalist. The representational system was coded according to whether it called for some form of proportional representation or for single-member districts. Countries which changed systems were given a fractional score.

In Chapter 2, concentration and centralisation of capital was hypothesised to be related to the degree of labour organisation. In attempting to assess the empirical validity of this argument, we ran into considerable difficulties. A number of processes are related to the centralisation and concentration process. According to Marx and most modern Marxists, the following are effects of these twin processes:

1. The average size of production establishments increases.
2. The average size of production enterprises (one or more establishments under common ownership) increases.
3. The number of individual capitals which dominate production in each branch of the economy decreases (monopolisation).
4. The number of individual capitals which dominate production in the economy decreases (conglomeration).
5. Ownership of industry becomes more concentrated and thus the distribution of wealth becomes more unequal.
6. Control in the economy becomes considerably more concentrated.

Points 1 to 4 are by and large correct, though the magnitude of change is not nearly as impressive as most contemporary Marxists assume (Pryor 1973: Chapters IV and VI).[2] Point 5 is only true if the expansion of collective ownership through the state and pension funds is ignored. Point 6, the concentration of control, is definitely correct, but only if one ignores the expansion of public control in cases where the labour movement is strong politically and economically. What is more important for the present analysis is that these aspects do not co-vary across the nations in our analysis. Thus individual measures for each must be obtained.

Frederic Pryor (1973) has developed measures for the first four of these aspects of concentration and centralisation. Establishment and enterprise size can be measured by the simple arithmetic average of the labour force in establishments or enterprises. Conglomeration, economy-wide centralisation, can be measured by the percentage of the labour force employed by the 200 largest enterprises. Pryor's measure for monopolisation or branch-level centralisation is a bit more complicated. The basic statistic used in the measure is the four-firm concentration ratio, that is, the percentage of employment, shipments or production that is accounted for by the four largest enterprises in a narrowly defined industry. Using pairs of similarly defined industries, for the United States and each foreign country, Pryor computes a weighted average of the overall concentration (centralisation, in Marx's terminology) of the two countries with the foreign country's average concentration expressed as a ratio to the United States. Unfortunately, Pryor was only able to find data on about half of the countries in our sample for all indices except average establishment size for which he presents complete data.

Comparable cross-national data on the distribution of wealth for a sufficient number of countries do not exist. Data for Sweden, the United States and the United Kingdom will be presented in the next chapter. Not only do no data exist for the distribution of control, it is almost impossible to develop a convenient quantitative measure for it. This is unfortunate for two aspects of our analysis. First, the relative balance of democratic and private control is one of the two main indicators of the state of transition to socialism. Second, the centralisation of control in the private sector which results from the separation of ownership and control in the modern corporation and the consequent usurpation of control by corporate directors, management and financial intermediaries may be related to the strength of the labour movement.

To measure trade union centralisation we used an indicator developed by Headey (1970). It is an additive index based on the central confederation's powers over bargaining and strikes, its financial resources and the size of its staff. Headey presents data for fourteen of the seventeen countries in our sample. Wilensky (1976) adds comparable data for the three remaining countries and corrects inaccuracies in Headey's data for two countries. Information on the degree of centralisation of bargaining for half of our sample can be found in Hibbs's (1976: 1049) discussion of strikes. He classifies countries according to three modal types: (1) decentralised systems – enterprise or establishment-level bargaining (for example, the United States) or 'anarchic' labour relations with some minimal multi-employer bargaining that imposes few restraints on local bargaining (for example, Italy); (2) centralised systems – industry-wide bargaining or multi-employer bargaining with industry-wide constraints (for example, the United Kingdom); and (3) highly centralised systems – economy-wide bargaining or industry-wide bargaining with economy-wide constraints (for example, Sweden). For our analysis, we coded the three types of bargaining 1, 3 and 5 respectively and gave a score of 4 to the countries which had moved from a centralised to a highly centralised system or vice versa in the post-war period (Belgium and Netherlands). We also complemented Hibbs's sample with information on the rest of the countries in our sample (Roberts 1968; Headey 1970; Reichel 1971; Yerbury and Isaac 1971).[3]

In his work on the causes of welfare state development in industrial democracies, Wilensky (1976) argues that the degree of 'corporatist democracy', along with the proportion of the population over sixty-five, are the main determinants of the expansion of social security spending. A corporatist democracy has the following four characteristics according to Wilensky:

1. Strongly organised and centralised interest groups, especially labour, employer and professional associations, interact with the government to come to a consensus on social and economic policy.
2. The peak bargains struck by these associations reflect a blurring of the distinction between public and private.
3. These associations produce a social contract.
4. Social policy is absorbed into general economic policy.

Wilensky (1976:21–4) develops an index of corporatism, or 'corporatist-technocratic linkages' as he calls it, by weighing equally the appointment powers of the central government and Headey's index of trade union centralisation.

Though Wilensky's hypothesis concerning corporatism should be seriously considered, his index does not measure what he claims it does. An absolute prerequisite for a country to be labelled corporatist according to Wilensky is that it be characterised by highly centralised bargaining. In two of the countries which are well above the mean on his measure, France and Italy, the establishment level is the most important point at which bargaining occurs. In this situation it is impossible to absorb wage policy into general economic and social policy and, in fact, governments of these countries have not been able to institute an incomes policy in the post-war period. Furthermore, the trade union centrals in both France and Italy are very weak and thus would be unable to enforce any centrally negotiated wage agreements. Headey documents that a moderate to high degree of trade union centralisation is a necessary condition for the development of an incomes policy. Wilensky's index should have been interactive instead of additive, both government centralisation and interest group centralisation are necessary for the formation of a unified national social and economic policy through bargaining between labour, capital and the government. The centralisation of labour and employers' organisations can be measured by Headey's index or by the centralisation of bargaining. This does not explicitly measure employers' federation centralisation but, of necessity, the power in both employer and labour organisations will be concentrated at the level at which the bargaining occurs. Since only those countries with economy-wide bargaining can be designated as potentially 'corporatist',[4] our scale of bargaining centralisation should be dichotomised on that basis, yielding seven countries with highly centralised bargaining: Sweden, Norway, Finland, Denmark, Austria, Belgium and Netherlands. These seven countries are also all of the countries above the mean on the index of union centralisation. Of the seven countries, only Belgium did not successfully institute an explicit or *de facto* incomes policy for a substantial part of the post-war period (Headey 1970). Furthermore, these were the only countries that managed to do so. In terms of government centralisation, federalism is perhaps the best measure. Austria is the only federalist government of the seven with highly centralised bargaining. However, Austrian federalism is very weak. The fact that the country did develop a wages policy through explicit bargaining between capital, labour and the government argues that the Austrian form of government is sufficiently centralised to qualify Austria as a 'corporatist democracy'.

To determine the relationship between social mobility and social inequality, data on social mobility were collected. Data on ten countries presented by S. M. Miller (1960) and Erikson (1976) on the degree of downward mobility as measured by outflow rates from non-manuals to manuals and on Miller's index of opportunity are the best mobility data now available. An index of equality of educational opportunity similar to Miller's social mobility index was constructed using OECD data on thirteen of the countries (OECD 1971). This index measures the relative advantage of middle-class offspring over working-class offspring in the probability of attending university. Even aside from the problem of missing data, the mobility measures leave much to be desired. The Miller data are not strictly comparable and by now are very old. The education data are more recent, mid-1960s, but do not measure comparable phenomena in the countries. In countries such as the United States, where university attendance is very high, university attendance gives the student sure entry into non-manual or at best upper middle-class status. In countries such as Switzerland, where university attendance is extremely restricted, a university education is a ticket into the élite.

The dependent variables proved somewhat more difficult to operationalise than the independent variables. Only the measurement of welfare state effort was straightforward. The percentage of GNI devoted to non-military public spending is our primary indicator of welfare state effort.

Since measuring the distribution of control proved impossible, the greatest possible effort was made to collect reliable, valid and comparable data for the distribution of the means of consumption. Unfortunately, even here complete information is not now available. Accurate empirical measurement and data collection of noneconomic aspects of the individual's class situation is now only in its infant stages.[5] Even on economic benefits, which are in principle quantifiable, roughly comparable data for industrial democracies are limited to income data. Total economic benefits are more than just income (earned income plus dividends plus transfer payments). They also include subsidies, imputed income and real values of paid vacations, expense accounts, free or subsidised consumption of particular goods (food, housing, schooling), income received in the form of fringe benefits and unrealised gains in capital assets (H. Miller 1964). To summarise, what we want to know is what a person consumes, plus his or her increase in net worth in any one year (see Kolko 1962). It is quite obvious that one researcher cannot collect data on all these items. However, one should get a reasonable idea of variation in the distribution of goods among capitalist societies by collecting data on the three main components of that distribution: the distribution of income, the effect of the public sector and the distribution of unrealised capital gain. Take the income of the family, subtract their taxes, add the use of public goods, and then add the effect of unrealised capital gains. One loses some detail excluding items like expense accounts, but this is unavoidable.[6]

However, figures on the distribution of capital gain are not readily available for most countries. We did go to considerable trouble to make some fairly accurate estimation for the United States, just in order to get some idea of how important a factor capital concentration is in contributing to the total inequality of the distribution of the means of consumption. To measure the degree of income equality we have used the Gini index, the most frequently used summary measure of income distribution. For the mathematical computation of the index, see Sawyer (1976). The index varies from 1 (complete inequality; one unit receives all income) to 0 (complete equality; all units receive the same income). With the addition of unrealised capital gains, the Gini index increases ·118 indicating a substantially greater degree of inequality. We bring this point up not only to point out some of the limitations of the measure that we will subsequently develop, but also to substantiate our claim that introduction of democratic collective ownership would decrease inequality in economic benefits as well as in power.[7] Because of lack of adequate data on capital distribution, the best measure of overall inequality of the distribution of means of consumption we could develop was the distribution of income adjusted for the distributive effects of the public sector.

Still another decision had to be made. Income distribution for the late 1960s or early 1970s was available for all but one of the countries in the sample. However, the data for some countries were not at all comparable to the others. It seemed wisest to limit our analysis to the countries where the most comparable data were available. Recently, Malcolm Sawyer (1976) surveyed all the income distribution data available for OECD countries and developed a data set of 'reasonably comparable' income distribution statistics through a combination of survey results and tax records.[8] Sawyer presents data for both income distribution among households before taxes (but including transfer payments) and income distribution after direct taxes have been levied as well as pre- and post-tax distributions adjusted for the varying size of households. Ten of the seventeen countries in our sample are included in Sawyer's study (see Table 4.1). Sawyer does not attempt to estimate the distributive effect of indirect taxes or the free or subsidised use of public goods and services. Since much of social democracy's programme of equalisation has focused on expansion of the public sector, we felt that some attempt should be made to estimate this effect. We opted for a method which would make conservative estimates of the distributive effect of public spending. We made adjustments in the post-tax income distribution based on' the assumption that half of public spending was distributed proportionate to household income and thus had no redistributive effects. The other half was assumed to be distributed equally among households.

Our estimates assume the same distributive effects for all countries, the only variation being the level of public spending. If anything, this biases our results against our hypothesis since all the evidence indicates that in countries with greater labour organisation, longer socialist rule and higher public spending the redistributive effects of public spending are much greater than in countries with weak labour organisation, brief or no socialist rule and low public spending. A considerable amount of empirical evidence supporting this contention will be presented in this and the next chapter.

TABLE 4.1   *Income distribution*

	Before tax		After direct taxes		
	Gini	Top 20*	Gini	Top 20*†	Gini†
Australia	·313	38·9%	·312	40·9%	·354
Canada	·382	43·3	·344	40·5	·348
France	·416	47·0	·414	47·1	·417
Germany	·396	46·8	·383	46·3	·386
Italy	NA	NA	·398	NA	NA
Netherlands	·385	45·8	·354	36·3	·264
Norway	·354	40·9	·307	37·7	·301
Sweden	·346	40·5	·302	35·0	·271
United Kingdom	·344	40·3	·318	39·3	·327
United States	·404	44·8	·381	38·1	·369
Mean	·371	43·1	·351	40·1	·337

SOURCE   Malcolm Sawyer, 'Income Distribution in OECD Countries', *Occasional Studies* (Paris: OECD, 1976)
* Percentage of total income received by the highest 20 per cent of households
† Adjusted for household size
NA   Not available

Results

Before examining the results of this analysis, some of the difficulties and pitfalls associated with analysis of cross-national data of this type should be mentioned. First, with so few cases it is difficult adequately to control for the effects of other variables. The countries fell together into several groups that have similar social and political structures and histories. It becomes impossible to separate out the effects of variables because very few cases fall into the deviant cells. Because of this, we usually avoided entering more than three independent variables in the regressions. We also carefully examined the residuals before and after each variable was entered into the regression in order to make sure that the variable added to the variation explained for the reasons hypothesised. Second, the direction of causality between two variables is rarely unambiguous. For instance, our basic argument is that higher levels of trade union organisation are associated with greater socialist hegemony which leads to greater electoral success of the left and thus longer socialist rule. But once the socialists are in office they routinely make trade union organisation easier. This factor is particularly important for the development of white-collar union-ism, especially in the public sector. For this reason, we have not used such techniques as path analysis and have avoided reference to direct and indirect effects as much as possible. By the same token, all of the regressions presented here should be taken with a grain of salt since some of the assumptions of regression analysis have been violated. Finally, some relationships revealed by cross-national analysis do not hold for time series analysis. For example, branch level centralisation (monopolisation) varies inversely with average establishment and enterprise size across nations, but they vary directly through time. For these reasons, we will complement this cross-national analysis with a brief historical overview at the end of this chapter as well as the in-depth comparative historical analysis in the next chapter.

The welfare state

As predicted, socialist rule was found to be a very important determinant of the level of welfare spending (Table 4.2). Economy-wide bargaining also proved to be an important predictor of welfare spending, confirming Wilensky's contention. Because socialist rule and bargaining centralisation have some common antecedents and because socialist participation in the government is a precondition for the development of an incomes policy (Headey 1970), it might be argued that the correlation between corporatism and welfare spending is primarily due to its correlation with socialist rule. The fact that the total variation explained increases by 9 per cent when economy-wide bargaining is added to the regression indicates that this is not the case. Apparently, the trade unions do get something in return for wage restraint. The percentage of total votes going to the socialist parties had no effect on the dependent variables independent of socialist rule. This indicates that it is effective power rather than left sympathies that counts. It can be argued that the more leftist labour leaders will devote more effort and resources to organising, but in the absence of the increased strength their radicalism will have little effect.

TABLE 4.2   *Determinants of welfare spending*

Independent variables	Beta*	r
Socialist rule	·89	·72
% Catholic	·32	−·15
$R^2 = ·59$		
Socialist rule	·52	·72
Economy-wide bargaining	·45	·76
% Catholic	·23	−·15
$R^2 = ·68$		

*The following notation is used in this and all subsequent tables: Beta = standardised regression coefficient; r = zero order correlation coefficient (simple correlation with the dependent variable); R^2 = multiple coefficient of determination (measures the variation in the dependent variable explained by all variables in the equation)

The relationship of the percentage of Catholics in a country to the level of welfare spending is complex. Our rationale for including this variable was that it seemed possible that anti-capitalist aspects of Catholic ideology – such as notions of a fair wage or prohibitions on usury – as well as the generally positive attitude of the Catholic Church towards welfare for the poor might encourage government welfare spending. An examination of the residuals before and after Catholicism was entered into the regression revealed that the relationship of Catholicism to welfare spending probably depends on the social and political setting of the country in question. When the Catholics are a centre party and have a substantial base in the organised working class, particularly when they have a strong trade union central of their own, then welfare state development will be encouraged by Catholic social and political forces. The contrast between Belgium and Netherlands on the one hand and Germany on the other is a good example of this contrast. The same argument probably holds for France in the Fourth Republic but not in the Fifth Republic. Often, the Catholic promotion of welfare state policies comes as a result of coalitions between Catholic centre parties and social democratic parties. But in other cases Catholic ideology finds its political expression through other paths. For instance, in the United States where most Catholics are working class and where the trade unions are heavily Catholic, the Church has often been a major active supporter of the expansion of the welfare state.

A number of other variables such as GDP per capita (logged and not), population (logged and not), age of the social security system, and percentage of the population over sixty-five were entered in this analysis. All of these proved to have very little effect once the variables in the equation were controlled. Thus, the finding that public spending is heavily influenced by the demographic and bureaucratic outcomes of economic growth does not hold for variation among industrial democracies.

The regression in Table 4.3 demonstrated the barriers to translation of support for socialist parties into political power for the left. The variable 'communist domination of the labour movement' is a dummy variable, with France and Italy coded as 1 and the rest of the countries coded as zero. What the high standardised regression coefficient for the variable obviously demonstrates is the effect of the systematic exclusion of the Italian and French Communist Parties from national political power. The development of Euro-communism and the softening of the cold war attitudes in social democratic and bourgeois left parties holds the promise that this barrier to working-class political power will soon be lifted.

TABLE 4.3   *Determinants of socialist rule*

Independent variables	Beta	r
Socialist vote	·54	·67
Communist domination of labour movement	− ·42	− ·24
Federalism	− ·33	− ·50
Single member districts	− ·16	− ·43

$R^2 = ·70$

The constitutional barriers to socialist incumbency may be more difficult to overcome. Federalism appears to be particularly disadvantageous to the left. The comparison of the actual values for socialist rule with the predicted values, before and after federalism was entered in the equation, reveals that the addition of this variable was especially important in bringing the predicted values for Switzerland and Australia closer to the actual values. In the period under examination, the Australian Labor Party out-polled the Country and Liberal Parties in three elections, achieving an absolute majority in one, yet received a minority of the seats in parliament in each case. In the Swiss case, it is the combination of federalism and the referendum system that prevents the Swiss Social Democratic Party from having much influence on policy-making. Most important social policy initiatives of the party have been rejected by the majority of Swiss voters following the recommendation of their respective parties. And when a majority of the electorate has been reached, the policy has usually failed to receive the support of a majority of cantons due to the weight of the thinly-populated Catholic conservative mountain cantons.[9]

The determinants of the average socialist vote in the post-war period are shown in Table 4.4. The most important independent

TABLE 4.4   *Determinants of socialist vote*

Regression

Independent variables	Beta	*r*
Membership in socialist unions*	·76	·79
European Catholicism	−·27	−·34

$R^2 = ·70$

* Percentage of labour force organised in socialist unions

variable in the regression is membership in labour unions closely associated with socialist parties in 1950. This somewhat underestimates the importance of socialist unions for the mobilisation of support for socialist parties since it ignores the development of socialist unions subsequent to 1950. But given the feedback effect of socialist incumbency on the growth of labour organisation, the results obtained by using trade union membership figures for later dates would be more difficult to interpret. So it was deemed best to use the 1950 figure. The 1950 figure for union membership is also distorted by the inflated figures for Italy and France. Because of the very loose definition of union membership and the low level of commitment (in terms of dues, etc.) involved in becoming a labour union member in those two countries, the actual level of membership is subject to large fluctuations from year to year and the official figures are subject to even greater fluctuations. The level of labour organisation in both countries dropped considerably in the years following 1950.

The variable, European Catholicism, needs some explanation. As Lipset and Rokkan (1967) point out, the outcome of the Reformation left a permanent stamp on the political systems of Europe. In countries in which Catholics remained a majority or a large minority, religion and the role of the Church became very politically divisive issues during the nation-building process. As a result of the counter-Reformation and the formation of Catholic trade unions during industrialisation, these divisions were also reflected in working-class politics. Thus the socialist movement had to compete with the Church in Catholic countries for working-class loyalties. This weakened the movement. The four non-European societies in our sample, all formerly British colonies, developed after the Reformation and all but Canada did not experience much Catholic immigration until the nineteenth century. Thus Catholicism has proved much less divisive to the working class in these countries. However, even there, such divisions are not completely absent. For instance, the break-off of the Catholic-based anti-Communist Democratic Labor Party from the Australian Labor Party prevented the Labor Party returning to power in the 1950s.

The divisions created in the working class in European countries by a strong Catholic presence explain why the zero order correlation between Catholicism and welfare spending is negative (see Table 4.2). Catholicism weakens socialist rule. But independent of its negative effect on socialist rule, it has a positive effect on welfare state development.

These findings support our contention that the changing distribution of power in civil society is an important cause of the development of the welfare state. Strong labour organisation and long socialist rule are strongly associated with high public spending. One reason that our results are at variance with those which emphasise the importance of economic and demographic variables is that the samples are different. Given that our sample is limited to developed societies, one would not expect economic and demographic variables to be of great importance. The differences in public expenditure between developed and less developed societies are explained by the economic and demographic variables which writers such as

Wilensky (1975) point to, though recent research (Hewitt 1977; Weiss and Williamson 1977) has shown that Wilensky under-estimates political effects due to methodological errors.[10]

It is our contention that social and political variables account for the *variation* among developed capitalist democracies. The argument that economic and demographic factors set some functional minimum on public spending in advanced societies can be accepted without damaging our position. However, Wilensky's (1977) analysis of variations in social security spending among industrial democracies does contradict our findings. This is in part attributable to the fact that Wilensky's dependent variable, social security spending, is limited to fewer programmes than ours. Two of the most important programmes in his measure are health care and pensions. It seems reasonable to assume that spending in any given legislated health or pension plan will rise as the proportion of the population over sixty-five rises. But using our independent variables and his dependent variable, we found the effect of the demographic variable to be small in comparison with the social and political variables. Thus part of the problem in Wilensky's analysis is linked to errors in measurement or corporatism (mentioned earlier) and working-class strength (left vote + voter turn-out + union membership). These errors led Wilensky to reject the hypothesis that political factors are important determinants of variations in public spending.

In a study developed at the same time but independently of our own, Cameron (1976) arrived at quite similar results.[11] His data cover the period 1956–73. Cameron's measure of socialist rule is quite similar to ours. His dependent variable is the growth of public spending between 1956 and 1973. He shows that socialist rule is the main determinant of the expansion of the public sector in that period. Cameron's data allow us to explain some of the deviant cases in our analysis. France and Germany were medium welfare spenders in 1970 despite only short periods of socialist rule. Cameron shows that the growth of spending in these two countries has been very slow since the mid-1950s. In both countries, the welfare state was expanded greatly immediately after the Second World War because the balance of power in civil society shifted suddenly and temporarily to the advantage of labour because a substantial portion of big business was discredited as collaborationist or fascist.

Björn's (1976, 1979) analysis of time series data for five countries (Sweden, the United States, Denmark, the United Kingdom and Australia) confirms Cameron's and our findings. Björn develops measures of the redistributive impact of government taxation and spending, labour cabinet influence, and the interaction of labour cabinet influence and strength in the legislature for the periods 1920 to 1939 and 1945 to 1970. He then compares the effect of the political variables and of economic growth on the change in redistributive impact of government activity for each country in both time periods. Only in one of the ten cases (pre-war Denmark) was economic growth a better predictor than the political variables, though in three cases (pre-war United Kingdom, post-war Australia and post-war United States) none of the variables had an effect on redistributive change.

Income distribution

The analysis of the determinants of the various measures of income distribution is presented in Table 4.5. Labour organisation explains between 50 per cent and 81 per cent of the variation in the income distribution measures, strongly supporting our hypothesis. Socialist rule explains about 25 per cent of the variation in the pre-tax indices, close to 50 per cent in the post-tax indices and over 50 per

TABLE 4.5 *Correlation between labour organisation, socialist rule and social inequality*

	Union	Socialist rule
Before tax		
Gini	− ·72	− ·48
Top 20	− ·74	− ·55
After direct tax		
Gini	− ·82	− ·72
Gini*	− ·73	− ·66
Top 20*	− ·76	− ·65
After public spending (estimate)		
Gini	− ·90	− ·81
Gini*	− ·71	− ·70
Top 20*	− ·76	− ·70

$N = 10$ (after tax) or 9
* Adjusted for household size

cent in the indices after adjustments for public spending have been made. This is consistent with our assumption that leftist rule would have its greatest influence by socialisation of income rights via taxation and public spending. Because of the small number of cases, and the high correlation ($\cdot 87$ for these ten countries) between the two main independent variables, we did not run multiple regressions but rather simply examined the zero order correlations of the independent variables with income distribution. Per capita GNP was found to have low and inconsistent correlations with the indices ($r = -\cdot 13$ to $\cdot 24$). This finding indicates that the arguments presented by Kuznets and his associates do not hold, at least once a country has entered the advanced industrial stage. The level of unemployment was somewhat correlated to the Gini indices ($r = \cdot 26$ to $\cdot 37$) but not to the proportions accruing to the richest groups. But, as expected, it was strongly negatively correlated to the proportion accruing to the bottom 10 per cent of households before taxes ($r = -\cdot 68$). Both socialist rule and union membership were negatively correlated to unemployment ($r = -\cdot 44$ and $-\cdot 37$ respectively). Thus part of the effect of these variables on income distribution seems to operate through the changing of labour supply and consequently changing economically-determined income rights.

The results of this analysis are confirmed by the studies conducted by Cameron and Hewitt. Both studies show that income distribution is strongly influenced by political factors and that it is not very strongly influenced by economic development. Neither attempts to analyse the effects of labour organisation.

The welfare state and equalisation

Leftist critics of the welfare state have claimed that it has no equalising effect. Though no accurate data on the exact redistributive effect of taxation and public spending exist, some evidence on this question can be found in this cross-national data. Welfare spending is not correlated with pre-tax income distribution. But it is negatively correlated with inequality of income distribution after direct taxes are levied ($r = -0\cdot 29$) and post-tax income distribution after adjustments for household size are made ($r = -\cdot 57$). Using the ratio of income taxes to indirect taxes·as a measure of the progressiveness of the tax system, the relationship between the welfare state development and the method of financing can be examined. It appears that the welfare state will be much more progressively financed when it is developed under socialist leadership than Catholic ideology or other influences. Progressive taxes are positively associated with socialist rule (·47) and labour organisation (·39) but negatively related to the Catholic percentage of the population (−·65). Economy-wide bargaining is not related to tax composition once labour organisation or socialist rule are controlled. Our measures here are crude but they all point in the same direction. Taxation and public spending will have the greatest redistributive effect when public spending is high and taxes are progressive. This situation occurs when the socialists control the government for long periods. Thus welfare state development under socialist leadership does represent a movement towards socialist distribution.

This is not to indicate that welfare state expansion effected by non-socialist forces has no redistributive effect. Our data on this point are a little ambiguous, but it does point in the direction of some redistributive effects of non-socialist (Catholic or independent) trade union strength on equalisation. The aggregate strength of trade unions explained an average of 57 per cent of the variation in the income distribution indices compared to 40 per cent explained by the strength of socialist unions alone. This finding has to be taken cautiously because it is largely due to how estimated corrections for household size affect the relative positions of the Netherlands and Australia. But the same finding can be shown for the effect of non-socialist unionism on welfare state expenditure: aggregate union strength explains 6 per cent more variation in welfare spending than socialist union strength.

Moving somewhat beyond our data, we would propose the following hypothesis for the effects of non-socialist unions on redistribution. Three different types of non-socialist unions can be distinguished: Catholic (for example, Belgium), independent blue-collar unions (for example, the United States), and independent white-collar unions (for example, Scandinavia). On 'bread and butter' wage and benefit issues, the non-socialist blue-collar unions, Catholic or independent, are probably almost as effective as their socialist counterparts. Indeed, the Catholic unions must be since they are often in competition with socialist unions. On the political side, the existence of strong Catholic unions exerts a leftward pressure on Catholic parties establishing the preconditions for a welfare state expansion by a Catholic – Social Democratic coalition. While this coalition involves compromises in the direction of less progressive taxation, it is clearly better than political isolation of the Social Democrats given the substantial redistributive effects of most public expenditure (see Chapter 5). Independent blue-collar and white-collar unionism has created similar leftward pressures on bourgeois left parties (for example, the US Democrats and the Scandinavian Liberals).

But to leave the reader with the correct impression it is important to emphasise that most of the redistribution that has occurred has been the product of the trade union and political strength of the socialist movement. Not only is the immediate political effect on redistribution of non-socialist trade unions less than that of socialist unions, the long-term effect of non-socialist blue-collar unionism on the growth of class consciousness and growth of labour organisation is very much less than that of socialist unionism due to the feedback effect of socialist rule on labour organisation, as we shall see.

Social mobility

As we indicated, the social mobility data available leave something to be desired, so no final conclusion about the relationship between social mobility and equality can be made on the basis of this analysis alone. The correlations between the measures of mobility and inequality are shown in Table 4.6. All of the correlations are in the hypothesised direction, but only the correlations between down-ward mobility and inequality are very strong. Even if these results are taken at face value, they cannot be given an unambiguous interpretation in the light of the present state of sociological re-search. We have argued that the causality between equality of distribution and social mobility goes both ways. Equality promotes social mobility and social mobility promotes equal distribution. Jencks (1972) has argued that the latter is not true. And he provides convincing evidence that the Great Society Program aimed at expanding higher education thereby changing supply relations on the labour market did not have the predicted result, an increase in equality of reward between educated and unskilled labour. A glut of trained personnel resulted but no decrease in high incomes fol-lowed. Jencks is concerned with only a very short period, so it might be true that things would be different in the long run. Two factors may account for the inflexibility of the income of educated personnel. First, the revenue component of their income is dependent on the market situation of capital, not educated labour. Second, it may be true that the meritocratic ideology that is propagated in defence of capitalism is so important to employers that it over-rides considerations of market conditions, counteracting the downward pressure on salary income. Obviously, the role of professional associations in defending current salary scales is of some importance here too. None of this, however, contradicts the central point we want to make here: there is no tension between equality and equal opportunity in the sense that promoting one means sacrificing the other. In fact, leftist governments usually try to foster both. Educational spending is positively associated with both social security spending (·37) and socialist incumbency (·39).

TABLE 4.6   *Social inequality and social mobility*

	(1)	(2)	(3)	(4)	(5)	(6)	(7)
(1) Downward mobility	10	−·41	·15	−·57	−·60	−·56	·34
(2) Mobility index	10	10	−·41	·20	·38	·14	·05
(3) Educational opportunity	9	9	13	·34	·32	·27	·20
(4) Gini before tax	7	7	7	9	·91	·81	·02
(5) Gini after tax	8	8	8	9	10	·96	−·29
(6) Gini after spending	7	7	7	9	9	9	−·49
(7) Welfare spending	10	10	13	9	10	9	17

NOTE The figures above the diagonal are correlation coefficients. The figures below the diagonal are the number of cases each correlation was based on

Labour organisation

Since the level of labour organisation is the key underlying cause of the movement to socialism according to our theory and has proved to be strongly related to the dependent variables in this analysis, it is obviously of utmost importance to examine the causes of labour organisation. In Chapter 2, we hypothesised that the degree of labour organisation is related to ethnic, linguistic and religious diversity, average establishment size, the level of technological advance, the strength of craft unions and the degree of economic centralisation.

In attempting to test our hypotheses concerning labour organisation, a number of methodological problems arose. We were not able to find adequate data for centralisation of control, craft unionism and the character of industrialisation. In addition, Pryor's data on economy-wide centralisation – conglomeration – cover only seven countries. This is unfortunate because his data on conglomeration and branch-wide centralisation, monopolisation, indicate that it is possible that the two phenomena may not be nearly as strongly associated as one might think ($r = \cdot 47$). This moderate correlation is primarily due to two deviant cases, Switzerland (low conglomeration, high monopolisation) and the United States (high conglomeration, low monopolisation). Pryor presents conglomeration data for only one of our highly unionised countries, Belgium, and it is the most centralised of all his seven countries (37 per cent of the labour force is employed by the 200 largest enterprises). Sweden is probably much more centralised since the 100 largest private firms employ 43 per cent of all employees in private manufacturing. If anything, with the inclusion of government firms this figure would be even higher. This leads us to believe that complete information would reveal that the association between conglomeration and monopolisation is much higher than Pryor's data show. This could be of some importance for the prediction of future trends in labour organisation.

Monopolisation data was only available for ten countries, but it was sufficiently strongly correlated with the natural log of the GDP ($r = \cdot 76$), a measure of the size of the domestic market, that we felt safe in estimating the degree of monopolisation in the remaining seven countries using the regression equation with the natural log of the GDP as a predictor.

In this analysis, the percentage of non-agricultural workers organised was used as the dependent variable in order to control for variation due to differences in the size of the agricultural sector and the urban petty bourgeoisie. The analysis was made on union membership data for 1930 and 1970. Given the feedback of socialist rule on union membership, it seemed wise to make an analysis for the earlier date also. The political effects are particularly important in the post-war period, so the 1930 data help control for the fact that the left has been stronger in the small (and thus highly monopolised) countries.

Table 4.7 shows the results of the analysis. Monopolisation and one of the diversity variables are strongly related to labour organisation at both dates. An examination of the regressions and the correlation coefficients suggests the following conclusions on the

TABLE 4.7   *Determinants of trade union membership*

Regression

Independent variables	Beta	*r*
Membership, 1970*		
Monopolisation	·58	·49
Ethnic diversity	− ·36	− ·48
Linguistic diversity	− ·25	− ·23
$R^2 = ·51$		
Membership, 1930*		
Linguistic diversity	− ·68	− ·51
Monopolisation	·49	·25
$R^2 = ·44$		

Correlation

	(2)	(3)	(4)	(5)	(6)	(7)	(8)	(9)
(1) Membership, 1970*	·41	·72	·68	·73	·49	·29	·05	·81
(2) Membership, 1930*		·33	·17	·13	·25	·19	·13	·25
(3) Membership growth 1930–70			·62	·71	·43	·17	·77	·69
(4) Union centralisation				·95	·36	·52	·55	·64
(5) Economy-wide bargaining					·63	·50	·59	·72
(6) Monopolisation†						·45	·47	·34
(7) Export, % GDP							·37	·17
(8) Conglomeration‡								·42
(9) Socialist rule								

* Union membership as a percentage of non-agricultural wage and salary earners
† Seven cases estimated on the basis of GDP (logged)
‡ Seven cases only

causes of variations in the level of labour organisation: diversity and monopolisation have roughly the same effect on the initial development of trade union organisation. Subsequent growth appears to be due to socialist rule, bargaining centralisation and union centralisation or some combination of these factors.

A number of other hypothesised predictors of labour organisation were found to be of little importance in the analysis. Average establishment size was somewhat related to labour organisation when monopolisation and diversity were controlled (Beta = ·21). This is a prime example of a relationship that differs in cross-national analysis from within nation or time series analysis. Larger workplaces are much more organised in every industrial society. Other indicators of technological and economic advance such as GDP per capita were not found to be related to labour organisation. The variation among these countries in the relevant by-products of technological advance, such as improved communication, is probably too small to have any effect on labour organisation.

The international and historical context

Socialist rule, bargaining centralisation and trade union centralisation a·e strongly related to the level of labour organisation. The four phenomena are all causally inter-related and the causal relationship in each case involves at least some feedback. Given the importance of highly centralised bargaining, strong labour organisation and socialist rule for the advance towards socialism some attempt should be made to unravel the causal links between these phenomena. For this we must move from regression analysis and its assumption of linearity, unidirectional causality, and no strong association between the independent variables to an historical overview and a more careful case-by-case comparative analysis.

The development of the labour movement

Though Marx's expectations on the speed of the transition to socialism were incorrect, his statements of the progressive phases of the class struggle have been proved largely correct. By the middle of the last century, the bourgeoisie in most of the Western world had consolidated an economy unfettered by the particularistic constraints of feudalism in which the mode of political rule was bourgeois parliamentarism, that is, *régime censitaire*, where there were property or income qualifications for voting. Labour organising followed closely on the heels of industrial development in Europe and by the last decade of the last century the labour movement was a social and political force to be reckoned with. At this point only a few countries were democratic in the sense that most did not have universal male[12] suffrage government responsibility to the parliament, and the secret ballot (see Hewitt 1977: 457; Therborn 1977). The first phase of the working-class struggle was 'to win the battle of democracy' (Marx and Engels 1848: 504). This struggle was won in most cases between 1898 and 1919. The organised working class was a major force behind the struggle for democracy in every case except Switzerland and the United States. In these two countries, democracy was the product of urban petty bourgeois and artisanal and peasant mobilisation in precapitalist agrarian societies dominated by small landholders.[13] Thus, democracy itself is a product of organised working-class struggle to transform capitalism. It represents a movement away from pure capitalism caused by the changing distribution of power in civil society.

But it is important to note that democracy was not won by working-class action alone. At this point (circa 1910), the organised working class was not sufficiently strong to carry out such a task alone (Therborn 1977). Where an important feudalistic large land-holding class was absent, as in Scandinavia, Australia and New Zealand, the working class found allies among smallholders and the urban petty bourgeoisie. Divisions in the bourgeoisie were important in cases such as the United Kingdom. But perhaps the most important factor was the First World War.

In many countries (Sweden, Finland, the United Kingdom, Denmark, Netherlands, Belgium, Austria, Germany, Italy), full democracy was accepted reluctantly by the ruling class as a direct or indirect consequence of the war. The war affected class relations, shifting power in civil society in the direction of labour in a number of ways. The mass mobilisation required by modern war necessitated some concessions to the people who were to fight the war. The arming of the working class posed a threat which the government could not ignore. The decline in unemployment in the war economy and the need for uninterrupted production also increased the power of labour. And the diminished threat of capital flight in wartime reduced the power of capital. Finally, in the defeated powers, the war created a power vacuum on the right by discrediting the old ruling class.

The First World War is an example of the type of international and historical factors which have been left in the background to this point in our analysis since we have focused on the causes of *differences* in labour movements. The international economic and political situation created common constraints on labour action and caused the development of various labour movements to exhibit some similarities. For instance, the structural constraints on policy-making, such as capital flight, are heavily influenced by the conditions in other capitalist countries. Thus, the danger of capital flight is much greater when the socialist movement in one country comes to power and attempts to move boldly ahead than in a situation where similar developments occur in other countries. To take another example, the bargaining power of organised labour depends in part on the strength of labour in other countries. The importance of key international developments such as the two world wars, the cold war, the depression and the rise of fascism[14] is that they have often created common reactions in the labour movements of various countries, thus shifting the distribution of power in the entire capitalist world. The mobilisation of the working class in almost every country in the wake of the two world wars is an excellent example of this phenomenon.

To return to our narrative, the working-class movement achieved its first goal with the advent of democracy. But universal suffrage did not result in 'the political supremacy of the working class', as Marx (1852: 200) had thought. Instead, everywhere the socialist movement found itself a political minority, partly because the industrial working class was a minority of the population, and partly because non-class loyalties cut into the socialists' class base. The end of the war brought a wave of leftist enthusiasm and a surge of organising in the new democracies (see Table 4.8). But this was short-lived and the labour movements faced the task of slow build-up of labour organisation and socialist hegemony in order to effect a transition to socialism, a task which many labour and socialist leaders still do not realise faces them.

The propertied classes who had resisted democracy found, much to their delight, that the socialists' minority position meant that they could be politically isolated and that their more radical plans posed no immediate danger. Up to the early 1930s, the compromises that the Western bourgeoisie had to make with the labour movement were miniscule. At this point, the similarities in the situations of various working-class movements are more impressive than the differences. True, there were important differences in the level of labour organisation due to the size of the petty bourgeoisie (compare the two parts of Table 4.8) and differences due to the degree of diversity and economic centralisation. But the latter tended to counteract each other, and leaving aside countries experiencing suppression of working-class organisations (Italy and Finland), the density of union membership (the second part of Table 4.8) was

TABLE 4.8   *Union membership*

As a percentage of the labour force

	1905	1913 –14	Post- war peak	1930	1935	1939 –40	1950	1960	1970
High monopolisation, economy-wide bargaining									
Sweden	5	6	11	20	24	36	51	60	75
Norway	2	7	13	12	17	26	34	49	52
Denmark	7	13	27	21	25	28	33	48	50
Finland	NA	2	11	1	2	3	17	19	45
Austria	3	3	39	25	—	—	40	46	51
Belgium	2	7	27	18	22	24	36	43	51
Netherlands	NA	11	25	20	22	22	31	33	34
Mean	3·8	7·0	22·9	16·7	18·7	23·2	34·6	42·6	51·4
High monopolisation, industry- or firm-level bargaining									
New Zealand*	8	15	19	17	13	39	38	38	35
Australia	10	25	30	38	33	35	50	45	44
Canada	NA	6	12	8	6	8	19	24	27
Switzerland	NA	5	12	17	19	19	29	28	27
Mean	9·0	12·8	18·3	20·0	17·8	25·3	34·0	33·8	33·3
Low monopolisation									
United Kingdom	11	22	43	23	23	31	40	41	44
United States	6	7	11	7	7	16	22	24	23
Germany	6	11	30	18	—	—	29	30	30
Italy	1	2	12	—	—	—	37	31	36
France	4	5	8	7	7	17	22	11	15
Mean	5·6	9·4	20·8	13·8	12·3	21·3	30·0	27·4	29·6
Grand mean	**5·4**	**9·2**	**20·6**	**16·8**	**17·5**	**23·8**	**31·0**	**33·5**	**37·6**

continued overleaf

TABLE 4.8—*continued*

As a percentage of non-agricultural wage and salary workers

	1930 –1	1935	1939 –40	1945 –6	1950	1960	1970
High monopolisation, economy-wide bargaining							
Sweden	35	44	53	55	69	73	87
Norway	21	33	42	51	54	62	67
Denmark	42	41	46	59	54	69	66
Finland	4	7	11	46	32	33	62
Austria	41	—	—	51	70	72	72
Belgium	35	40	40	41	51	58	65
Netherlands	35	48	44	44	45	44	41
Mean	30·4	30·4	33·7	49·6	53·6	58·7	65·7
High monopolisation, industry- or firm-level bargaining							
New Zealand*	36	21	67	60	60	54	45
Australia	57	49	53	63	63	61	53
Canada	14	15	17	24	29	31	33
Switzerland	26	30	28	35	40	36	31
Mean	33·3	28·8	41·3	45·5	48·0	45·5	40·5
Low monopolisation							
United Kingdom	31	29	34	45	47	45	49
United States	11	13	25	31	32	31	28
Germany	26	—	—	—	44	39	37
Italy	—	—	—	—	81	61	57
France	18	21	43	85	47	17	20
Mean	21·5	21·0	34·0	53·7	50·2	38·6	38·2
Grand mean	**28·5**	**27·7**	**36·1**	**49·3**	**51·1**	**49·1**	**50·8**

*Unions registered under New Zealand's Industrial Conciliation and Arbitration Act only. Excluded are many public servants, mine-workers, chemical fertiliser workers and agricultural workers
NA   Not available

remarkably similar in Europe. And the political situation of the socialist movement in all countries at the end of the 1930s was remarkably similar. No party had achieved a sufficiently stable position in government to even make important welfare statist initiatives, much less advances toward socialisation of control.

The depression brought on different responses in different countries. In countries in which the nation-building coalition had included a large landholding élite under whose wing a politically dependent bourgeoisie had developed (Austria, Germany and

Spain), the response of the ruling classes was to accept authoritarian or fascist rule often by movements based in petty bourgeois strata rather than a compromise with the labour movement and continuation of the democratic rule they so detested.[15]

In countries in which democracy did survive, the crisis of the 1930s and the high employment levels of the war brought on a growth of labour organising and in most cases necessitated a compromise by the capitalists with the labour movement. In some cases, such as the United States – where the labour movement became a significant force but was still weak – the concessions of capital only involved a recognition of the labour movement's existence, the routinisation of collective bargaining, and acceptance of some minimal expansion of the public sector. Where the labour movement became very strong and the social democrats entered the government, as in Scandinavia, the concessions of capital were more far-reaching. But the depression and the war delayed significant welfare state build-up until after the war. So, when the defeat of fascism and the discrediting of the old ruling coalitions in those countries brought similar compromises between the labour movement and the formerly intransigent bourgeoisie, the concrete achievements of the labour movements of the West still appeared quite similar. Welfare state effort as indicated by non-military public spending varied little at this point in time.

Patterns of welfare state development

In the post-war period, industrial capitalist societies became increasingly different not only in terms of welfare state effort but also in terms of the underlying distribution of power in civil society. The patterns of welfare state development can be analysed with the help of Table 4.9. The countries in the table are divided according to the degree of monopolisation, and the high monopolisation group is subdivided according to the degree of bargaining centralisation. The monopolisation division also divides the countries by population size and GDP. They fall neatly into two categories, the small democracies and the large democracies, with a large gap between the countries on all three variables. The division of the small democracies by bargaining centralisation also coincides with the division by trade union centralisation and level of welfare spending. And with only a few exceptions it divides them by length of socialist rule and degree of union organisation.

TABLE 4.9   *Antecedents of welfare spending*

	Monopolisation	Union centralisation	Union membership	Socialist rule	Welfare spending	% Catholic
High monopolisation, economy-wide bargaining						
Sweden	1·55	30	75%	24	44%	0%
Norway	1·60*	30	52	20	45	0
Denmark	1·54*	15	50	16	49	1
Finland	1·62*	25	45	9	38	0
Austria	1·55*	35	51	10	43	89
Belgium	1·52	30	51	9	37	93
Netherlands	1·25	33	34	6	43	40
Mean	1·52	28·3	51·1	13·4	42·7	31·8
High monopolisation, industry- or firm-level bargaining						
New Zealand	1·72*	0	35	7	30	14
Australia	1·37*	5	44	4	23	23
Ireland	1·79*	0	35	2	36	94
Canada	1·35	0	27	0	35	41
Switzerland	1·68	5	27	0	24	43
Mean	1·58	2·0	33·6	2·6	29·6	43·0
Low monopolisation						
United Kingdom	1·13	0	44	12	35	9
United States	1·00	0	23	0	21	40
Germany	·92	5	30	3	35	45
Italy	·86	0	36	2	31	91
France	·95	3	15	4	37	82
Mean	·97	1·6	29·6	4·2	31·8	53·0
Grand mean	**1·38**	**12·7**	**39·6**	**7·5**	**35·6**	**41·0**

TABLE 4.9—*continued*

	Ethnic diversity	Linguistic diversity	% agriculture	Tax composition	Population (millions)	Socialist vote
High monopolisation, economy-wide bargaining						
Sweden	·08	·12	8%	1·56	8	51
Norway	·04	·19	12	1·31	4	52
Denmark	·04	·12	11	1·04	5	46
Finland	·16	·35	20	·89	5	47
Austria	·13	·01	14	·85	7	47
Belgium	·55	·51	5	·70	10	38
Netherlands	·10	·04	7	1·29	13	35
Mean	·16	·19	11·0	1·13	7·4	45·1
High monopolisation, industry- or firm-level bargaining						
New Zealand	·37	·07	12	1·57	3	45
Australia	·32	·03	7	·91	13	47
Ireland	·04	·44	25	·28	3	10
Canada	·75	·48	7	·52	21	18
Switzerland	·50	·50	8	1·25	6	29
Mean	·40	·30	11·0	·91	9·2	29·8
Low monopolisation						
United Kingdom	·32	·04	3	·83	56	46
United States	·50	·25	4	1·25	203	0
Germany	·03	—	8	·80	61	36
Italy	·04	·09	16	—	54	42
France	·26	·14	13	·31	50	43
Mean	·23	·13	8·8	·82	84·8	33·4
Grand mean	**·25**	**·21**	**10·5**	**·98**	**30·7**	**37·2**

*Estimated by GDP (logged)

Let us begin our attempt to discover the causal links between the various independent variables with an examination of the high spenders. Based on detailed knowledge of the Swedish case, we would argue that the following would hold for the Scandinavian countries. Labour organising and the formation of a socialist party with close ties to the unions occurs soon after the development of industrial production. In the beginning, the national trade union centre is weak. Because of the high degree of industrial centralisation and product specialisation these countries are characterised by a small group of non-competing oligopolistic firms who unite to support each other in their struggle against the unions. The trade union federation is then forced to centralise to provide mutual financial support during strikes and to organise almost all of the larger firms adhering to the employers' federation. The centralisation of bargaining finally develops after the Social Democrats enter the government on an apparently permanent basis either alone (Norway) or in coalition with a farmers' party.

The Austrian case is somewhat different. Labour was already well organised in the First Republic but neither the labour federations nor the employer federations were centralised. The union movement was divided on ideological grounds into three competing central organisations. But this can have been only a minor contribution to the lack of overall centralisation since the Free Trade Unions (actually social democratic) were by far the largest. And though craft unionism was moderately strong, the Free Trade Union federation was composed of only fifty-seven separate national unions, not many more than the number (48) of the Swedish movement at the time centralised bargaining developed. It is possible that a centralising movement would have developed given the proper political conditions (Social Democratic government). In any case, the Dolfuss *coup* and the subsequent repression of the trade unions under the Catholic–Conservatives and the Nazis broke the link with the past and allowed the Austrian trade union leaders to change completely the organisational structure of the trade unions when they were reconstituted after the war. The pre-Dolfuss and resistance leadership met on one side of Vienna while fighting was still going on on the other side of the city and decided that the then memberless Austrian trade union movement would be organised entirely on the industrial principle with only fourteen (later sixteen) national organisations and that the central organisation, the ÖGB, would have very strong powers. A year later the ÖGB could already claim 625,000 members and, by 1949, 1,279,000 members, almost 70 per cent of non-agricultural wage and salary earners. The discrediting of German nationalism and fascism and Catholic authoritarianism forced the Catholic right to accept the Social Democrats in the system after the war. The centralisation of the employers' federation and bargaining came in 1947 when, by legislative fiat, the Chamber of Commerce was made the bargaining partner of the ÖGB.

While the temporal sequence of union centralisation and heavy labour organisation depends on whether one counts pre-Dolfuss membership, both clearly pre-date the centralisation of the employers' federation and bargaining. The Austrian case differs on the question of employer federation centralisation but is similar to Scandinavia in that the centralisation of labour unions, high levels of labour organisation and a stable socialist (coalition) government precede and are necessary for the development of centralised bargaining. The necessity of trade union centralisation for the proper operation of highly centralised bargaining is obvious. High levels of labour organisation are needed because if the blue-collar workforce in significant sectors of the economy are not organised, the employers in those sectors will have a very high incentive to break out of the system leading to a system of industry-wide instead of economy-wide bargaining. Or in order to keep the unorganised employers in the national system, wage increases would have to be so low that organised workers would become dissatisfied leading to a break-up of the system or sufficiently high levels of wage drift that the economy-wide bargain would mean little.

The comparison of Sweden and Austria shows that the sequencing of union centralisation and employers' federation centralisation are variable features of the countries under examination. But the development of bargaining centralisation is an absolutely invariable feature of welfare state development in these seven cases. First, it does not occur until the trade unions have organised virtually all of the blue-collar workers in larger firms. The percentage of non-agricultural wage and salary earners organised at the time of the adoption of a highly centralised bargaining system is between 44 per cent and 59 per cent. Since blue-collar workers are more heavily organised than white-collar workers, especially in earlier periods, and since larger firms are more heavily organised, it is safe to say that the level of organisation among blue-collar workers in the larger firms is substantially higher than these figures indicate. Second, bargaining centralisation never develops before the dominant socialist party has formed a stable government with a parliamentary majority either alone or in coalition with a Catholic (on the continent) or centre party (in Scandinavia). This may be a coincidence. But if Headey is correct in contending that socialist participation in government is a prerequisite for trade union acceptance of a wages policy, then the development of 'corporatism' is dependent on socialist incumbency. Actually 'corporatism' is a bad word because of its co-optative connotations. Centralised bargaining is the result of strong labour organisation. The organisational representative of the capitalist class, the employers' federation, becomes willing to bargain centrally with the labour federation only when it becomes apparent that the labour movement is too strong to be defeated and thus compromise is necessary. And 'corporatism', as indicated by the trade unions' acceptance of an incomes policy, only comes about when the trade unions feel that they can get something in return for wage restraint, such as price control and social legislation. For this, socialist participation in the government is necessary. Thus the effect of economy-wide bargaining on welfare state expenditure can ultimately be traced to working-class economic and political power.

A legally enforced or a *de facto* incomes policy is characteristic of all of these seven countries except Belgium. Many leftist critiques of social democracy consider this to be strong evidence that the labour movements of these countries have become a tool of the capitalists to control the workers' demands. It can be argued that even under the best conditions, such as in Sweden where the 'social contract' is based on expansion of social services, progressive taxation, price and profit controls, and where the incomes policy is based on voluntary agreement on the part of the trade unions, that ultimately wage restraint means that workers pay for capital investment and thus enrich the capitalists at their own (the workers') expense. Unfortunately, the primary alternative suggested by the left, a return to free bargaining in a decentralised system, is worse. In countries with a high level of labour organisation and a heavy dependence on exports, the end of an incomes policy and wage restraint would lead to high levels of inflation, a deterioration of the country's competitive position in foreign markets, capital flight and a drying up of internal investment sources. Furthermore, in a decentralised bargaining system, employees in strongly organised, highly profitable sectors would benefit at the expense of consumers, or rather employees in less profitable sectors and particularly unorganised workers. The result would be a breakdown in working-class solidarity, a growth of narrow group egoism and the development of a dual labour market. In fact, only in countries like the United States where organisation is weak and export dependency low can the trade unions bargain without any restraint and not have a major impact on the economy – and then only at the cost of the consumer and the development of a dual labour market. In countries with very high levels of labour organisation, labour leaders are forced to consider the broader economic impact of wage demands because the connection of the wage settlement to prices is so intimate in these cases. Economic policy, wage policy and social policy then become indistinguishable and the trade unions of necessity stay politicised. Though the suggestion to reject an incomes policy altogether is unrealistic, the problem of workers sacrificing for capital growth remains a dilemma for social democracy. We will return to this point in the last two chapters to suggest a solution.

The fact that centralised bargaining is dependent on working-class power calls for a complete re-evaluation of the concept of corporatism which dominates the present discussion of the phenomenon. Schmitter's (1974) connotation of co-optation of the working class in the transition from pluralism to corporatism is extremely misleading. The alternative to corporatism found in other capitalist democracies is not pluralism. Rather it is the class rule of the capitalist class. Corporatism represents a deadlock in the class struggle in which working-class economic and political power is sufficient to force substantial concessions from capital but insufficient actually to take control of the accumulation process. The substantial redistribution accomplished through taxation and public spending in countries like Sweden is also strong evidence that such a pattern of policy-making is much more democratic in its result than policy-making in supposedly pluralist countries like the United States.

Examining the group of countries under consideration, two main paths to high welfare state development can be identified. When the welfare state is developed under a purely social democratic government (Norway and Sweden) or with the social democrats as strongly dominant members of a coalition government (Denmark and Sweden 1951–7), it will be progressively financed. When it is developed by a social democratic/Catholic (Austria, Netherlands and Belgium) or a social democratic/centre coalition (Finland), public spending is not so progressively financed. Less progressivity is the price the labour movement has to pay in the compromise.

Netherlands seems to be a deviant case among these countries by its lower level of labour organisation and shorter period of socialist rule. This is part reality and part appearance. It may be that the Dutch system of bargaining centralisation owes more to the combination of very heavy export dependency and the 'politics of accommodation' (Lijphart 1968) than to the political and economic strength of the labour movement. On the other hand, the Dutch labour movement was moderately strong fairly early. The socialist party was included in many inter-war governments and the labour unions had organised 44 per cent of wage and salary earners when centralised bargaining was adopted right after the war. Labour organisation has stagnated at that level. And though the Netherlands is much lower than the other high spenders on the index of socialist rule, the social democrats have been minority participants in most post-war governments. It is interesting to note that in every country characterised by economy-wide bargaining, the social democrats have participated in the government in over 60 per cent of the post-war period while socialist participation in governments does not exceed 50 per cent in any other country included in this analysis.

The countries in the second group are also characterised by a high degree of oligopoly and small populations but not by centralised bargaining, centralised trade unions and long socialist rule, and as a consequence are medium to low welfare spenders. Though it appears that there are different factors in each case which prevented the left from moving into a position as a more or less permanent participant in government, one thing is striking: all of the countries with economy-wide bargaining systems have effective systems of proportional representation, while all of the countries in the second group (except Ireland) lack such a system. The Swiss system is proportional formally, but in fact the importance of referenda in policy formation and the federalist structure has effectively excluded the Social Democrats from major political influence. As a tentative hypothesis for further investigation, the influence of the left on the shaping of the electoral system could be the explanatory factor. In the cases of Switzerland, Australia and New Zealand the representation system seems to have been decisive in preventing them from following a pattern of vigorous welfare state development. All three countries were as well organised in the late 1940s as the high spenders, yet the political threat was absent.

The contrast of these three countries with the high spender group also highlights the importance of socialist incumbency and, perhaps, centralised bargaining for the development of labour organisation. Every country which experienced a substantial increase in labour organisation between 1950 and 1970 has a highly centralised bargaining system. And in every country in which organisational density exceeded 60 per cent of non-agricultural wage and salary earners, socialist parties have been participants in government cabinets for two-thirds of the 1945–70 period. The reasons for the effects of socialist incumbency on labour organisation are quite obvious; the socialists use their governmental position to pass legislation facilitating union organising and their role as state employer to encourage public employee unionisation. The growth of public employment that occurs with welfare state development makes the latter factor particularly important. And since state employees are heavily white collar, socialist incumbency is critical for the breakthrough of the labour movement to white-collar ranks. Without a breakthrough to non-manual employees, union membership density will automatically decline, as it has in the United States, Germany, Switzerland and Australia, due to changes in workforce composition. The relationship of bargaining centralisation to labour organisation is less clear. Tentatively, we would argue that centralisation of employers' federations and of bargaining reduces the incentive of employers to resist unionisation since their wage bill will not be greatly affected by the presence or absence of a union in the enterprise. The factor is of greatest importance for small enterprises and multi-establishment enterprises where each establishment is small (for example, retail sales chains, hotel and restaurant chains). To achieve the density of unionisation reached in Norway or Sweden, especially in the virtual absence of union shops, the labour movement must organise these small establishments. The difference in unionisation in these small establishments is almost certainly the primary reason for the difference in the density of organisation in the United Kingdom as compared to Norway,

Sweden and Austria. As Price and Bain (1976) show, UK public employees are very well organised; almost 90 per cent of them belong to unions. It is in the small establishments and in the private service sector that the UK labour movement is weak.

The argument that Australia and New Zealand did not develop centralised bargaining systems because of the lack of political threat from the left is considerably weakened by the fact that it depends on the employers' ability to foresee the fall of the Labor Party from power. Two additional factors help to explain why these countries showed no tendency toward the type of corporatist policy-making pattern characteristic of the high spenders despite high degrees of monopolisation. First, the single-member district system leads to a different political strategy on the part of employers and other political actors. Switching of power rather than compromise at each point in time is the most effective way to ensure one's interests are represented in the long run. Perhaps more important is the fact that New Zealand and Australia developed collective bargaining systems at a very early stage which were characterised by high degrees of legal interference. Compulsory arbitration, the legal extension of negotiated agreements to unorganised workers in the sector, and legal registration of trade unions impeded the development of a centralised system despite high levels of unionisation in both countries at an early point in time. In New Zealand, national unions of workers were actually prohibited until 1936. In addition, Australian labour legislation was developed on a regional basis thus preventing centralised bargaining. The organisational complexity created by the peculiar historical development of the labour movements of New Zealand and Australia is indicated by the large number of separate unions: over 300 in both cases. A further factor in the Australian case is the low degree of export dependency; only 14 per cent of GDP goes to exports. Thus the employers can more easily pass on wage raises in price increases without the adverse effects on the economy that would occur in a heavily export dependent country like the Netherlands.

Canada is probably misplaced in Tables 4.8 and 4.9. The high degree of integration of the Canadian and US economies and the consequent integration of the labour movements indicates that the degree of oligopoly in North America as a whole and not just Canada is the more important factor shaping the Canadian system of bargaining. If this is the case, then one would expect less centralised bargaining. The fact that the development of labour organisation in Canada follows the US pattern rather than the pattern of any of the highly monopolised countries indicates that this is the case.

Ireland is clearly a special case. The decisive factor influencing the formation of the Irish party system was the struggle for independence. This has impeded the development of a strong labour party. Moreover, the Irish economy is much more heavily agricultural than that of the other countries analysed here.

All five large democracies are characterised by low monopolisation, decentralised unions and decentralised bargaining. Only in the United Kingdom does the working class gain sufficient economic and political power in the immediate post-war period such that one might expect pressure for bargaining centralisation and an incomes policy to occur. The primary factors in preventing union centralisation are probably: (1) the complexity of the union organisational structure inherited from the technical complexity of the UK market during the initial organising period and (2) the lack of centralisation and solidarity of UK employers. The latter is linked to the lower levels of monopolisation, Ingham argues. In addition, the absence of proportional representation may influence the political strategy of various actors, as was previously mentioned. The British Labour Party actually has done comparatively well which is more of a negative comment on the fortunes of social democracy in other large democracies than it is a positive comment on British labour.

As we pointed out earlier, France and Germany spend more than one would expect given the length of leftist rule or level of labour organisation in the two countries. Aside from the post-war power vacuum on the right mentioned earlier, specific historical causes can be pointed to in both cases. In the German case, the unions would not have accepted the wage restraint necessary for the rapid capital accumulation required by the plan for economic reconstruction had they not received expansion of social benefits in return. In France, the immediate post-war period and the Popular Front period account for most innovations in French social legislation. Both periods were characterised by communist/social democratic co-operation in the government *and* tremendous and temporary increases in the level of trade union membership. Thus the balance of power in civil society tipped in the direction of labour in both cases giving the leftist governments substantial social support. However, the lack of a strong long-term institutional commitment, such as regular dues paying and participation, made these jumps in union membership short-lived bursts of enthusiasm rather than permanent gains for the labour movement.

In Italy and France, the exclusion of the communists as 'legitimate' government partners during the cold war shortened socialist rule and thus impeded the growth of the welfare state. In the French case, the main effect of conservative dominance of the government may be the tremendously regressive tax system and widespread tax evasion, particularly among the self-employed. The French welfare state is so regressively financed that it is possible that it redistributes income from the working class to the more well-to-do (see Chapter 5). Again, this is not unusual for welfare state development under Catholic influences and/or administration of the developed welfare states by conservative governments.

In Italy, as compared to France, there is a greater disparity between the level of labour organisation and the length of socialist rule. This is because the Italian Communist Party is larger than its French counterpart and because Italian labour unions are much stronger. The decline in Italian union membership shown in the second part of Table 4.8 is misleading. The 1950 figure is inflated and the decline that did occur has been reversed since 1968. This difference between France and Italy is important in terms of the future prospects of the left in those two countries.

The United States falls into a pattern one would expect given the analysis presented here. Being a large, ethnically divided country with a strong federal system, it is characterised by decentralised unions and bargaining, weak labour organisation, no socialist rule and low welfare spending.

5

Labour Organisation and the Welfare State: a Comparative Historical Analysis

In this chapter we will take a closer look at the development of the welfare state and the ideology and programmes of the labour movement in four capitalist democracies: Sweden, the United Kingdom, the United States and France. These countries were chosen because they exemplify variant patterns of welfare state development. They differ not only in the level of spending and the method of financing of the welfare state, but also in the antecedent variables which were found in the last chapter to be related to welfare state development. After surveying the historical development of the welfare state in each country, the redistributive impact of the public sector in the four countries will be compared.

Sweden[1]

Sweden emerges as a polar case in our cross-national analysis. There, the welfare state has been developed by a strongly organised and highly centralised trade union movement in co-operation with a social democratic government which remained in office for forty-four years. Under these conditions, the welfare state is characterised by high levels of expenditure and progressive financing and thus represents a transformation of capitalism towards socialism.

Swedish conditions clearly favoured the development of a labour movement with these characteristics. Sweden is a small, ethnically and linguistically homogeneous, Protestant country which experienced late and rapid industrialisation in comparison with other European countries. As a consequence of its size and thus the size of its domestic market and the pattern of its industrial development, Swedish industry was (and is) characterised by a small group of non-competing firms engaged in product-specialised industrial production. All these factors led to the development of a politically

unified, well organised and highly centralised trade union movement closely associated with a social democratic party.

Sweden entered a period of rapid industrialisation in the 1870s.
Vigorous labour organising began in the next decade. German
socialist ideas also found their way to Sweden via Denmark, and
socialist agitation began in earnest in this decade. The Social
Democratic Party was founded in 1889. Fifty of the seventy organisations founding the party were trade unions (Korpi 1978b: 61),
establishing the close association between the trade unions and the
party which has continued to the present. In the beginning, the party
also functioned as a central body for the trade unions. An organisationally distinct trade union central, LO, was formed in 1898. After
some dispute on the matter, it was finally decided that trade union
locals (not the national unions) would have the right to affiliate with
the Social Democratic Party. Today about 60 per cent of all party
members are affiliated through their trade union local.

Though the earliest trade unions were craft unions, the Swedish
pattern of industrialisation favoured the development of industrial
unions. Korpi (1978b: 64) shows that in 1908 46 per cent of all LO
members were organised in industrial unions and 26 per cent were
in craft unions with the remainder in mixed unions. In 1912, LO
made industrial unionism its main organising principle, thus ensur-
ing the dominance of industrial unions and industry-wide bargaining in Sweden. However, this alone did not lead to the concentration of power to LO and the development of industry-wide bargaining. As we pointed out previously, this evolved as a result of
employer organisation.

By 1902, the Swedish labour movement had already organised
roughly 15 per cent of all non-agricultural workers and a quarter of
all workers in the metal-working industry (Korpi 1978b: 62). In
that year, the unions conducted a nationwide strike for universal
suffrage. This alarmed employers and led them to organise a central
federation of employers, SAF, to fight the unions. To re-emphasise
a point made in the last chapter, the structure of Swedish industry, a
small group of non-competing oligopolistic firms, obviously facilitated this effort at co-operation among employers. The members of
SAF acted solidaristically, supporting each other financially and
otherwise, and waged an aggressive struggle against the labour
movement with frequent use of the lock-out weapon in an effort to
crush the unions. This stimulated the progressive centralisation of

LO and constant organising drives as part of an effort merely to survive.

At the Social Democrats' first congress in 1891, the party voted to co-operate with the Liberals in their drive for universal suffrage which was to be the main focus of the party's reform work. In 1897, the party adopted its first real programme, a slightly moderated version of the German Erfurt programme. These two events typify the ideology of the early leadership of the Swedish Social Democratic Party. They were reformist Marxists, heavily influenced by the rather deterministic version of Marxism held by the Germans at this time. Their image of the transition to socialism did not differ greatly from that of Karl Kautsky. But they were faced with different conditions. In purely formal terms, the Swedish labour movement was more excluded politically than the German once the German socialist laws lapsed because they had to struggle for *both* universal suffrage and cabinet responsibility to parliament (the German Reichstag was elected by universal suffrage). However, the class structure of Sweden was very different from that of Germany and, consequently, the Swedish labour movement had greater possibilities for alliance. The Swedish countryside was dominated by family farms though there were some large estates in the south. The old aristocracy dominated the bureaucracy and army but had a much smaller independent economic base than the German Junkers. Because an alliance with landholders would have been too weak the Swedish nation-building élite allied itself with the urban commercial and industrial classes. German economic development was directed by the state and thus the bourgeoisie fell under the political dominance of the Junker military bureaucratic authoritarian ruling coalition. Sweden was industrialised through foreign demand for her products, especially timber, and thus the bourgeoisie developed autonomously of the state and some sections were open to liberal political ideas. In summary, though the national bureaucratic military élite in Sweden was as authoritarian as the German élite, its social base was much narrower and, correspondingly, the alliance possibilities for the labour movement much greater. This difference had important consequences. The Swedish Social Democrats were more reformist than the Germans, because they could realistically expect more returns from their activity. So despite deterministic elements of their ideology, the Swedes were engaged in practical activity aimed at the gradual transformation of society from the inception of the movement. In consequence of this, deterministic Marxism never played the role of an ideological fetish which functioned to maintain solidarity in the absence of opportunity for practical activity among activists in the movement as it did in Germany (Roth 1963). For this reason, Marxist ideology probably never penetrated to the base of the party to the extent that it did in the German party.

But the leadership was Marxist and remained so, at least until the change of leadership after the Second World War. This is not to say that the party did not undergo important ideological evolution in this period. It did and it is our thesis that this can be linked directly to two deficiencies in classical Marxist theory – the projection of the evolution of the class structure and the development of class consciousness. The shift of policy emphasis from production politics to consumption politics in the inter-war period and then back to production politics in the 1970s can be understood against the background of a gradual build-up of the hegemony of the labour movement and the shifting class alliances in Swedish politics resulting from changes in the class structure.

Their first programmatic changes came at least as early as 1911. By that time, it had become apparent that the agricultural sector was not undergoing the same centralisation process as the industrial sector. The 1911 programme thus eliminated the demand for nationalisation of land and replaced it with a policy whereby ownership of small farms was to be protected, co-operative farming encouraged, and only large monopolies of rural resources transferred to the state. Obviously this change was made not only to conform with the reality of social structural development but also for reasons of political strategy. The party did not want to alienate the large rural class of small farmers.

This change to accommodate the small farmers can hardly be said to have been of major significance for Social Democratic ideology and policy at the time, though it foreshadowed some important later changes. The major transformation came in the period between the First World War and the depression. The Social Democrats and their allies had succeeded in getting an extension of suffrage in 1909. With the German defeat in the First World War, the Conservatives and the crown finally capitulated to the demand for universal suffrage and cabinet responsibility to the parliament. The Social Democratic–Liberal coalition dissolved with the victory of democ-

racy. The Social Democrats then began to concretise their programme for a gradual transition to socialism. The first Social Democratic minority government came to power in 1920 and proceeded
to set up two parliamentary investigation commissions, one on
socialisation and the other on industrial democracy. This brought
the issue of socialisation to the centre of political debate. In the
1920 election, the Social Democratic Party suffered its first electoral setback. The Swedish Social Democrats, like many other reformist socialists in this period, were faced with something they had
never counted on in the pre-war period. They had won 'the battle
for democracy' but it had not 'raised the proletariat to the position
of ruling class'. The voice of the people had been heard and it had
not supported the socialists. During the 1920s, the Social Democrats groped for a strategy to deal with the situation. In 1928, they
attempted to put a more radical programme on the agenda, this time
sharply increased inheritance taxes. Again the party was met with
electoral defeat. At this point, the leadership made a fairly definite
decision to put aside the issue of socialisation. Fortunately, the
party had something to put in its place which would respond to the
current economic crisis. Ernst Wigforss, Swedish Social Democracy's most brilliant theoretician, had developed a programme based
on a combination of Marxist theory and his readings of Keynes'
early writings. The programme called for deficit spending and an
expansion of public sector spending and employment to reflate
the economy. Wigforss convinced the rest of the leadership that his
programme would work and it was adopted as the party's policy for
the 1932 election campaign. The election proved to be a great
victory for the socialist block. The Social Democrats garnered 42
per cent of the vote and the two left socialist parties another 8 per
cent.

This did not give the socialists a majority in parliament, since the
small leftist parties were under-represented and since only a quarter
of the upper house was replaced at each election. The Social
Democrats needed bourgeois support for their programme. In part
because small Swedish farmers were hit hard by the Depression, the
Agrarian Party ultimately agreed to support their programme in
return for support of a protectionist farm policy. This farmer–
worker coalition – sometimes concretised in the form of a coalition
government (1936–9, 1951–7), sometimes not – dominated Swedish politics until 1957. The reform programme of this coalition

focused on common factors in the class situation of small farmers and workers, low income, little education, and thus low mobility chances for their offspring. The achievements of this period were the expansion of the welfare state services and the transformation of the Swedish educational system from the elitist European model to the more egalitarian American model of universal secondary education.[2] The coalition with the farmers also necessitated a de-emphasis of the factor which separates farmers and workers, the ownership of productive property. In terms of our typology of strategies for equalisation, the Social Democratic programme moved from production politics in 1920 to mobility and consumption politics in the coalition with the farmers.

What caused this change? The historical record not only for Sweden but also for social democracy in other countries gives a clear answer. Marx was wrong about the development of the class structure and the development of class consciousness. Actually, the latter only becomes a problem because the former prediction did not prove true. Had the development of the class structure approximated his projections, socialist parties in most capitalist democracies would never lose an election given the levels of support in the industrial working class which they now enjoy. But with the exception of Britain, the non-agricultural manual working class has rarely comprised much more than half the population. Thus the socialist parties have always had to look outside their core support to get their programmes passed. This has led to compromise of their programmes, either before elections to gain their own majority or after the election in a coalition with a party based outside of the working class.

Changes in the class structure are only part of the answer. According to the model proposed in Chapter 2 the proportion of the population with an objective interest in socialism is much larger than the non-agricultural working class. For instance, when the Swedish Social Democrats suffered a setback in the 1920 election, 71 per cent of the labour force were propertyless employees (non-agricultural workers, 42 per cent; agricultural workers, 17 per cent; non-manual employees, 12 per cent). However, the socialist block received only 36 per cent of the total vote. Class consciousness was obviously poorly developed. Why? Because the distribution of power in civil society was unfavourable to socialist forces. At this time, only 11 per cent of the population was organised in trade unions. Thus the opinion-making power of the bourgeoisie with domination of the media and all sorts of institutions, public and private, was much greater than the one the socialists had through their weak press and the union and party organisations and the resultant network of personal contacts. In short, the labour movement had not developed sufficient control over civil society. It had not developed a hegemony.

The hegemonic position of the bourgeoisie at this point in time is also indicated by the figures on differential turn-out. Two-thirds of upper class men and 60 per cent of upper class women voted in the 1921 election, compared to 58 per cent of working class men and 44 per cent of working-class women (Särlvik 1974:391). This also demonstrates the effect of sexism on the strength of the left. The isolation of women from worklife makes it more difficult for the socialist movement to reach them. And their role as guardians of traditionalism makes women more subject to voting cross-pressures on religious and traditionalist (for example, the royalty) issues. While there is no hard evidence that the Swedish women who did vote voted more conservatively than men in the 1921 election, the best guess is that they did.

The accession of the Social Democrats to power in 1932, along with continued growth of labour organisation, led to a reassessment of strategy on the part of the leading elements of the bourgeoisie as represented by SAF. As it appeared that the Social Democrats might stay in office a long time, compromise was necessary. In 1936, LO and SAF entered into negotiations that concluded in the signing of an agreement two years later that established the routinisation of collective bargaining and labour peace in Sweden. This agreement also laid the ground for the subsequent development of economy-wide bargaining between SAF and LO and later TCO, the white-collar union central organisation. Swedish 'corporatism' was the result of the labour movement's strength rather than an absorption of the labour movement into the capitalist system or a demonstration of some mystical 'Swedish spirit of compromise' (for example, see Tomasson 1970).

By the time the Swedish economy had recovered and the socialist block had achieved a parliamentary majority, the war intervened to halt temporarily the development of social policy of any sort, welfare statist or socialist. Plans for post-war expansion of the welfare state and some moderate socialisation of industry were developed by LO and the party and published as the 'Post War Programme of the Labour Movement'. The war coalition with all bourgeois parties dissolved as the war's end approached and the Social Democrats, who now had a commanding parliamentary majority, formed their own government.

The bourgeois parties' offensive against the Social Democrats took a pattern which was (and is) typical for the European right in the post-war period. Their first line of attack was the (very limited) socialisation programme. At this point the effectiveness of the propaganda of the Swedish right was increased by the unpopularity of rationing which the Social Democratic government had introduced to deal with the unexpected post-war inflation. But the spectre of communism was more important, not only for this period but the whole post-war period, and not only for the Swedish right but also for conservative forces in the entire capitalist world. Our point here is not to blame the development of the cold war entirely on the Western bourgeoisie. Clearly, the Soviet Union was totalitarian and the takeover of Czechoslovakia seemed to indicate it was expansionist. Our point is that anti-communism served a very important domestic function for the bourgeoisie in their fight against the labour movement's effort to expand democratic control of the economy. However absurd it may seem to claim that the prime mover in the development of democracy was preparing to do away with it, this claim was made with some effectiveness not only in Sweden but everywhere in Europe.

The bourgeois parties' second line of attack was to accept introduction of basic welfare state services but to push for less progressive financing. Again this was typical for most of Europe. Basic welfare services such as pensions, unemployment insurance, national health care and housing and family subsidies have proved popular everywhere the labour movement is even moderately strong. And once they are passed, these programmes are so popular that it is political suicide for conservative parties to reduce spending on them more than marginally.[3] So in election campaigns, the right generally promises to maintain services while lowering taxes and/or 'shifting the burden of taxation so that marginal taxes in certain groups do not reduce the incentive to work'. In practice, since it is impossible to reduce the tax burden substantially without cutting services, conservative parties in power have usually shifted the burden of taxation away from capital and high income earners to lower income groups while maintaining or slightly reducing the level of expenditure. The most common formula is a reduction of direct taxes on capital and of marginal rates in income taxes for the higher brackets and an increased reliance on indirect taxes such as sales or value added taxes.[4]

A third effective issue for the right has been traditionalism. As we pointed out earlier, this has been particularly important in influencing the voting behaviour of women. This has been especially important in Catholic countries, but, even in the United Kingdom, the Labour Party would have won every election since 1945 had women voted like men (Anderson 1965: 276). In Sweden, sex differences in voting in the late 1940s were less than in the United Kingdom (3 – 4 per cent versus 6 per cent) but still significant.

Despite their retreat on the socialisation issue under heavy opposition pressure, the 1948 election was a setback for the Social Democrats though the socialist block still had a majority in both chambers of the Riksdag. The election marked the Social Democrats' final retreat from the issue of socialisation. The party immediately began to make overtures to the Agrarian Party for a renewal of the coalition. A new coalition government was not consummated until 1951, but policy in the whole period to 1957 reflects this worker – farmer alliance, a suppression of production politics and an emphasis on mobility and consumption politics.

The cold war and the post-war economic control are only part of the explanation for the Social Democrats' final retreat on socialisation and the 1948 election setback. Though the distribution of power had changed dramatically due to the growth of labour organisation since the 1920s, the white-collar sector was not yet heavily organised. In 1945, 45 per cent of the Swedish labour force belonged to unions. LO accounted for 37 per cent; TCO, 7 per cent. Unorganised white-collar workers remained firmly under the political hegemony of capital, so it was impossible to appeal to them for support for increased democratic control of capital. And even in the working class, the labour movement had not reached maximum penetration as indicated by the turn-out figures for the 1948 election. Ninety-three per cent of upper-class men and 92 per cent of upper-class women voted in the 1948 election, compared to 82 per cent of working-class men and 78 per cent of working-class women.

A final factor in the lack of public support for socialisation demonstrates a general dilemma of social democracy. Survey evidence shows that even the Social Democrats' own supporters were at best lukewarm to the issue (Stephens 1976:219–41). Because the party had suppressed the issue of socialisation, it was unable to propagandise for it even among its own loyal supporters. Not only did the party leadership fail to convert its electorate to its point of view, it also failed to educate thoroughly the new recruits to the lower- and middle-level leadership, many of whom developed a social reformist rather than socialist ideology. As the Hansson/Wigforss generation gave way to a new generation of leadership in the late 1940s and early 1950s, the leadership of Swedish Social Democracy passed out of the hands of a thoroughly socialist group to a group that included some moderate socialists, such as Erlander, and some social reformers, such as Sträng.[5] The long-term effects of this change in leadership should not be overemphasised. It did not prevent the party from going through an ideological reorientation which had its root in the pension struggle of the late 1950s and culminated in the workers' control and collective ownership programmes of the 1970s. But this is the story of the next chapter. Let us now assess the record of Swedish Social Democracy as it stood at the beginning of the 1970s. Since social democracy has been most successful in Sweden, this brief overview will give us an idea of achievements and limits of an equalisation policy which does not include socialisation of industry.

The Swedish Social Democrats have created one of the most well-developed and perhaps the most progressively financed welfare states in the world. The record of the Swedish labour movement on unemployment has also been good, particularly given the unprecedented expansion of women's participation in the labour force. Not only were the Swedes the first to apply Keynesian policy to reduce the level of unemployment, they have gone beyond that policy to develop a comprehensive labour market and wage policy aimed at reducing the inflation–unemployment trade-off while equalising wages (Meidner 1974). This policy was developed by LO economists under the leadership of Gösta Rehn and later Rudolf Meidner. The policy was a unique response to the following conditions. In the late 1940s, the high levels of employment in Sweden combined with very high levels of blue-collar unionisation (about 75 per cent of blue-collar workers were organised, Korpi 1978b:62) meant that any wage gains by workers would be translated into increased inflation and deterioration of Sweden's export market, which would have had very serious consequences for a small export-dependent country like Sweden. The Social Democratic government asked for and received wage restraint from LO. As Martin (1975) points out, LO considered this policy unviable for a trade union in the long run so it sought to develop an alternative. What emerged was a policy for structural change in the economy. Through fiscal policy and trade union wage pressure, profits were to be squeezed. LO would demand equal pay for equal work across the economy regardless of the ability of the company to pay. This policy is known as the wage policy of solidarity. This would obviously force some low-wage companies out of business. The workers released by these companies would be provided alternative jobs through an 'active labour market policy' consisting of job retraining, provision of unemployment benefits and moving costs, facilitating information on employment possibilities and public works jobs. The effect of these policies was to reduce structural unemployment through increasing labour mobility and to shift workers to high-productivity and high-wage sectors. Thus the policy would upgrade average wages and the overall productivity of the Swedish economy while reducing the inflationary impact of high employment. Such a policy can hardly be carried out under conditions very different from those in Sweden, since it requires a high level of labour organisation, centralised wage negotiations and socialist participation in the government.

Though we have emphasised that the Swedish Social Democrats turned away from production politics, it is incorrect to assert that no inroads in the control of capital were made at all. Some control rights of capital have been socialised. Overall Keynesian management of the economy through fiscal and monetary policy has been complemented with selective socialisation of decision-making rights such as in the areas of manpower policies, access to corporate information, pollution control and job safety. Furthermore, collective savings and, to some extent, ownership in Sweden has expanded in the form of the supplementary pension (AP) fund which accounts for almost half of total gross savings and half of the credit supply in Sweden. The fund has recently begun to buy stock in various Swedish corporations. Aside from the pension fund, collective ownership in Sweden is limited to the usual state ownership of monopolies, such as railroads, utilities and telephone; state ownership of the largest bank in the country; and co-operative ownership of substantial shares of the retail trade and housing sectors.

The level of collective ownership and direct public control of investment is the primary limitation to the extent of equalisation achieved in Sweden by 1970. The government and trade unions have a large amount of indirect control over investment through the credit sources provided by the pension fund, the state bank and special counter-cyclical investment funds. But the final investment decision remains in the private sector. Private ownership of productive capital was greater in Sweden than many other European countries such as the United Kingdom, France or Italy. The effects of private capital ownership on distribution are obvious if often understated by the exclusion of unrealised capital gain from calculations of distribution in capitalist society. Only slightly less apparent is the social power associated with capital which limits the effectiveness of all other efforts at equalisation. As long as the capitalists own a substantial share of total capital and retain the right to sell that capital, the efforts of a government to socialise income or control rights associated with the capital in question will be limited by the necessity of maintaining an adequate rate of return on the capital. Similarly, a social democratic government's exercise of control rights once they are socialised will be constrained by this need to prevent capital exit. Social democracy has been able to reduce distributed profits and increase reinvestment, but the resultant capital growth still accrues to the capitalist. The efforts of Swedish trade unions with the aid of the government to achieve high wages and employment without excessive inflation and export deterioration has also been limited by the need to provide for adequate reinvestment. In practice, this has resulted in a *de facto* incomes policy the result of which is that capital growth is paid for by wage restraint.

Britain

Britain is a case of medium welfare state development under social democratic auspices supported by a moderately strong trade union movement. The Labour Party has been in office approximately half of the post-war period and the welfare state is not as well developed as in Sweden. Nor does it appear to be as progressively financed as the Swedish welfare state.

Britain is similar to Sweden in that it is an overwhelmingly Protestant country which established a national church at the time of the Reformation and in that it experienced a long smooth history of state and nation building. Wales, Scotland and Ireland (before 1922) introduce an ethnic diversity in Britain absent in Sweden but this has differentiated the two countries politically only before 1922 and very recently. Two primary factors differentiate Britain and Sweden which explain the difference in their social and political configurations. Ingham identifies one of them, the industrial infrastructure (see Chapter 2). The second is the pattern of political mobilisation of the working class.

Britain is a larger country than Sweden and consequently, the centralisation of capital is lower and production is less specialised. Britain industrialised before any other nation and developed at a moderate pace. These factors explain the difference between the British and Swedish trade union movements. The British labour force is less organised than the Swedish despite the fact that closed and union shops are common in Britain and absent in Sweden. The difference in organisational density is all the more impressive when one considers that two-thirds of the British labour force work in manual jobs compared to one-half in Sweden. The TUC is much less centralised than LO. And the craft unions are stronger in Britain than in Sweden, which is probably why the TUC has some 155 affiliates compared to LO's 25. The difference in the characters of the trade union movements is the single most important factor accounting for the difference in the success of social democracy in Britain and Sweden.

The magnitude of the difference in electoral success is greater than it might appear at first glance. In the post-war period, the Swedish socialists outpolled the British Labour Party by an average of 5 per cent despite the differences in the size of the working class. When these figures are broken down by class, the difference is greater. Then the Swedish lead is about 15 per cent in the working class and 10 per cent among non-manuals. If the British Labour Party had enjoyed the level of support in both groups which the Swedes did, it would have won every election since the introduction of universal suffrage.

The effect of the level of trade union organisation on the political fortunes of social democracy and thus on welfare state development needs no further comment here. But the differences in organisation are not the whole story. While the level of labour organisation is the resource base of the socialist movement, the utilisation of the resources will depend on structural characteristics of the movement as well as leadership ideology. The opinion-making power and capacities for political action of the labour movement are dependent on the degree of centralisation of resources and decision-making. Centralisation also affects the degree and character of politicisation of trade unions. Centralised trade union movements are more likely to take a more leftist class-wide perspective rather than a narrow group-interest view. They are more likely to become and remain committed to political action. And they have the resources to translate this leftist politicised orientation into action. The well-known differences between craft and industrial unions are only a special case of this general principle. To exaggerate the differences between Britain and Sweden a little, let us compare the point of view of the officials at the centres of power in the two movements, the local official in Britain and the head of LO. To best further the interests of his constituency, which is the whole working class, the Swedish leader will contribute to the financing of the Social Democratic Party and of Social Democratic newspapers. He will promote a policy of wage solidarity and will be willing to consider wage policy as one part of a total package to promote the interests of the working class. For the British local official, none of this will be done if he attempts to promote his constituents' interests in the most rational way. The immediate returns he would get for setting up a newspaper or even contributing to the Labour Party would not justify the outlay. A solidaristic wage policy makes no sense from the point of view of the British official whether he is in an unprofitable or profitable firm. In one case his members will be without a job and in the other, they will end up with lower wages. And in the case of the official in a craft union, the pressure towards narrow group egoism is even greater. From the point of view of the general secretary of the TUC, supporting newspapers and the like may be rational, but he lacks the power and the resources to carry out this policy.

Anderson (1965) has outlined the dimensions of hegemonic presence of a labour movement and documented the weakness of the Labour Party and the TUC on all of these dimensions. Without going into detail on all aspects, it appears to us that the Swedish labour movement is stronger than the British labour movement in every respect. For instance, about 20 per cent of the Swedish press is Social Democratic (much of it LO owned or supported), while there is no real party press in Britain, though a few papers do support Labour at election time. On other measures of hegemonic presence such as individual party membership, membership in women's and youth groups, trade union journal circulation, movement-linked study groups and rank-and-file propaganda campaigns, the Swedes appear to have a substantial edge on the British. In analysis of survey data, we found that the social penetration of the Swedish labour movement explained variation in voting behaviour independent of trade union membership.[6] Scase (1977) also found that unionised Swedish workers were more leftist in their voting behaviour than a matched sample of English workers. Moreover, he found that among those who voted Social Democratic or Labour, the Swedes were more radical and more class conscious.

This evidence on the Swedish/British differences indicates that another interpretation of some of the results of the data analysis in the last chapter is possible. The effect of economy-wide bargaining on welfare spending may not be entirely due to absorption of wage policy into a more general social policy package. Since the centralisation of trade unions and the centralisation of bargaining are strongly related, and since trade union centralisation seems to increase labour movement hegemony, some of the variations explained by bargaining centralisation may be due to its covariation with hegemony.

The second factor which accounts for differences in the electoral strength of the Swedish Social Democrats and the British Labour Party is the historical differences in the political mobilisation of the working class. The Labour Party was a late comer on the British political scene relative to the Conservatives and Liberals: substantial sections of the working class were first mobilised by the Conservatives and Liberals. In Sweden, the political mobilisation of the working class was almost entirely the work of the Social Democrats. Pointing to the intergenerational inheritance of party preferences, Butler and Stokes (1976) attribute part of the Conservative voting in the British working class to this factor. Our cross-national analysis of Swedish and British data confirms Butler and Stokes's argument (J. D. Stephens 1979). The difference in political mobilisation patterns accounts for one-third of the difference in leftist voting in the working class and one-half of the difference in the middle class. The differences are almost entirely concentrated in the older generation.

The nature of the opposition to the labour movement varies between these two countries, but the effects on the strength of the movement probably cancel each other out. On the one hand, the Swedes face a fragmented political opposition, while the UK Labour Party faces perhaps the best organised conservative party in any capitalist democracy. This factor contributes to Labour's relative disadvantage. On the other hand, the Swedish trade unions, unlike the British, are faced with a highly cohesive centralised group of employers on the labour market. This may explain why some British trade unions seem to have been more successful than the Swedes in gaining a higher degree of shop-floor job control through bargaining.

With these differences and the Swedish historical development as a background, the development of the welfare state in Britain can be explained with a very brief historical sketch. The pattern of industrialisation in Britain led to the initial development of strong craft unions. The lag between the development of union organising and the final development of the Labour Party was very long. The openness of the British political system may have been partially responsible for this. It is true that the first working-class movements for political and social rights were repressed. But later, political competition between two sections of the propertied classes resulted in partial suffrage extensions in 1867 and 1883. As Moore (1966) points out, the precondition for this pluralistic competition between the landed upper class and the industrial bourgeoisie was the early development of a 'non-labor repressive' form of commercialised agriculture in England. In Germany, by contrast, the Junker form of agricultural production required more political control of the peasant population. The economic situation of the landed class and the development of a politically independent industrial bourgeoisie prevented the development of a German-style bureaucratic statism in Britain and set the stage for competitive struggle among the two factions of the ruling class. As in the Swedish case, it seems that class relations rather than formal political structures were of critical importance in determining the openness of the political system.

In explaining the late development of the Labour Party, the role of the strength of craft unions – which tend to be liberal rather than socialist in the early phases of organising – should not be ignored.

And it is no accident that the Railway Workers' Union, an industrial union, was a prime mover in the formation of the Labour Representation Committee in 1900. After the 1906 election in which the committee was able to get twenty-nine MPs elected with the help of the Liberals, the Labour Party was formed. The membership was made up of organisations, primarily trade unions, but also socialist societies such as the Fabians and the Independent Labour Party. From the beginning the party was very reformist, to the point of focusing almost all political action on parliamentary politics. Until the adoption of the *Labour and the New Social Order* programme in 1918, the party was not formally committed to socialism. While some would claim that even that programme is not socialist and the party never was socialist, we think it is fair to characterise the early Labour Party leadership as moderate reformist socialist though obviously not Marxist. With the introduction of universal male suffrage in 1918 (female suffrage came in 1928), the party turned its full energies to the promotion of its new programme. The period to 1929 is similar to the same period in Sweden; Labour was a minority in Parliament, so any of its more radical programmes could not be promoted because it needed Liberal support. The 1929 election victory and the subsequent Labour government marks the point of divergence of the British from the Swedish case. By rejecting Keynesian reflationary policies, the Labour Government failed to respond creatively to the crisis and a section of the leadership finally deserted the party to form a government with the Conservatives to carry out an austerity policy. The Conservatives then won the next two elections in a row.

In no election before the war was Labour able to garner more than 38 per cent of the vote, which it reached in 1929 and 1935. Like the other antagonists in the war, Britain experienced a brief spurt of trade union growth immediately after the First World War and then a sharp decline in the early 1920s (see Table 4.8). Throughout the remainder of the 1920s to the mid-1930s, British trade union membership declined constantly. For the reasons given in the last chapter, the Second World War brought about a sharp increase in the density of organisation. Since the war the level of labour organisation has grown somewhat. Given the level of labour organisation in the inter-war years, along with the historical disadvantages the Labour Party was faced with, its electoral fortunes and the low level of support for its more radical programmes are not surprising, even given the favourable class structure it was operating in.

As in Sweden, the plans for the development of the welfare state were laid during the war in Britain. And, as in Sweden, the legislation establishing basic welfare services was passed by the Labour government in the immediate post-war period. Similarly, the opposition in Britain agreed to the expansion of services but wanted less progressive financing. Britain and Sweden also entered the post-war period with similar levels of labour organisation. Thus it is not surprising that the Labour Party leadership underwent an ideological transformation similar to that of the Swedes. The British case differs from the Swedish (and all others) in that no alliance with the rural petty bourgeoisie was necessary. But the hegemonic strength of the socialist movement is the critical factor in both cases.

The expansion of welfare services had displaced socialisation as the core of the party's programme. Reform of the educational system was added later. Consumption and mobility politics took the place of production politics. Around 1950, the ideologies of Swedish and British social democracy were more similar than they had been before or would be subsequently. The major difference in policy orientation is that Labour maintained its commitment to a modified socialisation programme in the form of selective nationalisation with compensation while the Swedish Social Democrats became thoroughly committed to socialisation of control rights as the more effective policy.

In the 1950s, the paths of development in the two countries began to diverge again. Both social democratic parties slipped electorally but this put Labour out of office and only reduced the Swedes' parliamentary base.[7] Because of bargaining centralisation and continued social democratic tenure, labour organisation grew much more rapidly in Sweden than in Britain. The Swedish Social Democrats responded to their sliding electoral fortunes by policy innovation and increased mobilisation, Labour by becoming more like their opponents. When returned to office in 1964, the Labour Party responded to inflation with a pure capitalist policy – wage restraint and deflation. Faced with a similar situation, the Swedes developed a policy of structural change of the economy. In short, Labour under Wilson had become a social reformist party, attempting to operate a capitalist economy with very limited tools of control in a way that it hoped would benefit the working class but could only to a limited extent. Its achievements were few and far between. At the same time, the Swedish Social Democrats had begun a process of ideological renewal that led to a return to a focus on production politics in the seventies.

How much of the Swedish/British differences are due to policy innovations on the part of the Swedes? Heclo (1974), in his comparison of Britain and Sweden, reduces the development of the welfare state to a search for technical solutions to problems and attributes the differences between Sweden and Britain to differential success in finding solutions. He explicitly denies that 'politics' have much to do with welfare state development. One reason Heclo can discount politics is that he uses an extremely limited definition of what is political. Political effects are said to exist if a policy is passed as the result of a change of government in which the party winning the election promised the policy in question while the other did not. Popular agitation, which Heclo admits stimulated policy development, is not considered to be political. Nor does Heclo consider the strength and centralisation of the labour movement to be political or apparently to be an important factor anyway, though he does admit that LO played an important role in Swedish policy developments. Another problem in Heclo's analysis is that it focuses on only three programmes: unemployment insurance, basic pensions and supplementary pensions. The first two may be functionally necessary for capitalism (or any industrial society) because all capitalist democracies have them. Thus we would have predicted that these programmes would be developed no matter who was in the government, though they would be financed differently. The only programme that Heclo studies which varies considerably across nations is supplementary pensions. And there he finds considerable 'political' effect.

The strongest point supporting Heclo's point of view is that the parties of the right favoured the introduction of most of the welfare state programmes in the immediate post-war period. (His argument receives additional support in the British case from the fact that Beveridge was a Liberal.) From our point of view, the reason for this is clear: the changed distribution of power in civil society caused by the growth of labour organisation. The response of conservative parties in a situation like this is to support the institution of welfare policies but to finance them regressively. Actually it is very rare for governments without a socialist party as at least a partner in coalition to promote a vigorous expansion of welfare spending.[8] But Heclo's argument is not simply that conservative parties sometimes increase spending. Rather he takes the more extreme position that incumbency makes very little difference at all. Not only is this contradicted by our cross-national analysis; the British case itself is a good example of what conservatives do when they administer a welfare state. The Conservative government of the 1950s slowed the expansion of welfare services and more important they made the tax system more regressive. Furthermore, they introduced fees for a number of services which were free before, and means tests for a number of previously unrestricted services.

While rejecting Heclo's assertion that the innovations of civil servants have been the critical factor in policy development, it is possible to raise the question of whether policy innovation by political élites does not make some difference. One can hardly help but be impressed by the differences in the responses of the social democratic élites in Sweden and Britain at a number of critical points. Martin (1975) argues that it is at least conceivable that, had the 1929–31 Labour government carried out the same type of social Keynesian policies in co-operation with Lloyd George Liberals that the Swedish Social Democrats did a few years later, they might have retained control of the state in the 1930s. He raises a similar point about the 1951 election defeat. Had the Labour Party adopted a policy of structural change to deal with the problem of inflation, things might have turned out differently. It is ironic that a party which prides itself on ideological openness as compared to its supposedly more dogmatic Marxist sister parties has actually been one of the least innovative social democratic parties in Europe. It has responded to a number of difficult situations with an odd combination of the prevailing capitalist economic logic and the most traditional of all socialist policies – nationalisation.

It is important to emphasise that the British leadership did not have one resource that the Swedes had – a highly centralised trade union movement. Though this would have had no effect in the case of the economic policy followed by the two movements in the 1930s, the decentralisation of English trade unions would have made it difficult for the Labour Party to introduce the same type of policy that the Swedish Social Democrats did in the 1950s. The wage equalisation and structural rationalisation policy was aided by the existence of a centralised trade union movement. Leftist critics might respond that that is exactly the point: local autonomy of English trade unions allowed them to resist capitalist rationalisation and assert more control over the immediate conditions of work. This critique correctly points out a cost of the Swedish policy of maximal growth through structural rationalisation: one by-product of a policy of ceding control of technological development to capitalists is the dehumanisation of work life. But resistance to capitalist rationalisation is a defensive response and is not a viable alternative to the Swedes' policy in the long run. The creative response would be to demand democratic control of technological development. Again, as in the case of wage restraint, the limit of social democratic reformism is precisely that it is not socialist.

To summarise the British situation as of 1970: a moderately strong trade union movement in alliance with a social democratic party that was in power half of the post-war period managed to build up a moderate-sized public sector which was financed through fairly progressive taxation. The trade unions in the heavily organised sectors had achieved a greater degree of job control than is the case in most capitalist countries. Socialisation of control rights of capital is much more limited than in the Swedish case. Consequently, even the fiscal and monetary manipulation of the economy by recent Labour governments has been carried out on terms dictated by the workings of domestic and international capital.

The United States

The United States is characterised by a very low level of labour organisation and the absence of a major reformist labour party. The result is minimal welfare state development. The United States, along with Japan, comes closest to having only a level of spending which is functionally necessary for the maintenance of a capitalist society. To say it has the minimum is probably an exaggeration, as there is good reason to believe that public spending would be even lower in the absence of organised working-class pressure.

The United States is a large, ethnically diverse country which industrialised at a pace greater than Britain but less than Sweden. The political system at the time of industrialisation was more open than in Britain or Sweden, thus one would expect a unified, moderate, weak labour movement. The absence of a labour party, a characteristic which is idiosyncratic among capitalist societies, could not be predicted from anything said to this point. Instead of creating its own party, the US labour movement has tried to influence and mobilise support for the more liberal of the two existing parties. Greenstone (1969) calls this relationship the 'partial equivalent' of European social democracy. Understanding why this alliance and not an independent labour party developed will help us understand the US pattern of welfare state development.

In the US case, the link between the form of labour organisation and political ideology and action again proves to be important. Early craft unions tend to be liberal not only in the sense that they are not socialist but also in the sense that they are much less interested in political action as a method of furthering their members' interests. Furthermore, their liberalism is demonstrated by their efforts to restrict rather than to expand state activity in the labour market. The political thrust of industrial unions has always been socialist – or more accurately, social democratic – which calls for more vigorous political action on the part of the unions and is directed towards expansion of the scope of state activity in the economy. And if industrial unions do not play a major role in creating a labour or social democratic party, their success in organising a significant portion of the working class is a necessary prerequisite for social democracy to become a major political force. This did not happen in the United States until the late 1930s. The US industrial working class was recruited from successive waves of immigrants. The ethnic diversity of the working class served to reinforce the narrow group egoism of the craft unions which dominated the AFL and contributed to its lack of organising zeal. The CIO was formed by some of the industrial unions in the AFL in 1935. The organising drive that ensued changed the character of the US labour movement. From 1936 to 1937, membership almost doubled and it increased substantially again the next year. With one-quarter of non-agricultural employees organised, the US labour movement became an important political force. It did not, however, set up an independent labour party.

One reason for this is the character of the US electoral system. Single-member districts, primaries and the presidential system create a situation where there is maximum incentive and opportunity for social groups to compete and coalesce within the structure of the two existing parties. Lipset (1967) argues, convincingly we think, that a parliamentary system of government in the United

States would have produced a labour party. The Canadian case is strong support for this assertion. The Canadian and US trade union movements are almost one and the same. When the AFL–CIO merger in 1956 put an end to trade union in-fighting, it was the prelude to the formation of a social democratic party, the New Democratic Party, in Canada in 1961 but to increased involvement of the trade unions in the Democratic Party in the United States.

The policy followed by the Roosevelt administration was also instrumental in convincing the CIO leadership to support the Democrats rather than create a labour party. Roosevelt began the first halting steps toward welfare state development and economic reflation along Keynesian lines well before the organisational burst of 1937–8. Furthermore, the union leadership owed a lot to Roosevelt because he put the prestige of the president behind union organising (Harrington 1972:258–9). Thus the openness of the Democratic Party in terms of the policies of a particular incumbent president, as well as the primary structure, helped channel the political activity of organised labour into that party.

In the Roosevelt administration, we see the beginnings of welfare state development in the absence of organised working-class pressure. Roosevelt owed nothing to organised labour for his 1932 election victory. But it would be wrong to infer that Roosevelt's policies were an expression of the capitalist state's recognition that some expansion of state activity was necessary to ensure the smooth functioning of the capitalist system. The business community hated Roosevelt and his social Keynesian policies. For instance, the newspaper baron Hearst said of Roosevelt's 1935 tax reform: 'The President's taxation program is essentially communism' (Harrington 1976:300). Roosevelt's reforms may have been functionally necessary for capitalism but US business certainly did not think so.

The events in the United States raise the question of whether the labour movement was successfully absorbed into a capitalist political party. The problem with this interpretation is that the Democratic Party is not a disciplined political party capable of formulating and carrying out a programme in the interests of anyone (see Martin 1973). It is a coalition of local groups with social bases varying from constituency to constituency which meets every four years to elect a presidential candidate. In the beginning this worked to labour's advantage as it tried to get a foothold in the party. But in the long run it worked against labour, since the lack of disciplined voting meant that the party could never be relied upon to produce on its promises. To counteract this, the labour movement would have to set up local organisations in every constituency and in alliance with like-minded groups (for example, minorities) run candidates pledged to a programme. In short it would have to create a disciplined party or faction within the Democratic Party. It has never been willing to go this far.

It should be pointed out that the Republican Party shares this characteristic with the Democrats. Thus the US capitalist élite has no coherent policy through either party. And it lacks this in any other form too. Because of the size and market structure of the US economy, the capitalist élite in the United States is very large in absolute numbers relative to the small capitalist systems. And, at least to some extent, it is divided through competition. Thus without a disciplined party to develop and focus its programme, it is unable to produce a coherent policy. Through the effect of numerous large corporations and local businesses contributing to local and national candidates and each lobbying for its own special interests, as well as through the usual latent threat of investment stops and capital flight, US capitalist interests and a few well-organised professions, such as medicine, have succeeded in preventing much progress on labour's programme and have created a system of concessions to particular interests and a web of corruption rather than a coherent programme. This situation impedes the development of the United States towards the principal viable alternative to socialism – corporate collectivism. The US capitalist class, much more than its European counterparts, still rules much more through economic domination in the market rather than political domination through the state. The decline of US dominance of world capitalism promises to make this an increasing problem for US capitalism in the future.

The cold war was more devastating to the left in the United States than it was in other capitalist democracies with the possible exception of those where the communists were strong. The labour movement itself went through anti-communist purges. Labour organising stagnated at one-third of non-agricultural employees and began to slide back with the growth of white-collar ranks. Reuther and the other leaders of the CIO expected a great organising drive when the merger with the AFL put an end to the inter-union raiding. This never materialised because of the climate of opinion in the United States and because the craft unions of the AFL were overrepresented in the AFL-CIO executive council. Furthermore, the overwhelming dominance of US capitalism in the world economy allowed US corporations to pass on labour costs to consumers and thus the unions were able to gain substantial concessions which reduced the incentive for massive organising efforts. With the dominance of the AFL in the new organisation, a CIO man did not succeed George Meany on his sixty-fifth birthday as had apparently been tacitly agreed on. Possibly because of the influence of the AFL and Meany, labour's political strategy never went beyond mobilisation of personnel and financial support for the Democratic candidate in the general election.[9]

Against this background, it is hardly surprising that the demands for welfare state expansion on the part of organised labour met with little success. The unions were never able to get a supplementary and comprehensive pension plan or national health insurance, two key welfare state programmes, passed by even a Democratic administration. Instead, they resorted to negotiating these for organised workers in the more dynamic sectors which left substantial sections of the working class partially or completely uncovered and usually left control of accumulated pension funds in the hands of the employers. And just when the mobilisation of Blacks and election of a new Democratic administration promised to alter the situation, the war in Vietnam intervened to halt the expansion of welfare programmes and shatter the unity of the left.

The weakness of the US labour movement, and the inadequacy of its chosen political instrument (the Democratic Party) raise the question of whether the US case does not represent a situation of complete capitalist control of state policy. Might not the low level of non-military spending in the United States be the absolute minimum functionally necessary for the survival of capitalism? Piven and Cloward (1972) argue that this is the case for public welfare. At first glance, their contention that public assistance is expanded in times of public disorder and contracted in times of political stability seems to be confirmed by the coincidence of the expansion of welfare in the 1930s and 1960s with the mass unemployment of the 1930s and the racial unrest of the 1960s. But the latter case does not hold on closer inspection. As Harrington (1976:304) points out 'The main innovations of the Great Society ... were initiated (and in most cases passed into law) prior to ...

1965. They were not, therefore, a response to the most violent of the ghetto explosions in Watts (1965), Detroit, New Haven and Newark (1967) and Washington, D.C. (1968).'

The empirical evidence indicates that state policy in the United States has not been entirely shaped in the interests of capital. The most comprehensive study of the redistributive impact of government activity in the United States shows that significant redistribution does result from taxation and spending (Reynolds and Smolensky 1977). Furthermore, the redistributive impact of government does seem to be due, in part, to the activity of labour unions. Hicks, Friedland and Johnson (1978) show that the variations in the strength of organised labour had a significant effect on interstate variations in the degree of government redistribution as measured by the ratio of net taxes to net benefits for households with incomes under $4000. Friedland (1977) finds similar effects for local funding levels of the War on Poverty in the 130 largest cities in the United States. Ratner (1977) shows that the level of labour organisation (but not the rate of increase in organisation) is related to the expansion of labour standards legislation. The results from research on the impact of the Democratic Party on redistribution are more ambiguous. In his time series analysis Björn (1979) found that Democratic incumbency affected the rate of redistributive change before the Second World War (that is, the Roosevelt administration) but not after the war. However, Hibbs (1977) shows that the Democrats did carry out a more pro-working-class macro-economic policy than the Republicans in the post-war period. Inflation was higher and unemployment lower during Democratic administrations. The research conducted by Hicks, Friedland and Johnson suggests an explanation for these apparently contradictory results. They show that 'Democratic Party strength has a positive effect on the level of state redistribution to the poor to the extent to which Democratic Party cohesion and interparty competition are simultaneously high' (Hicks *et al.* 1978: 305). This confirms our contention that the effect of the Democratic Party on redistribution is contingent on the degree to which it approximates a mass-based disciplined party along the lines of a European labour party.

Even given the effect of Democratic Party strength and labour organisation on the institution of various policies, it still might be argued that these policies were functional for capitalism. Since the function served by a given institution can never be invoked as an explanation for its origin, the argument cannot be dismissed. For instance, Roosevelt introduced counter-cyclical economic policy over the loud protests of the business community, yet helped them in the long run. And though it would be a revision of the traditional orthodox Marxist argument, it could be claimed that the redistributive effect of public spending is necessary if it is to serve its legitimation function. But this argument cannot be supported because there are clear functional alternatives that are even more pro-capitalist than the ones now existing in the United States as a whole. The US tax system could be much more regressive, as the example of France shows. And the substantial interstate variation in government redistribution shown by Hicks, Friedland and Johnson indicates that US capitalism as a whole could continue to function with lower levels of redistribution.

What is the optimal level of public expenditure from the capitalists' point of view? Clearly it is not the absence of public spending. Internal and external order must be maintained, some public goods such as highways must be provided. Beyond that, it is impossible to say what would be necessary. The 'legitimation expenditure' (for example, pensions, public assistance) necessary in the absence of labour organisation would depend entirely on the trade-off between the costs of spontaneous disruptions of production and the costs of the governmental expenditure itself. Primary education may be a necessity for the functioning of the system, to provide the labour force with some minimal level of literacy. It would be more beneficial for higher income groups for the higher educational system to be paid for on a fee-for-service basis. Not only would that make it easier for them to pass their social position on to their offspring, it would also be cheaper unless taxes were extremely regressive, more regressive than, say, a sales tax. This brings up an important point: ultimately, it is impossible to say what level of expenditure is optimal from the capitalists' point of view unless one specifies how it will be financed. While it is very difficult to achieve a balance where the public sector distributes income to higher income groups (the tax system must be very regressive and benefits structure highly skewed towards the rich, as we shall see), it is theoretically possible. In this hypothetical case, it would be in the capitalists' favour to increase spending.

To summarise the situation in the United States, the weakness of

US labour and the left has resulted in a system of financing of public expenditure which is at best proportional to income. Public spending does create some marginal redistribution in favour of the very poor. The collectivisation of control on the other hand has largely benefited capitalists. Regulatory boards are filled with industry spokesmen and fiscal and monetary policies have been operated in a way most beneficial to business. Even Democratic presidents have cut taxes rather than increased spending in order to reflate the economy. Workers in strongly organised sectors have succeeded in getting some measure of shop-floor job control but they are a small minority of all employees.

France

France has a divided and weak labour movement and has experienced little socialist control of the government. Yet the French public sector is somewhat larger than average among capitalist democracies. But it is very regressively financed. France is a good example of what happens when public sector build-up is carried out by socialists in coalition with Catholic or centre parties, but then administered by conservative forces for a long period of time. The result is corporate collectivism.

To understand the French case, we have to account for the emergence of a divided labour movement faced with a conservative coalition in which the petty bourgeoisie plays an important part. Italy and Spain also have these characteristics, so it is instructive to look at what these countries have in common. They are large Catholic countries in which the nation builders and the church were at odds and in which small-scale production was dominant in the initial period of democratic mobilisation and formation of the labour movement. And they experienced a fascist interlude, either through internal development or conquest.

All Catholic countries developed Catholic labour unions which competed with the socialist-controlled unions.[10] In France, Italy and Spain – but not in The Netherlands, Belgium, Germany or Austria – the dominant ideology of the socialist unions was anarcho-syndicalist rather than social democratic. They were not necessarily more radical; but they differed in their view of the state. Critically, they stood apart from the social democratic parties who reluctantly respected their autonomy. This pattern was maintained even when the unions later moved from syndicalism to socialist reformism as the CGT (General Confederation of Labour) did in France after the first World War. Organisationally, the unions in these countries were much less centralised than the unions in other countries. Even in the industrial unions, the focus of power (and, to the extent it occurred at all, of bargaining) was the local level. As Shorter and Tilly (1974: 15) point out, in France, 'only a fraction of all workers in any given manufacturing establishment became union members in these years (1900–1914); but this handful constituted itself in most industrial enterprises'. And to this day in France and until recently in Italy, the dues structure is very loose, members are often not required to pay regular dues and no check-off system exists. Consequently membership can fluctuate radically from year to year.

The syndicalist ideology and the organisational structure are related and have a common antecedent, an economic situation characterised by few large dynamic enterprises and the dominance of stagnant small business. The decentralisation of bargaining and unions follow from this. Syndicalism's focus on the immediate enterprise is consistent with this organisational form of decentralised industrial unionism. But unlike the liberalism of craft unions, it is radical. The radicalism is due not only to the fact that it is industrial unionism but also to the small enterprise size. Small enterprises, especially family-operated ones, tend to be characterised by archaic, paternalistic labour relations. Mann (1973: 39–45) attributes the radicalism of French workers to the 'feudalistic' attitudes of French employers toward their employees and their consequent extreme hostility to unions. In the industrial field as in the political field, inclusion generates moderation; exclusion, radicalism. The labour relations in small-scale stagnant enterprises amount to exclusion. For example, the overwhelming majority of employers refused to recognise unions or to enter into negotiation with employees at all. Industrial disputes were generally solved through government intervention (Shorter and Tilly 1974: 33–9). The radicalism of French unions was reinforced by the fact that so few employees in each enterprise were members. It is a safe guess that the few workers who were members were among the most militant.

Not all French workers were radical: some accepted the paternalism of the employers. The role of the Church comes in here;

workers from family backgrounds which remained religious in the state/Church struggle accepted paternalism and later Catholic unionism. Thus the French working class was and is divided between socialist radicals and a smaller segment of Catholic moderates.

Since the membership of the French trade unions in times of social and political stability consists of a few militants in the majority of enterprises rather than a combination of militants and passive members as in the United Kingdom or Sweden, the level of labour organisation in such times grossly underestimates the hegemonic presence and mobilisation potential of the French trade unions. However, the substantial portion of the French working class who do not come into personal day-to-day contact with these militants remain largely outside the sphere of influence of the labour movement because they lack the formal organisational links (and thus contact with trade union journals, etc.) that the Swedish worker in an equivalent position would have. This situation at the same time increases the potential for revolutionary explosions and reduces the potential for socialist reformism in France.

The importance of the organisational structure and the autonomy of the trade unions for the development of a strong Communist Party in France can be seen by the fact that the French Communists did not become the major working-class party until they took over the CGT, which they accomplished during the Resistance. Though the political control exerted by the foreign powers after the war in Germany makes any definite conclusion on this matter impossible, it seems likely that social democratic rather than communist control of the German unions would have been re-established anyway. In the inter-war years, the German and French communists' electoral performance was similar, between 7 and 15 per cent in most elections. Only after the war did the French communists manage to gain over 20 per cent of the votes cast.

The French and Italian Communists benefited greatly from their activity in the Resistance. Their effectiveness was in part due to the structure of their party organisation, which, after all, was developed to carry on political activity in a hostile and authoritarian society. Not only were they able to capture the trade unions, they were also able greatly to expand their political base and gain some measure of legitimacy for their efforts at national liberation.

The Church and the market structure also made its mark on the socialists' opposition. The dominance of the petty bourgeoisie, small businessmen and farmers, in the economic structure of Third Republic France meant that virtually every government would have to be led by their representatives, the Radicals. Naturally, the Radicals were not prepared to carry out any economic modernisation programme as that would destroy their base, at least the urban wing of it. Instead, they supported the petty bourgeoisie through tax advantages and tolerated widespread evasion of taxes. This impeded economic growth and the centralisation of capital, slowing the development of both a stronger labour movement and a big bourgeoisie. The Church comes into the picture in several ways. The secularisation struggle resulted in a position of militant secularism among French civil servants, especially teachers, which eventually led them into the socialist camp. As a result, the petty bourgeoisie became indispensable to the big bourgeoisie, who replaced the petty bourgeoisie as the hegemonic economic and political force as a consequence of the post-war economic boom in France. The French civil servant could not be relied upon by the conservative forces like the German Beamte could, so it was politically necessary for the French capitalists to continue the policies aimed at the maintenance of the petty bourgeoisie.

Parliamentary (male) democracy came to France with the reform of the upper house in 1884, though the secret ballot was not introduced until 1913. The Socialists were more radical than one would expect given the degree of openness of the political system because of the exclusion in the industrial sphere, if the argument just laid out is correct. They were committed to a parliamentary path to socialism but were opposed to any collaboration with a bourgeois party. Given the large agricultural and urban petty bourgeois sector, this precluded any socialist participation in government. After the First World War, this policy was modified to permit collaboration with, but not entrance into, a bourgeois cabinet.

This policy was modified again in the face of the growing fascist threat, which also led the Soviet Union to direct the communists to support the socialists in the Popular Front government of 1936. Since the petty bourgeois Radicals formed the third partner in the front, no direct attack on capital could be made. Thus the reforms of the front were welfare statist. The reforms of the Blum government were considerably helped by a sudden and tremendous surge in union membership. French union membership had been very low previous to this point, never more than 20 per cent of non-agricultural employees. The advent of the Blum government was followed by a wave of strikes and factory occupations by both unorganised and organised workers. This terrified the employers and made them willing to sign the Matignon Agreements, when Blum called them in to discuss the situation. The agreement gave the workers wage raises and full bargaining rights. The signing was followed by another surge of organising. The trade unions claimed to have 5½ million members by 1937, some 71 per cent of all non-agricultural employees. Though French (and Italian) union membership statistics are notoriously bad, partly because of the vagueness of the commitment involved in membership, it is safe to assume that a very substantial jump in membership did occur. Blum followed the agreement up with legislation guaranteeing a forty-hour week, vacations with pay, and the establishment of a public works programme. Due to a sudden shift in the balance of power, the French working class was able to gain substantial victories.

However, the victories were not the prelude to further progress. The Blum government was already out of office by mid-1937. The limitations of the coalition with the Radicals was one cause of his fall. Like the Swedes at this time, the French Socialists had to make concessions to the farmers in the form of price supports and no movement towards socialisation. But unlike the Swedes the French had to make concessions to the urban petty bourgeoisie. Thus no reform of the tax structure was possible. And it made price control impossible with the consequence that the workers' wage gains were cancelled entirely by inflation (Cole 1960: 109). In truth, it would have been difficult to control prices even if it had been politically possible given the decentralised nature of the French economy. An enormous control apparatus would have been necessary. For the same reason it would have been difficult to do anything about the capital flight and investment slowdown which occurred during the Blum government.

The surge in union membership proved to be short-lived. Membership dropped by one million in 1938, by the same amount the next year, and back to its pre-1936 level by the conquest. Instead of being a permanent change in the distribution of power in civil society the unionisation surge of 1937 represented a temporary burst of enthusiasm. The organisational structure of French trade unions and intransigence of French employers ensured it would be no more. While it is doubtful that the jump in membership would have been so great had membership involved a greater commitment, it does seem likely that it would have been more permanent and thus represented a more important contribution to the transition to socialism.

It is interesting to note that almost all of the problems of the Blum government are in some way or another related to the low degree of centralisation of French capitalism. The political necessity of the coalition with the urban petty bourgeoisie, the reaction of the paternalistic French employers to the unionisation drive and the reforms, the difficulties of establishing control over such a decentralised economy, and even the immediate backslide of union membership are connected, to some extent, to the lack of capital-centralisation.

The period from the liberation to the Communists' movement into the opposition in May 1947 was the second and last period of rapid welfare state development in France. Plans for the social reforms were laid by resistance forces before the Liberation. In addition to enacting basic welfare services and benefits, collaborationist enterprises were nationalised and the economy was structurally reorganised laying the basis for post-war modernisation. The reforms were carried out under conditions very favourable to the left. Business had been discredited by its policies under Vichy. The Communists had gained prestige in the Resistance and were willing to co-operate in the government and the Socialists were willing to work with them in this interlude between the hot and the cold war. With business discredited and enthusiasm for the left high, workers flocked to the unions. According to union figures, 85 per cent of all non-agricultural employees were union members in 1945–7 (Ross and Hartman 1960:203). Even if this figure is inflated, all indications are that union membership was very high. The Communists and Socialists even had their own majority in the assembly of October 1945–June 1946, the only time in French history that this has occurred. The Catholic MRP which had a substantial trade union base in the CFTC had replaced the Radicals as the dominant centre party. The first two governments (to June 1946) were led by de Gaulle, and included all parties. The reforms passed by these governments represented a national consensus on indispensable economic reconstruction, though of course, a consensus which did not include the discredited sections of business. The reforms of the next year were carried out by a Communist–Socialist–MRP alliance. The exit of the Communists from the alliance in 1947 ushered in the period of political paralysis for which the French Fourth Republic is so well known. It is an exaggeration to say that nothing was achieved in this period. Notably a pension plan was passed by a Socialist government in the third parliament. But on balance, the achievements were indeed small. In particular nothing was done to change the tax system which was very regressive. The political strength of the petty bourgeoisie in France made changes in the system impossible politically. It is even questionable whether much could have been done had the cold war not intervened to divide the left. Both the Communists and the Socialists attempted to gain peasant support and the MRP depended on the Catholic petty bourgeoisie for many of its votes.

In some ways, the pattern of economic and political control in the Fourth Republic was similar to that which exists in the United States. The structure of the parties and the political system prevented any coherent policy from emerging from parliamentary politics in either case. But one important difference allowed the French state to plan economic and social development. All higher French civil servants share a common socialisation experience (education at the Ecole nationale d'administration) and a very large number of them come from families engaged in the higher civil service. This combination of the cohesion of the higher civil service and party paralysis permitted the development of corporate collectivist planning by the French bureaucracy. Thus, the Fourth Republic is a case of the 'relative autonomy of the state' dependent on party political paralysis and the autonomy and cohesion of high-level state bureaucrats.

In the Fifth Republic, France emerges as one of the best cases of the development of corporate collectivism. With a solid parliamentary base, the Gaullists were able to expand the policy of co-ordinated corporate capitalist development initiated by the civil service. The nationalisation of industry, carried out for reasons unrelated to this policy, and the further collectivisation of control, carried out specifically for that purpose, were used by the French government to further the interests of corporate capital. Add this to a tax and spending pattern whose net distributive effect is probably to the working class's disadvantage and you have the corporate collectivist pattern.

The welfare state and redistribution

To substantiate our claim concerning the redistributive effects of taxation, spending and labour organisation, let us now turn to a careful inspection of the data available on this account for the four countries in question. For France, the reliable data is largely limited to that cited by Sawyer, but for the other countries data on redistribution, wealth distribution and trends in distribution are available.[11]

Let us begin with the Sawyer data presented in the last chapter (p. 98). The reader should keep in mind that this data is the only data on income distribution which is reasonably comparable across these countries. The other data which we will cite to trace the trends in each country and so forth is comparable for the different time points within a country but not across countries. The Sawyer data does have one drawback for our purposes. The pre-tax income distribution refers to money income, which deviates from factor income as it includes government cash transfers (Reynolds and Smolensky 1977: 36). Thus the Sawyer figures cannot be interpreted as representing differences in income distribution due solely to the strength of labour and capital in the market. Income distribution before tax but including transfer payments shows that inequality is greatest in France, somewhat less in the United States and substantially less in the United Kingdom and Sweden. These differences are what we would predict given the strength of the labour movement with the exception of the fact that the United Kingdom and Sweden exhibit the same amount of inequality. The latter is probably a statistical artefact due to the greater number of one-person households in Sweden, which are known to have much lower incomes than larger households. Sawyer made no attempt to adjust for this factor in the pre-tax data, but the change in the relative positions of the United Kingdom and Sweden can be seen by comparing the post-tax distribution before and after adjustments are made. Because of under-reporting of property income in all four countries, the true figures would probably be somewhat higher; but this would not affect the relative ordering of the countries. In fact it would increase the differences, since the under-reporting is much greater in France than the other three countries; Sawyer estimates that only one-third of property and entrepreneurial income is included in the French figures. We would interpret these differences in income distribution before taxes are levied to be largely a result of labour strength in the market. Trade union organisation is the primary factor but the maintenance of lower employment levels also plays a role here. But it must be remembered that these data do include transfer payments, thus government redistribution does account for some of the differences. A final factor here is that dividends and interest income are lower in Sweden than in most capitalist countries. They are about 5 per cent of net national income, which is about half of the usual figure.

Trend data are available for the United States, the United Kingdom and Sweden. There is a strong trend in Sweden toward equalisation of household incomes. The Gini index declines from ·54 in 1935 to ·44 in 1948 to ·36 in 1970. The change since 1948 may be due largely to the entrance of women in the labour market, since one recent Swedish study found that income distribution among males between the ages of nineteen and sixty-six was stable from 1951 to 1972 (Statistiska Centralbyrån 1974). The study did not control for level of employment and included even those who were not working, so it is probable that income distribution among full-time employed men did become more equal. In all probability the increase in the student population has caused an increase in part-time employment and a decrease in labour force participation among men. But it must be remembered that the working class in Sweden was very heavily organised in 1951 and density of organisation in the manual ranks has increased only gradually since then. Unemployment was low by this time too. So given that our two predictors of before tax income do not vary much, it is not surprising that the dependent variable does not change much either.

The UK pattern is one of decline in inequality in household income between 1938 and 1957, relative stability to 1961 and some increase in inequality since then. The US data show a decline in inequality from 1929 to the end of the Second World War and a relatively small increase since then. One study based on census data shows an increase in inequality in personal income among males from 1958 to 1970, so it seems that the entry of women into the labour force prevented a greater increase in inequality of household incomes.

The trend towards equality that occurred in these countries has often been attributed to structural changes in the economy, such as the decline in the rural sector and the decline in domestic employment, to climbing GNP, or to some unspecified factors simply referred to as the special conditions associated with the crisis of the depression and war. These may have had some effect but it seems plausible that the changes in income distribution between the early 1930s and early 1950s might be due to the growth in the strength of the labour movement in this period. Where the labour movement was not crushed by fascist forces, it generally went through an organising spurt from the mid-1930s to the late 1940s. The distribution of power in the whole capitalist world changed in this period. Our finding – that labour organisation is a much better predictor of before-tax income distribution than the percentage of the labour force in agriculture or the growth of per capita GNP – does indicate that the latter factors might not have been so important in the changes through time. It can hardly be an accident that the changes in income distribution in these three countries begin and end with the rapid growth of blue-collar labour organisation in the 1930s and 1940s.

The extent of redistribution effected by public spending depends on how progressive taxes are, which groups benefit from transfer payments, the use of free or subsidised public goods and services, and the size of the public sector. In the debate on the redistributive effects of the welfare state it is often forgotten how little has to be accomplished for the public sector to effect some redistribution. For instance, if taxes are proportional to income and each income bracket receives an equal share of the cash payments, goods and services dispensed by the state, then substantial redistribution will result. A public sector which follows this pattern and accounts for 40 per cent of GNP will reduce the variation in income by 40 per cent (that is, 40 per cent of GNI will be distributed equally, 60 per cent in proportion to pre-tax income). If taxes are proportional and the public cash payments, goods and services do not accrue to the wealthier brackets in proportion to their income, then the net effect will be at least some redistribution.

Estimation of the distributive effect of public spending is the most difficult problem in answering the question of whether and to what degree the welfare state redistributes income. Only cash transfers pose no problem here. The effects of free or subsidised use of public goods and services are very difficult to estimate. Some services, such as education, tend to be used by higher income groups disproportionately. Others, such as national health services, tend to be used somewhat more equally. And some, such as subsidised public transport, are used by medium-income groups more than the wealthy or the poor. On balance, it does appear that the use of public goods and services is directly related to income because middle and upper income individuals have the time, money and knowledge to make use of them. However, the differential use is not so great as to be proportional to income differences. In fact, they are not nearly that great, if the UK pattern is at all indicative. The UK Central Statistical Office collects data periodically on the use of certain public goods and services.[12] The lowest income group, £260 or less before taxes (or £500 after taxes and benefits), received a total of £136 in benefits in kind in terms of education, health services, welfare foods and subsidised housing. The highest income group, £3104 or more before taxes (or £2997 after taxes and benefits), received £276 in benefits in kind. Thus the top income group received twelve times the income of the bottom but just twice the benefits in kind. In point of fact, Nicholson shows that all of the benefits measured in this survey taken individually – even education – had a net progressive effect. The figures just cited compare the extremes and tend to give an exaggerated picture of the redistributive effects of the UK welfare state. Working with the same data, Nicholson calculates the 'vertical' redistributive effects of taxation and benefits. That is, he controls for family size and eliminates pensioners in order to eliminate the confounding effects of 'horizontal' distribution from households of one size to households of another size and from one generation to another. The Gini index for 1971 drops from ·34 before taxes and benefits to ·25 after taxes and benefits. Thus the welfare state in the United Kingdom does redistribute income. Aside from the magnitude of the redistributive effect, it is important to note that the primary source of the redistribution comes from the benefits not the taxes. Of the ·09 drop in the Gini index, ·08 is accounted for by the provision of public benefits. The tax system actually created very little redistribution.

Aside from other studies based on the British Family Expenditure Survey, the only attempt to estimate the distributive impact of all government taxation and expenditure is Reynolds' and Smolensky's study of the United States. Their study is at the same time more comprehensive and less precise than Nicholson's study. They attempt to measure the incidence of all government expenditure and taxation but are forced to rely on estimates based on household characteristics more often than Nicholson. But with some adjustments, the results of the two studies can be compared.

Reynolds and Smolensky provide three different estimates of the effect of taxation, one based on the standard assumptions about the incidence of various taxes, one with slightly more regressive assumptions, and one with more progressive assumptions. Nicholson's study excludes death duties and capital gains taxes, which Reynolds and Smolensky assume fall in the highest category, while Nicholson assumes that all indirect taxes fall on consumption, which is consistent with Reynolds' and Smolensky's assumptions in the more regressive estimates of incidence. Thus, the regressive assumptions appear to be most appropriate for the comparison.

Reynolds and Smolensky give two estimates for the redistributive impact of expenditure: one assumes that half of the benefits of general expenditure are distributed according to pre-tax income and half equally; the other estimate assumes that it is distributed according to pre-tax income. The largest component of general expenditure is defence, but it also includes police, parks, libraries and administration to name a few items. All of these items, as well as highway expenditure and agricultural subsidies, are not included as either direct or indirect benefits in Nicholson's study; thus they have no redistributive impact in his study. Consequently, the Reynolds' and Smolensky's estimates which assume that general expenditure benefits are proportional to income are most comparable to Nicholson's results.

A final problem in the comparison presents greater difficulties. The US study includes pensioners and makes no control for family size. Thus it does not measure vertical redistribution only. We can partially adjust for this by subtracting the redistributive effects of social security payments from the US figures. As a result of government taxation and spending, the US Gini index drops ·06 when all benefits and taxes are included and ·03 when all except social security are included. Despite problems of comparability, the difference between the US figure and the UK figure is large enough that it is safe to conclude that the UK welfare state is much more redistributive than the US welfare state.

Tables 5.1 and 5.2 and Sawyer's data allow us to make some comparisons of the tax systems of all four countries. Table 5.1 shows that income taxes are least progressive in France followed by the United States then Sweden and the United Kingdom. The relative

TABLE 5.1   *Effective income tax rates for a married taxpayer with two dependants, 1961*

	Yearly wage and salary income					
	$3000	$6000	$10,000	$20,000	$50,000	$100,000
United States	–	8%	11%	16%	27%	38%
United Kingdom	–	6	16	24	37	57
Sweden	15%	21	27	40	54	63
France	–	2	5	10	20	29

SOURCE   Richard A. Musgrave, *Fiscal Systems* (New Haven: Yale University Press, 1969) p. 183

TABLE 5.2   *Kinds of tax revenues as percentages of total tax revenues, 1971*

	United States	United Kingdom	France	Sweden
Direct				
Individual income tax	35·1%	32·1%	10·8%	45·8%
Corporate income tax	12·7	8·0	5·9	4·4
Employees' social security contributions	8·8	6·8	11·5	7·1
Other	1·8	2·8	2·1	1·4
Total	58·4	49·7	30·3	58·7
Indirect				
Excise, sales, customs taxes	19·1	29·1	35·8	28·4
Property tax	12·1	9·5	1·5	–*
Employers' social security contributions	10·4	7·1	28·9	11·8
Other	–	4·6	3·5	1·1
Total	41·6	50·3	69·7	41·3

SOURCE   Arnold J. Heidenheimer *et al.*, *Comparative Public Policy* (New York: St Martin's, 1975) p. 232
* Less than 0·05 per cent

position of Sweden and the United Kingdom is reversed in Sawyer's data. This could be due to changes in the tax systems of the two countries between 1961 and 1972 or it could be due to statistical errors in estimating the effective rates. Whatever the case may be, it is probably safe to assume that overall the Swedish tax system is more progressive. Schnitzer calculated that the share of the top 20 per cent of British households of the national income drops from 42·5 per cent to 38·7 per cent after taxes are accounted for, a drop of 3·8 per cent. The corresponding drop in Sweden is 7·5 per cent. While the data are not strictly comparable, there is no indication that the statistical discrepancies account for the difference. The difference in the two tax systems is due to the greater reliance of the British on indirect taxes, which are regressive. In particular, local government in Sweden is financed by a proportional income tax amounting to 15 per cent of income, while local government in the United Kingdom relies on the regressive property tax.

The United States relies more heavily on direct taxes than the United Kingdom but its income tax is less progressive. And as Sawyer's data shows, overall its direct taxes effect less redistribution than the UK direct taxes. In fact, according to Reynolds' and Smolensky's estimates, the US tax system was somewhat regressive as of 1970. After taxes were subtracted, the Gini index increased by ·008 under standard assumptions of incidence or ·018 under more regressive assumptions.

France's tax system is clearly much more regressive than the US system. It relies less on direct taxes and its income tax is less progressive than the US income tax. Since direct taxes resulted in no income redistribution, it is safe to assume that total taxation in France is quite regressive in its effect on income distribution.

As for the redistributive effect of benefits, good data are only available for the United States and the United Kingdom. The redistributive impact of benefits in the United Kingdom has already been stated. Based on Reynolds' and Smolensky's estimates, the benefits more than offset the regressive nature of the US tax system resulting in significant redistribution. The fact that some redistribution occurs even when one excludes social security payments suggests that the US welfare state redistributes income between classes at least to some extent. Given the lack of data for Sweden and France, the best we can do is to make an educated guess. Comparing the United Kingdom and Sweden, the incidence of direct cash benefits is not as progressive in Sweden, since more benefits are means-tested in the United Kingdom. But the incidence of indirect benefits is probably not very different, the total volume of all benefits is greater, and the tax system is more progressive. So it is probable that the Swedish welfare state effects more redistribution.

France and the United Kingdom spend equivalent amounts but the French tax system is much more regressive. To make an educated guess on the effects of spending, transfer payments can be compared. The top 20 per cent of UK income earners receive 7·2 per cent of transfer payments while the bottom 20 per cent receive 47·3 per cent. The corresponding figures for France are 24·3 per cent and 17·8 per cent (Sawyer 1976: 34−5)! So despite similar levels of expenditure, the UK welfare state is surely much more redistributive than the French. The US/French comparison is much more difficult. The United States spends much less than France but its tax system is less regressive. If transfer payments are a general indicator, then US spending benefits are more equally distributive than the French: the top 20 per cent receive about the same as the bottom 20 per cent (Sawyer 1976: 35). Other factors of the spending pattern indicate offsetting effects: the United States spends relatively more on education and spending on transportation is concentrated more on highways than collective transport. On balance, it seems to us that the net effect of the US pattern is more progressive than the French, but this is no more than an educated guess. Another educated guess is that the *short-term effect* of the French welfare system is some equalisation – but not very much.

Trend data on the effects of taxes and benefits on income distribution are available for the United Kingdom, the United States and Sweden. The Swedish data for the earlier period include only the effects of direct taxes and benefits. The Gini index declines from ·52 in 1935 to ·41 in 1948 to ·30 in 1972. Comparing these figures to the ones cited earlier, there appears to be an increase in the redistributive effect of the direct taxes and benefits. The Swedes have increased indirect relative to direct taxation since the beginning of the 1960s, but the concurrent expansion of benefits has probably more than offset the negative effects of this tax.

The UK figures on the effect of direct taxation indicate substantial changes toward equality from the late 1930s to 1953 or 1954 and then some increase in inequality until about 1963 followed by some decrease since then. The changes in the effect of direct taxation on income distribution follow closely the changes in government. The Conservative tax changes partially offset a trend toward slight equalisation of pre-tax income in the 1950s, while Labour's changes partially offset a trend in the opposite direction in the 1960s. For the 1960s, the UK surveys of the effect of benefits and taxes allow us to estimate trends in the effect of the whole public sector on income distribution. There is no doubt that there is a strong coincidence of the changes in the redistributive effect of benefits and taxes with the change of government. In the period 1961–4, the taxes and benefits reduced the Gini index of inequality by 22 per cent; in 1970–1, by 26 per cent (Nicholson 1974:79). There is some disagreement about whether the change offset the increase in inequality caused by the rise in unemployment in the same period. Nicholson claims that it did, based on the stability of the Gini index. Westergaard and Resler say that it did not, based on a comparison of the income of the top and bottom quintiles. The discrepancy seems to be a matter of measurement differences. The bottom 20 per cent of households, those hit hardest by unemployment, lost relative to those immediately above them.

Reynolds and Smolensky make estimates for the redistributive impact of government spending and taxation for 1950 and 1961 as well as 1970. The redistributive effect of the government increases somewhat. The Gini index drops ·042 in 1950, ·048 in 1960, and ·062 in 1970 after the effect of taxes and benefits are adjusted for. The magnitude of the changes does seem to follow changes in governments (Republican in the 1950s and Democratic in the 1960s) but the overall difference is small. The change from 1950 to 1970 is surprisingly small given the 57 per cent increase in government spending in the period. The reason is that the tax system became increasingly less progressive both because of a greater reliance on regressive taxes like the social security tax and because personal income taxes became less progressive. In fact, based on standard assumptions of incidence, the tax system, which was slightly progressive in 1950, had become slightly regressive by 1970. As a result, the increase in public expenditure barely offset the slight increase in inequality of pre-tax income distribution such that distribution after taxes and benefits shows a very slight, statistically insignificant, decline from 1950 to 1970 (·01 on the Gini index).

These figures on distribution of income do not include the distributive effect of unrealised capital gain. Westergaard and Resler make the same sort of calculations for the United Kingdom that we made for the United States with the same result, the inclusion of unrealised capital gain increases inequality substantially. The same could be shown for Sweden and France. However, the inclusion of capital gain is unlikely to change the relative position of the four countries and, if our data for the United Kingdom, Sweden and the United States are indicative, the magnitude of the differences in inequality in the four countries would remain the same. The reason is simple: the variations between countries and through time in the distribution of wealth affect variations in income distribution only among the very highest income earners because wealth ownership is so concentrated. This is particularly true of non-agricultural productive property. The distribution of stock ownerships is more concentrated in Sweden than in the United States or the United Kingdom but in all three countries the top 10 per cent of stockholders own all or almost all of privately-held stock. Other forms of wealth are less concentrated; overall, the top 1 per cent of wealthholders own about a third of all wealth in the United Kingdom and about a quarter of all wealth in the United States. Since capital gains accrue overwhelmingly to the top 10 per cent of income earners, the question arises as to how this factor affects the progressiveness of taxation and spending. Since unrealised capital gains are rarely taxed directly and only lightly taxed indirectly, especially in the case of corporate stock, there is little doubt that taxation would appear to be more regressive were this factor counted. It may be objected that estate taxes are often quite high, and this should be counted in, but it is well known that a very large amount of inherited property escapes taxation. The redistributive impact of public benefits would logically be greater if capital gains were counted as income since the initial degree of inequality would be greater. But the net result would be less redistribution.

Let us take a hypothetical but not unreasonable case to demonstrate this: assume taxes are proportional to income when capital gains are not counted, that half of the benefits accrue equally and half proportional to income, and that 50 per cent of all income goes to taxes and is returned in benefits. If the richest 10 per cent gets 30 per cent of income, its share after taxes and benefits will be 25 per cent $[30-15+(2 \cdot 5+7 \cdot 5)]$ which is 83·3 per cent of its pre-tax income. If the bottom 10 per cent gets 1 per cent before taxes, its final share will be 6·5 per cent or 650 percent of its pre-tax income. If we now add capital gains equal to 10 per cent of national income and assume they go entirely to the top 10 per cent, the pre-tax share of the top 10 per cent is now 36 per cent $(40 \div 110)$. The tax rate is now 37·5 per cent for the richest 10 per cent and 50 per cent for everyone else. But benefits make up 25 per cent of pre-tax income instead of 33·3 per cent for the top deciles. The final share of the richest group is now 32 per cent [(40 − 15 + (2·5 + 7·5))/110], or 88·9 per cent of its pre-tax income. The bottom 10 per cent now has 0·9 per cent of national personal income before taxes and 5·9 per cent after taxes and benefits which is 650 per cent of its pre-tax income.

This example makes it clear that the inclusion of untaxed capital gains reduces the redistributive impact of the welfare state. But it also demonstrates that their inclusion would not necessarily negate the redistribution caused by taxation and spending. The estimates used in the example are drawn from the UK case but purposefully biased to show less redistribution. In the hypothetical case, the top 10 per cent gains 6 per cent by the inclusion of capital gains compared to Westergaard and Resler's estimate of 5·5 per cent; taxes are assumed to be proportional rather than somewhat progressive, and so on. Thus even with the inclusion of capital gains, welfare state taxation and spending causes some redistribution in the United Kingdom and even more in Sweden. In the United States and France, the question is more problematic.

Left critics of the welfare state claim that it primarily effects a generational transfer not redistribution between classes. They correctly point out that such generational transfers would appear to equalise in most measures of income distribution even in the absence of a redistribution between classes. Westergaard and Resler have argued this point of view with particular forcefulness, substantiating their argument with data from the previously mentioned UK surveys. But their contention is not supported by a more careful inspection of these data. Nicholson's analysis on this matter is very convincing, since he controls for family size and eliminates pensioners and still finds substantial redistribution. On the other hand, there is no doubt that the redistributive impact is reduced. Again, lack of data prevents us from drawing any definite conclusions, but we think that once the effects of unrealised capital gains and generational transfers are accounted for, the US system would show little redistributive effects and the French none at all. And since French taxes fall so heavily on wage and salary earners, it seems almost certain that the French working class is a net loser, while small, low-income property-holders come out ahead.

The data presented here strongly support our central argument.

The welfare state, when developed by a social democratic government in alliance with a strong labour movement, has redistributed
income. Critics of the welfare state have made a number of errors in
their arguments. Sometimes they present no data or misinterpret
the data they do present. But more often they infer characteristics of
the welfare state from a single case. The analysis here shows that this
is illegitimate. The welfare state has very different effects in different countries. In France, the development of the welfare state,
largely by accident rather then design, has led to corporate collectivism and little or no redistribution. In Sweden, a strong labour
movement and a long period of socialist incumbency has led to the
extension of democratic control and very significant redistribution.
There the welfare state is part of a transitional political economy
between capitalism and socialism.

The leftist detractors of the welfare state have also failed to think
realistically about what the capitalist world would look like without
an organised labour movement. This is hypothetical since it is
probably impossible to have capitalism and no organised labour,
but it is a useful intellectual exercise. First, no labour movement, no
democracy. Almost everywhere the labour movement was a driving
force in the battle for suffrage. Most leftists would not deny this.
What they would deny is that the labour movement has changed the
economic structure of capitalism. The coincidence of the organising
surge with the redistribution that occurred in the 1930s and 1940s is
ignored. The stability of pre-tax income in post-war United Kingdom and the United States is assumed to demonstrate that trade
unions have achieved nothing. But is it not more reasonable to
assume that income distribution would have become more unequal
in the absence of labour organisation, that Marx was correct on this
account? Furthermore, why should we expect more redistribution
given the fact that power relations in the market have not changed
much in the post-war period due to the stagnation of blue-collar
labour organising? In their defence, the critics of social democracy's
record have not had access to much of the material on the countries
where that record is best, since they are all small countries and most
have esoteric languages. But as dismal as Labour's record has been,
it is hard to believe that the UK welfare state would be as well
developed or as redistributive as it is today if Labour had not been in
office part of the post-war period and the labour movement had not
been as strong as it is. It seems unlikely that a Conservative

government faced by a labour movement the strength of, say, the US labour movement would have expanded welfare services as much as did Labour in 1945–51. But it is almost certain that it would not have been as progressively financed. Even if we accepted the argument that the UK welfare state effects no redistribution between classes (which we do not), the question would arise as to why it does not effect a redistribution in the opposite direction, if it is a creature of the capitalists' interests. The French case shows that this is possible. And, if Wilensky (1976: 32) is correct, it is actually politically easier to get people to accept hidden regressive taxes like the value-added tax than it is to get them to accept progressive direct taxes, like the income tax.

If the achievements of organised labour and social democracy are clear, so are the limitations of its programme, which has focused on the socialisation of income rights and, to some extent, control rights, but not the socialisation of capital itself. Socialists like Westergaard and Resler have correctly pointed out that this not only results in the maintenance of basically capitalist control relations in the economy but that it also limits efforts at redistribution. But this latter factor can be exaggerated. Calculations of the distributive effect of unrealised capital gain on income distribution, like those made by us or Westergaard and Resler, overstate the degree to which the distribution of *consumption* could be equalised by socialising capital. If the economy is to grow at all, a substantial portion of that capital gain would have to be reinvested. This is not to say there would be no return; some capital gains are turned into consumption and often in ways that escape taxation. There would also be substantial equalisation through redistribution of revenue income and some through redistribution of dividends and realised capital gains. And clearly one of the great distributive injustices of the strong social democratic pattern, as in Sweden, is that workers' wage restraint pays for capital growth which accrues to capital owners. Our point here is that it is unlikely that the socialisation of capital will have more impact on the distribution of consumption than taxes and benefits do in the United Kingdom or Sweden. Nicholson's estimate of the change in the Gini index brought about by taxes and benefits in the United Kingdom is roughly the same as our estimate of the change due to the inclusion of capital gains. But most capital gains will have to be reinvested even in the long run. Thus the equalisation of consumption effected by the redistribution of revenue income, dividends, realised capital gain or capital gains that are unrealised in the short run would probably not be greater than that effected by taxation and welfare spending in places like the United Kingdom and Sweden. On the other hand, socialisation of capital would effect much greater gains in societal control of the economy and employee control in the workplace than has been achieved by social democracy anywhere, at least as of 1970. Of the four cases examined here only the Swedish labour movement was able to make much more than insignificant gains through socialisation of control rights.

6

Beyond the Welfare State: the Swedish Case

In this chapter, we will see how the Swedish labour movement turned from welfare state reformism that had dominated its policy for almost forty years back to the original programme of the party – democratic ownership and control of production. Two structural changes allowed this policy shift. First, the decline in the farming population and the growth of the non-manual working class and the upper middle class weakened the objective class base for consumption and mobility politics and strengthened the base for production politics. Second, the growth of white-collar labour organisation decisively changed the balance of power in civil society, making a direct attack on capital possible.

The pension struggle

Actually, the discussion of wealth and ownership concentration at the end of the last chapter painted a slightly misleading picture. If public pension funds are counted, the distribution of wealth is much more equal than indicated and the trend is towards more equality in both the United Kingdom and Sweden (Spånt 1973; Atkinson 1975). If private trade union pension funds are counted, the United States is moving in the same direction. One author has gone so far as to say that the United States was (or at least will be) 'socialist' because by the mid-1970s a third of all equity capital was held by employees pension funds (Drucker 1976).[1] In all cases, it is true that the development of pension funds does represent a redistribution of wealth in the employees' favour because the income rights of the capital in these funds belong to the employees and, in fact, the income cannot be appropriated by anyone else.

But the monetary benefits accrue to individuals entirely in the form of the pensions themselves. Thus, unlike privately held wealth, pension funds are not a source of potential consumption. They are, of course, a source of credit and investment and thus of control in the economy. In fact, the development of pension funds along with insurance funds, public and private, represents a very profound change in the control relationships in the political economies of capitalist democracies. But the results are quite different depending on the country in question. In the United States, the new collective ownership remains largely under corporate control contributing to the development of a corporate collectivist political economy. In Sweden, the pension funds are publicly controlled and represent an expansion of democratic control of the economy and thus a step towards socialism.

The struggle for supplementary pensions marks the Swedish Social Democrats' first step beyond the welfare state not only because it resulted in an expansion of collective ownership but also because it was the beginning of the political alliance that brought production politics back to the centre of the Social Democrats' programme, an alliance between organised blue- and white-collar workers. The attempt to find new sources of political support, not the attempt to raise the socialisation issue again, was one of the motivations of the Social Democratic leadership at that time. On the contrary, the pension fund itself was only a small part of the whole programme and, taken as a whole, the Social Democrats' posture on the pension issue might be seen as a de-radicalisation of the party since benefits were to be earnings-related not equal. The party leadership once even offered to eliminate the fund in order to get a compromise. In fact, this period – the late 1950s and early 1960s – was the party's most conservative period as indicated by the party programme which was revised in 1960. The 1960 programme eliminated much of the Marxist language of the 1944 programme and was ambiguous on the subject of the future of private ownership. And the Social Democrats increasingly relied on more regressive, indirect taxes to finance public sector expansion.

During the 1950s the electoral fortunes of both partners in the Swedish coalition government, the Social Democrats and the Farmers' Party, deteriorated. Both parties attributed this partly to the decline in their respective social bases – manual workers and farmers. And both parties wanted to appeal to the growing ranks of non-manual employees. The pension question gave the Farmers' Party, which subsequently changed its name to the Centre Party, an opportunity to go its own way and it left the coalition.

In 1947, a parliamentary investigation on the pension question had been appointed.[2] Two proposals emerged from the investigation. The Social Democratic, LO (Swedish Federation of Trade Unions) and TCO (Central Organisation of Salaried Employees) members supported comprehensive, public and obligatory earnings-related pensions. The SAF (Swedish Employers' Association), Liberal and Conservative members supported the development of private pensions through negotiation between the trade unions and employers. The Centre Party later developed its own position, an increase in basic pensions, with further supplementary pensions voluntary. As was pointed out, the one radical aspect of the Social Democratic plan was the build-up of huge pension funds designed to offset the decline in private savings and private insurance funds which the plan might cause. The fund was vigorously attacked by the Liberals and Conservatives as a 'secret socialisation' plan.

The Social Democrats hoped to break through to the increasingly organised non-manual ranks on the pension issue. The results were mixed. The TCO members of the parliamentary investigation did side with the Social Democrats and LO. However, in the pension referendum of 1957, strong elements of TCO supported the bourgeois alternative. But after that point TCO moved increasingly into the Social Democratic camp on the issue. This began to create tensions in the Liberal Party, as indicated by the fact that the Social Democrats' pension proposal was finally passed in 1958 when a Liberal member of parliament broke party discipline and abstained on the vote on the pension question. Furthermore, the two leading Liberal papers, which had urged the Liberals to compromise with the Social Democrats, refused to support the Liberals in the autumn 1958 election when the party failed to follow their recommendation. By the 1960 election, TCO was solidly behind the new pension plan and the Liberals agreed to accept it. Thus, as TCO changed its position, the Liberals were quick to follow. Probably for this reason, the Social Democrats did not make a disproportionate breakthrough to the non-manual ranks in 1960, despite its victory at the polls. Its victory was apparently due to increased mobilisation in all strata.

The pension struggle demonstrates the consequences of changes in the class structure and changes in the distribution of power in civil society for Swedish politics. The growth of white-collar labour organisation (see Table 6.1) made it impossible for even the bourgeois left to line up solidly behind capital. Swedish bourgeois forces had to compromise with labour to a much greater degree than in, say, the United Kingdom where white-collar organisation is much lower than in Sweden.

TABLE 6.1   *Growth of union membership in Sweden*

	Percentage of labour force organised		
	LO	TCO	SACO/SR
1900	2%	–	–
1910	4*	–	–
1920	11	–	–
1930	19	1%†	–
1940	32	4	–
1945	37	7	1%‡
1950	41	9	1
1960	46	12	2
1965	46	12	3
1970	49	21	3
1975	56	28	5

LO   Landsorganisationen – Swedish Federation of Trade Unions (primarily manual workers)
TCO   Tjänstemännens Centralorganisation – Central Organisation of Salaried Employees
SACO   Sveriges Akademikers Centralorganisation – Swedish Confederation of Professional Associations
SR   Statstjänstemännens Riksförbund – National Federation of Civil Servants
* LO lost a general strike in 1909 which resulted in the loss of half of its membership. Consequently the 1910 figure is not reflective of the general trend
† 1931. TCO was reformed in 1944 through a combination of DACO and old TCO. The figures for 1931 and 1940 refer to both organisations
‡ 1947

The effect of incumbency of Social Democratic parties on the development of the political economies of Sweden, the United Kingdom and the United States can clearly be seen in the patterns of pension development. Without the support of a labour party, the American labour movement was unable to get a statutory pension plan to supplement Social Security and thus negotiated separate private plans for their members, firm by firm. The huge majority of the pension funds built up under these plans are investment funds managed by the trust departments of large banks, by insurance companies or by a professional staff of their own (Rifkin and Barber 1978). Only a few are actually controlled by the unions themselves. Even these are now constrained by legal provisions that they must be invested where the potential rate of return is highest. These funds are a tremendous source of investment capital for US capitalism, and the funds, unlike the Swedish pension funds, carry little danger of democratic control with them. Thus, it is correct to say that contemporary US capitalism is characterised by a separation of ownership and control, but with the opposite results to those hypothesised by people like Berle and Means. The very large corporate investors, especially financial intermediaries such as banks, gain control of collectively-owned capital in pension funds.[3]

The UK case lies somewhere between the US and Swedish cases. Supplementary pensions became a big issue in the United Kingdom in the late 1950s just as they did in Sweden. The Labour Party's position was very similar to the Swedish Social Democrats'. They favoured a statutory earnings-related plan with a fund build-up roughly the size of the Swedish fund in relative terms (Heclo 1974:265). The British Conservatives reacted like their Swedish counterparts with screams about Labour's socialisation plans. The difference was that the British Conservatives were in power. They responded to Labour's plan with legislation in 1958 providing for meagre earnings-related benefits. Furthermore, as Heclo (1974:270–1) points out, the Conservatives desired to 'leave private insurance schemes unhindered' as much as possible, thus their plan allowed 'for generous terms for contracting out ... to private pension programs'. Most employees did contract out and the plan proved to be a great shot in the arm for the British insurance business. It took Labour five years to produce a new plan after its return to office in 1964. The plan was hardly as comprehensive as the plan proposed in the 1950s. Because the private schemes were now too big to be eliminated and because they had been outmanoeuvred on the fund issue, Labour's plan accepted a partnership between state and private insurance and proposed a much smaller state investment fund. Even this plan never became law. The Conservatives returned to office as a result of the 1970 election and subsequently passed a more modest version of Labour's bill. The net result in the United Kingdom in terms of control patterns in the economy is closer to the US case than the Swedish case. The biggest difference between the United States and the United Kingdom is that most unorganised US workers, particularly in low-wage sectors of the economy, are almost entirely dependent on basic pensions (social security), which does not even cover subsistence in their old age.

Industrial democracy

In Sweden, the 1960s saw a tremendous acceleration of white-collar labour organising. By 1970, around 70 per cent of all non-manual employees were members of unions. Seventy per cent of the Swedish labour force were members of either TCO or LO. This decisive change in the distribution of power in civil society laid the basis for the reorientation of Social Democracy's programme back to production politics. The organisation of non-manual employees in Sweden caused, or at least indicated, a release of that group from the one-sided social and political hegemony of capital. A new, specifically white-collar style of politics emerged: apathy about income equalisation, active opposition to high marginal taxation, but support for programmes expanding employee control in the enterprise.

Beginning with the pension struggle and culminating in the industrial democracy programme of the early 1970s, this new coalition of organised white- and blue-collar workers came to dominate Swedish politics. As the old farmer/worker coalition had resulted in policies which united the two groups, the new coalition has resulted in a re-focus of the Social Democratic programme on the condition which unites LO and TCO members, their role as propertyless employees. In short, the growth of TCO allowed the Social Democrats to bring democratic ownership and control of production back to the centre of its programme. As Olaf Palme put it in his speech introducing the new, more radical party programme of 1975, the Swedish labour movement then moved to the third stage of its long struggle to transform capitalist society. The first two stages were political democracy and social democracy (that is, welfare statism). Now the struggle was for economic democracy.[4]

The changing balance of power in civil society was a precondition for the success of the Social Democrats' shift to production politics, but in itself it did not bring the shift about. The first phase of the new attack on capital entailed a socialisation of control rights in the enterprise. While a number of purely situational factors, such as a generational change in LO leadership and party competition with the Liberals (J. D. Stephens 1976:276–7), helped to bring the workers' control issue to the foreground, it is worth mentioning that the most important causes of the shift can be directly linked to the undesirable by-products of past Social Democratic policy (Martin 1977). First, the policy of promoting maximum growth through structural rationalisation carried out under capitalist direction had resulted in the dehumanisation of work life and had blocked any significant expansion of direct employee influence on the conditions of work. The findings of a large-scale survey of living and working conditions, the Level of Living Survey; the high level of labour turnover in industrial production; and a wave of wildcat strikes in 1969 all highlighted this problem. Second, the highly centralised nature of the Swedish trade union movement and bargaining process, which had facilitated the carrying out of past policy, actually hindered any advance on control issues in the immediate workplace since these were difficult to deal with in a central bargain. Local bargaining carried on after the central bargain was agreed upon proved ineffective since the workers could not strike if they were dissatisfied with the employer's offer.

The movement of production politics to the centre of the Swedish labour movement's programme can be dated from the 1971 LO congress which adopted a report on industrial democracy recommending legislation to increase substantially employees' control in the enterprise. In the following two years a group of laws expanding workers' control was passed by the Social Democratic government. The Law on Improvement of the Working Environment substantially increased the power of the local safety officer, giving him or her the right to stop work when conditions are believed to be hazardous to workers' health, the right to take part in the planning of production changes and access to corporate information pertaining to his or her duties. Three laws, known as the Åman Laws, increased employment security and strengthened the powers of shop stewards and the local Labour Market Boards. In order to increase public information about corporate activities, two public representatives were placed on boards of all insurance companies and banks and two worker representatives were placed on the boards of all other corporations. To help these worker/directors perform their duties, LO demanded that the employees be given the right to appoint auditors to examine the company books. Faced with the threat of legislation on the matter, SAF agreed to give access to company books of all companies with more than fifty employees to worker-appointed auditors.

In the 1975 Social Democratic Party congress, Ingemund Bengtsson, the Minister of Labour, presented the government's proposal for the revision of labour legislation along the lines of the 1971 LO programme. The proposals were hailed by *Aftonbladet*, the left Social Democratic afternoon daily, as 'the most concrete plans for transferring power from capital to labour to date'. Before examining the provisions in the government's bill, let us look at the coalition formations within the parliamentary investigation committee on 'paragraph 32', the Labour Legislation Committee. Our general hypothesis that the distribution of power in civil society is the key factor in determining the possibilities and limits of social change as well as our contention that TCO holds a critical position in Swedish civil society today are confirmed by events in the work of this committee in the autumn of 1974.

The Labour Legislation Committee was appointed in 1971 to draft proposals for a revision of labour legislation concerning labour relations so as to broaden the sphere of negotiations to include such matters as the distribution and organisation of work, etc., which had previously been restricted by paragraph 32 of SAF's statutes. The composition of the committee was: three Social Democrats, one Conservative, one Liberal, one Centre, two representatives from SAF, one from the government employers, two from LO and two from TCO. Ordinarily, great effort is made to achieve the widest possible consensus on these investigations. Up until the autumn of 1974, this committee was working on a report that would be approved unanimously. At that point, the LO and TCO members of the committee decided that they wanted a more radical reform. They wanted the priority of interpretation of contracts in the case of a dispute to be shifted from the employer to the local trade union. They wanted the duty of the employer to open negotiations when he was planning changes that would affect the employees to be more binding than the committee was intending to suggest. And they wanted the right to strike during an ongoing contract period to be more inclusive than the committee as a whole was prepared to suggest. Also, on several other points, the trade union representatives wanted to go farther than the committee as a whole. When the trade union members made their position clear, the whole work of the committee was disturbed. By this time the text for the legislation, some 1000 pages, was practically written and, if the Social Democrats voted with the trade unions, the report would be defeated thus delaying the passage of the law considerably. Furthermore, the Liberals and the Centre were not about to be isolated from TCO on this important issue, so they announced their support of the trade union position on the important issue of interpretation of contracts and indicated that they would vote against the report as a whole. In order to avoid delay of the legislation, the Social Democrats voted for the report along with the employer and Conservative representatives while the trade union and middle parties' representatives voted against the proposal. Upon receipt of the proposal, Bengtsson announced that his ministry would rewrite the legislation along the lines of the trade union reservations. The political manoeuvring on this committee not only shows the influence that the trade unions have on the middle parties when LO and TCO unite on an issue, but also the consequent great isolation of the employers and the Conservatives on such issues. Thus, the changing distribution of power has affected the policy of the bourgeois parties as well as that of the Social Democrats. With the organisation of white-collar workers and the consequent weakening of capitalist hegemony, the Liberals and Centre cannot represent the interests of capital in an unqualified way.

The proposal presented by Bengtsson at the party congress and passed by the parliament in 1976 is so comprehensive that we can only afford to outline the most important points here. The basic principle underlying the new legislation is that the employers will now be liable to negotiate on any issue which the trade union demands. When the employer is considering virtually any changes that affect the employees, he must take up negotiations with the local trade union. If no agreement is arrived at, the employees have the right to resort to industrial action (for example, strike action) during an ongoing contract period. Priority in the interpretation of contracts will belong to the local trade union except on wage disputes according to the new law. In the latter case, the interpretation right goes over to the employees after ten days unless the employer asks for central negotiations. Finally, the bill stipulates that, in order to exercise its greater responsibilities effectively, the trade union must be given all the information that it desires on the company's activities.

These reforms are so comprehensive that most trade unionists in Sweden think that it will take years for the trade unions to exploit fully the possibilities opened up by them. For one thing, successful utilisation of the laws requires massive education among the lowest-level trade union officials, who are to have major responsibilities and autonomous power in the new system. Previously, these people were mainly communication links between the membership and leadership in the highly centralised Swedish trade union movement.

Is the path shown by this reform a path towards socialism in and of itself? Probably not, because in the last analysis, people are not going to invest in companies that are not controlled by people sharing their interests. To a certain extent, the present public control in the credit and savings market will help. In addition to publicly-controlled pension funds, the largest bank in the country, the publicly-owned PK bank, provides substantial public control of investment sources though not the investment decision itself. The government has also set up a counter-cyclical investment fund whereby companies get tax breaks by placing a certain amount of their profit in a fund which is government controlled. Though this public participation in the credit market helps, it is hard to imagine that investors are going to consider favourably any further expansion of employee-self-management. At some point, advances in employee power are going to become heavily dependent on increases in collective ownership. In fact, a programme for this key element of a socialist transformation of society did begin to crystallise in 1975.

Leadership ideology: 1972

In 1972, after the industrial democracy programme had been formulated but before the collective ownership discussion began in earnest, we conducted a number of interviews with Social Democratic politicians and leading LO officials about the sources of inequality in Swedish society and the respondents' political strategy and policy suggestions for remedying the situation. The ideology that emerged from these interviews sheds some light on the argument advanced by radicals and conservatives alike that the Social Democrats are no longer ideological and certainly not socialist.

The respondents' analysis of the sources of societal inequality was quite similar to the one we advanced in Chapter 2.[5] The concentration of capital into the hands of the few was a basic source of inequality. But in today's society, differences in skill and education were also quite important. They emphasised that the mechanism of market forces, which helped translate these differences of resources into differences in consumption levels, did not result in distribution based on contribution to the social order, as the Liberals claimed. No such measure existed, they claimed, and most of the respondents went on to maintain that, if such a measure existed, it should not be a distributive criterion anyhow. Another common theme in the interviews was that the only way to create equality of opportunity was to equalise the conditions of life. Thus, the party ideology has been broadened to include the stratifying influence of skill as well as capital. This is also clear from the party programme and other party tracts. After laying out this analysis of the causes of social inequality, most of our respondents went on to say that they thought that all or almost all inequalities of the present social order could be eliminated but that new inequalities would arise and that reform work would have to continue.

Using Tingsten's (1973) definition of ideology as 'a collection of political concepts that are developed into a systematic whole and are meant to give a general and definite directive for action', the values, social analysis and goals for the future of our respondents clearly formed a 'systematic whole'. The policies they suggested were fully consistent with and, indeed, could be derived from their values and analysis of society. Furthermore, their strategy was clearly consistent with their analysis as they wanted to emphasise to the electorate the class nature of Swedish society and that politics were a reflection of class interest. It is this class analysis that separated Swedish Social Democracy, even in its most conservative periods, and probably social democracy in general, from liberalism. Their class analysis of society meant that most Social Democratic reforms were steps, however small, on a path leading to socialism, even in a period when the party had no clear strategy for the transition to socialism. In this sense, the 'end of ideology' argument is wrong. Thus our answer to the question of whether or not the Swedish leadership is ideological is an unequivocal yes, but it is another question as to whether their ideology was a socialist ideology. If the question is whether their goal was a classless society, then the answer is yes. Furthermore, when we did our interviews, the leadership was emphasising a programme that focused on production politics. The modal opinion on this problem was that the powers of capital should be progressively transferred to the employees on the one hand and to the state and local government on the other. However, the respondents' positions on the question of ownership can not be considered to be clearly socialist. Only a third of the respondents favoured dramatically increased socialisation of industry in the long run. Our conclusion was that, as of 1972, one could only give an equivocal yes to the question of whether the Swedish labour movement's ideology was socialist for the following reason. While the plans for increased employees' and social control over capital provided the Social Democrats with a definite programme to attack capital, there are, as we have pointed out, limits beyond which such a programme cannot go without aggravating strong resistance on the part of investors in the form of capital flight and investment strikes. As was mentioned previously, when those limits are reached, the programme for increased employee and social power must be complemented by a programme of increased collective ownership. Having rejected state ownership, the Social Democrats lacked such a programme in much the same way that they had lacked a programme for unemployment in the 1920s. They knew they did not like the great concentration of ownership, but they did not have a practical programme to do anything about it.

Employee investment funds

In the autumn of 1975, an LO study group headed by Rudolf Meidner came out with a proposal that filled the vacuum in the labour movement's programme on the question of ownership. The group had been appointed by the 1971 LO congress to study some of the negative effects of the wage policy of solidarity and suggest some solutions to the problem. By demanding equal pay for equal work, the policy contributed to higher profits in the strongest sectors of the economy than would be the case under a system of more decentralised bargaining. This contributed to increased concentration of the already skewed distribution of wealth. Or to the extent that wage drift in these companies covered some of the excess profit, the wage policy itself was undermined. The central directive that the congress gave the Meidner group was that they should develop a proposal to complement the wage policy of solidarity in some way which would counteract the concentration of wealth. The group was given additional directives, the most important of which were that the proposal should provide for new sources of capital formation and that it should reinforce the employees' influence in the enterprise – gained in the recent labour legislation – through participation in ownership. The other directives were less controversial in the Swedish situation: full employment, a high rate of investment, low inflation and preservation of trade union autonomy.

Given the directives from the congress, the Meidner group had to come up with a proposal for collective ownership of the principal means of production, a proposal for socialism. They were faced with a problem which is central to the capitalist model of the operation of the economy. Marx identified this problem as the fact that surplus value gained from unpaid labour time paid for capital accumulation. We have pointed to this as the main limitation of the programme of even the most successful social democratic parties: wage restraint pays for capital accumulation. The only solution to this problem is to let the capital growth accrue to workers as a collectivity. In the long run, this means collective ownership of most productive capital in the economy.

The LO group's proposal, the principles of which were adopted by the LO congress in 1976, would in fact entail the socialisation of the Swedish economy in the long run. Companies with more than 100 employees, which account for two-thirds of all private employment, would have to transfer a portion (10–30 per cent) of their profits in the form of newly issued shares of stock to 'wage earner' or 'employee investment' funds administered by the unions. The transferred portion of profit would be new equity capital and would remain in the firm for investment. The voting rights of the stocks would go to the unions with the first 40 per cent split between the local and the national union. Thereafter the national body would appoint additional board members in consultation with the local. Dividend income would not be distributed individually but used for various collective services. At present rates of growth, the more profitable firms would come to be employee-controlled in twenty or thirty years. In fifty or sixty years, the Swedish economy would be essentially socialist because the huge majority of equity capital would be collectively owned.

Meidner himself has often pointed out that the proposal was emergent in the directives that his group was given. He goes so far as to say that their work was practically technical. Alternatives such as the individual share system proposed in Germany as a compromise solution between the Social Democrats and Free Democrats would not work according to the LO group's analysis. First, it would not increase employee power in the workplace. Second, since the shares can be sold after a certain period of time, it would lead to higher consumption and a drying-up of business capacity for investment. And finally, since lower income earners would be most likely to sell their shares the effect of such a system on the distribution of wealth would be small. Consequently, a system of collective ownership is necessary.

The LO proposal is a brilliant solution to the political and tactical problems of social democracy in its attempt to go beyond the welfare state towards socialism. Though it represents a fundamental change in the future organisation of the Swedish economy, it has an element of gradualism in it that makes it politically feasible. In terms of gradualist strategy, it has substantial advantages over nationalisation. First, it costs nothing. It can be argued that the proposal involves forced savings on the part of employees, particularly if it is revised so that part of the plan is paid for through a payroll tax as has been suggested. But to argue this line is to ignore that the alternative is to continue with the present system where the 'forced savings', that is, the results of wage restraint of workers, accrues to the capitalist. Second, unlike nationalisation, the plan would result in some short-term benefits to the employees in the form of increased control in the enterprise.

Unfortunately, the brilliance of this policy innovation in terms of the overall strategy of the labour movement[6] was almost matched by the poor political handling of the issue. LO and the Social Democratic leadership failed to co-ordinate their actions. The Social Democrats put together a parliamentary investigation on the issue in 1974, completely to LO's surprise. More important, the Social Democratic leadership was caught by surprise when LO proposed such a thoroughgoing plan as that which emerged. To a certain extent, the issue took on a life of its own. The directive given to the Meidner group in 1971 determined the outline of the proposal they were to present at the next congress in 1976. When the proposal was issued and sent to trade union locals for discussion, even Meidner and the LO leadership were surprised at the enthusiasm for the proposal that emerged from the local leadership and rank-and-file activists. The proposal was passed by the LO congress of spring 1976 without opposition.

This put the Social Democrats in a difficult position. The LO proposal was both radical and complicated. The party had little time to prepare the issue before the elections in 1976. SAF and the bourgeois parties took the offensive with charges that the plan amounted to 'confiscation', that it would set up an 'east state [that is, Eastern European] type socialism' and even that it would result in the end of democracy in Sweden. The Social Democratic leadership took a defensive posture, claiming that the parliamentary investigation would not be finished until after the 1979 election, thus they had no set position yet.

The Social Democrats lost the 1976 election, ending forty-four years in office. The critical question for our analysis is the extent to which the election was another defeat for the socialisation issue like the 1920, 1928 and 1948 elections. It seems that the employee investment funds issue played at most only a very small role in the defeat. In a poll in the March before the elections, respondents were asked to name the three issues which interested them most. Only 4 per cent named employee capital funds and only 5 per cent more named other socialisation issues. Furthermore, those interested in socialisation were concentrated in the Conservative and Communist Parties, not among the middle-of-the-road voters who decide Swedish elections (SIFO 1976:12).[7] On the other hand, it cannot be denied that the LO proposal on employee capital funds did not help the Social Democrats. Opinion polls show that more people favoured an individual share plan – such as the one proposed by SAF – than favoured the LO plan (SIFO 1976:27, 35). Thus *given the distribution of public opinion as of 1976*, this issue points to a bourgeois victory in 1979 since employee investment funds will certainly be the dominant issue in the election.

But as should be clear at this point, the Social Democrats do not have to take the present distribution of public opinion as a given. People have a hard time imagining a system very different from the *status quo*, so the onus is always on the left to mobilise opinion for change. The mobilisation on the collective ownership issue had just begun when the polls mentioned were taken since the LO proposal did not even appear until the autumn of 1975. And only LO was able to act on the issue since the Social Democrats were incapacitated by their decision to take a defensive posture in the election. A parallel here with the labour legislation of the early 1970s is instructive. When employees' control in the workplace first became an issue, a number of polls were taken asking employees how much decision-making rights they desired in the enterprise. The respondents answered conservatively, favouring co-determination only on distribution of work issues and some consultation on long-term planning. Many decisions were considered by the respondents to be the management's alone. Yet the labour law reform of 1976, which provided for a much more radical shift of decision-making rights in the enterprise, enjoyed such broad support by 1976 that the Liberal and Centre parties by and large supported it. The point is that the connection of the distribution of power in civil society to public opinion is very concrete. It operates through social mobilisation around an issue. The change in opinions on the expansion of workers' control was a result of the mobilisation of TCO and LO around the issue.

Consequently it is important to look at how the major political actors line up on this issue. Here the prospects for some system of collective ownership look better. Unlike 1920 and 1948, the Social Democrats did not move to bury the issue after the election. On the contrary, by the autumn of 1977, Palme, now the opposition leader, was calling the introduction of employee capital funds 'necessary and inevitable'. Gunnar Nilsson, the president of LO, was saying that it was not a question of whether the funds should be instituted but of how they should be constructed. Even in the initial stages of the discussion in 1976, the electorate was aware of and hostile to the concentration of wealth in Sweden (Zetterberg 1976:29). In 1977, LO sought to broaden this knowledge and translate it into support for employee capital funds in a campaign in which every member was to be reached with a booklet containing information on the question.

The Social Democratic Party began to commit itself to the wage earner fund concept in February of 1978 when a joint LO–Social Democratic work group produced a revised version of the LO proposal. The new proposal modifies the old one on several points. The formal ownership will now lie with the wage earners as a collectivity rather than with the trade unions. The voting rights of the collectively-owned shares will be exercised by the local trade unions and regionally elected representatives of wage earners. Only companies with more than 500 employees would be covered by this fund. The proposal also states that a number of development funds financed by a 3 per cent tax on the wage bill and controlled by the local trade union and public representatives should be set up to provide credit sources for new investment. In an obvious effort to soften the blow of these changes in the ownership structure, the work group suggests that the system be re-evaluated every five years. Whatever the modifications of this plan *vis-à-vis* the old LO proposal, the central thrust is the same: the principal means of production in Sweden would be gradually socialised.

TCO is the key to the success or failure of the proposal for collective ownership. It has trodden soft ground on the issue, since 60 per cent of its members vote bourgeois and the bourgeois parties launched an all-out offensive on Meidner's plan in 1976. The 1976 TCO congress was faced with a report on the problem which recommended collectively-owned funds. The report emphasised the need for new sources of capital formation much more than the LO report, but its conclusions were the same: the only way to aid capital accumulation without increasing the concentration of wealth is to institute collective funds. Interestingly enough, two Liberal members of the TCO study group reportedly did their best to come up with an alternative, but once they accepted the premises concerning capital formation and distribution they were locked into the conclusion that collective funds were the only solution. The TCO congress carefully avoided endorsing the report. Rather it passed a resolution making the report the foundation for further TCO work on the issue and making the ambiguous recommendation that, if the funds are instituted, they should be collectively owned, leaving open the question as to whether they should be instituted at all. The TCO leadership appears to support the plan but recognises the necessity of getting broad membership support before pushing it publicly. To this end, TCO began an educational campaign in the autumn of 1977 which strongly supported collectively-owned funds. Early in 1978, the organisation took another step towards full commitment to collective ownership when it issued a follow-up report which reconfirmed the principles contained in the first report. If TCO formally endorses collective ownership, which seems likely, the Liberal and Centre parties will be in a bind. Since they get the majority of their voters from LO or TCO members, they will be hard put to oppose LO and TCO. It seems absurd to suggest that bourgeois parties may help institute socialism, but this may well happen.[8]

In this chapter, we have seen how the shift in the distribution of power in Swedish civil society put production politics back on to the immediate political agenda. The growth of white-collar labour organisation and the release of non-manual employees from the hegemony of capital brought first employee power in the enterprise and, ultimately, collective ownership to the centre of the labour movement's programme. Though the question of collective owner-ship is yet to be decided, we think we have established conclusively that the transition to socialism has not and will not be prevented by the absorption of the Social Democratic labour movement into the capitalist system. The inability of Social Democracy in Sweden to move forward on production politics in earlier times was the result of a deadlock with capital, not a sell-out. Even if the 1979 election does not bring the Social Democrats to power, the future of socialism in Sweden will not be decided. The events of the last few years show that some immediate problems of the Swedish labour movement require a socialist solution, thus the issue is likely to be raised again. Furthermore, the renewal of socialism in Sweden shows that it is at least possible for other reformist socialist parties to bring socialism back on the agenda given the right conditions.

The transition to socialism depends not only on what the labour movement does but also on what capital does. Will the introduction of employee capital funds spark capital exit and investment stops by domestic capital? And will international capital perceive the Swed-ish model as a threat and orchestrate some kind of censure? Any assessment of these future problems involves speculation which we leave to the conclusion.

7

Conclusion

Marx's faulty predictions on the questions of the development of the class structure and consciousness formation led him to think that the transition from capitalism to socialism would occur much more rapidly than it has. The development of the new middle class and the more gradual decline in the petty bourgeois sector, particularly the rural portion, has meant that even under the best of conditions the development of labour organisation and class consciousness has proceeded at a much slower rate than the early Marxists imagined. They also underestimated the strength of religious, ethnic and linguistic ties and, like virtually all academics to date, failed to recognise the substantial differences in the economic structure of various countries. Because of variation in ethnic and linguistic diversity, the strength of religious ties and economic centralisation, Western capitalist countries vary substantially in the level of labour organisation and the strength of the socialist parties. Consequently, the political economies of various countries vary considerably. Countries where labour and the left are weak are moving toward a corporate collectivist pattern. Where labour and the left are strong, the political economies are transitional forms between capitalism and socialism.

Despite the fact that the Western labour movement has not yet fulfilled the historic role assigned to it by Marx, there is no denying that its achievements have been substantial. In almost every country, the working class has been a major actor in the struggle for political democracy. Though the introduction of democracy did not lead to socialism, it did ultimately lead to a compromise on the part of the bourgeoisie, albeit after an authoritarian interlude in some cases. The welfare state was the essential element of that compromise.

The expansion of the welfare state was a post-Second World War phenomenon, but in every country that experienced even medium welfare state build-up, plans were laid before the end of the war and the alignment of political forces destined to be instrumental in welfare state expansion was already determined. In every case except the United Kingdom, the welfare statist coalition contained the organised industrial working class in coalition with urban or rural petty bourgeois elements.[1] In the 1930s, the Danish and Swedish Social Democrats formed a stable coalition government with a petty bourgeois party. The Norwegian Social Democrats followed a similar pattern though without formal cabinet collaboration. The Social Democrats in Belgium had already entered a coalition with the Catholics in the 1920s, a pattern which was followed much later by the Dutch. In Scandinavia, the Netherlands, Belgium, and to some extent the United Kingdom, the growing strength of organised labour also necessitated significant concessions from employers.

The French situation, as we have seen, was somewhat different. A coalition between working-class and petty bourgeois forces did initiate welfare state development. But the decentralised nature of the French economy and the resultant paternalism on the part of employers and the erratic character of French unionism impeded any compromise in the industrial sector. In the long run, these factors, particularly trade union character, undermined the strength of the French left.

Similarly, the defeat of fascism and the discrediting of the old ruling coalitions in those countries brought compromises between the labour movement and the formerly intransigent bourgeoisie. The most dramatic case of compromise was Austria, where Catholic conservative forces that had eliminated democracy rather than compromise with the labour movement, now agreed to rule in an uneasy coalition with their former enemies. This coalition, which dominated Austrian politics until the Social Democrats won a majority in the 1970s, was responsible for very substantial expansion of the welfare state.

The point of this historical sketch is to reinforce several points made throughout this book. First, the class structure and the weakness of labour organisations prevented the socialist movement from pushing through its more radical programmes in the inter-war period. The coalition with petty bourgeois elements forced socialisation off the immediate programme during the inter-war period and the 1940s and early 1950s. The cold war contributed to keeping the issue in the background. Second, the social and economic rights associated with the welfare state are products of class struggle. After their attempt to limit the gains of the working-class movement to mere political rights failed, the bourgeoisie either compromised or aided the downfall of democracy. When the latter strategy was discredited by military defeat and the holocaust, the bourgeoisie everywhere settled for a compromise.

But the terms of the compromise varied substantially according to the strength of organised labour and the socialist parties. Moreover, the variation among capitalist countries increased in the whole post-war period. Immediately after the Second World War all countries stood at the beginning of welfare state development and the levels of expenditure were similar. By 1970, the differences were striking with some countries spending less than a quarter of GDP on non-military public goods and services and other countries spending almost one-half. Differences can be seen in the variation in control patterns in the economy, too, as our discussion of pensions in the United Kingdom, the United States and Sweden showed. Furthermore, as Table 4.8 showed, the variation in labour organisation indicates that the underlying distribution of power in capitalist democracies is increasingly different from country to country. Thus the character of the political economies has diverged too, some countries moving towards a corporate collectivist pattern, others, towards democratic socialism.

The inability of the left to move beyond the welfare state has been due to its weakness more than anything. There is a certain amount of truth to the Downsian model of democracy: parties do compete for the middle-of-the-road voter. But what determines where the middle of the road is – where the mean opinion lies – is the distribution of power in civil society. Yet even accepting the prevailing distribution of opinion, the electoral record of socialist parties has been poor. Looking back at Table 4.9, one can see that only in Scandinavia does the socialist period of incumbency exceed that of the centre and right in the period 1945–70. Given this, it is not surprising that only a few countries have moved much beyond the welfare state. Taking the Swedish case as a model, we would expect the labour movement to bring production politics to the centre of its programme when (1) the political necessity of a coalition with petty bourgeois forces is ended; (2) white-collar employees are thoroughly organised; and (3) the socialists have experienced a substantial period alone in the government. The only other country which fits these three criteria is Norway. Even Denmark does not qualify, because, as Esping-Andersen (1978) shows, continuation of the coalition with the petty bourgeoisie has prevented the Social Democrats from going beyond welfare statism.

This is not to say that the reintroduction of socialism to the centre of the left's programme in the future is limited by the same three conditions. There is no reason to think that past incumbency *per se* should limit future possibilities to that extent. And most structural trends favour the labour movement. Religious divisions in the working class are declining because of the reorientation of the Catholic Church in the wake of Vatican II, the jettisoning of militant secularism by the socialist parties and the general process of secularisation. Where it is not supported through subsidisation for political reasons as in France and Italy, the petty bourgeoisie, particularly in the rural sector, is declining rapidly. And capital centralisation is increasing everywhere. On the other hand, the cases of Belgium and Canada show that ethnic and linguistic divisions are still strong bases for group loyalty.

This brings up a topic which we can only touch on here. It has often been claimed that a number of ongoing changes in the class structure, the most important of which is the relative decline in the proportion of manual industrial occupations, will undermine the social bases of support for socialist parties. Our own research on the Swedish and UK cases as well as that of a number of other authors on other countries show that this argument received little support when tested empirically.[2] For one thing, forced mobility into the non-manual ranks created by changes in the class structure increases the number of non-manuals from socialist backgrounds and thus, given the strong intergenerational correlations in party preference, the proportion of non-manuals voting socialist tends to increase. Furthermore, the universalisation of secondary education is reducing the educational differences between lower non-manuals and workers and thus decreasing closure of mobility between the manual and non-manual working class. The emergent social division, as both our work and Hamilton's show, is between the upper middle class and the working classes as defined in Chapter 2. The decline in status consciousness, an essentially pre-capitalist element of class relations, contributes to this process. In Sweden the decline in closure has been furthered by an equalisation of consumption levels and class desegregation of living patterns. This has contributed to the decline in class voting. The socialists have lost some support in the working class and gained substantially among non-manuals. Consequently, the expansion of non-manual ranks is not likely to weaken the socialists' electoral base.

The increasing labour force participation of women also favours the left. The expansion of the white-collar ranks in the post-war period led to an inflow of women into active economic life. This is the material base on which the women's liberation movement grew. The increase in sexual equality, the greater contact with work life and thus the labour movement, and the general process of secularisation has eliminated sex differences in voting in Sweden and promises to do so elsewhere. In the Swedish case, the growth of sexual equality has already made crucial electoral contributions to the cause of socialism: the Social Democrats would certainly have lost the 1973 election and probably the 1970 election had the small sex differences in voting that characterised the country in the 1940s not been eliminated by the mid-1960s.

With these trends as a background, it seems at least possible that the left in the other 'corporatist' democracies could follow the Swedish pattern and bring socialism back on the immediate agenda. In Norway and Austria, there are no obstacles to doing this. In the Netherlands, the limited white-collar organisation is a problem, but the recent ideological renewal of the Labour Party and the break-up of the politics of accommodation are encouraging signs in the other direction. In fact, the Labour Party has shown some interest in instituting collective funds along the lines of the Swedish plan. Given the co-operation between the Social Democrats and the People's Democratic Union (the Communists) and the continued decline in the agricultural population, the Finnish left's future prospects look good. The Danish Social Democrats have the support of a fairly strong labour movement, but the severe economic problems combined with political fragmentation of the left's support make the future of Danish Social Democracy hard to predict. The Danes are discussing the introduction of a collective ownership scheme similar to the Swedish plan with the exception that it is to be developed through a payroll tax (Lykketoft 1977).

Among the other small democracies, the possibility of ideological renewal comes into question only in the cases of New Zealand and

Australia. In the rest of the countries labour organisation is too low and thus the weakness of the labour movement's hegemony and the parliamentary position of the social democratic parties make the passage of any socialist programme completely out of the question. The Australians face an unfavourable political system. But more seriously, the trade unions failed to break through to the non-manual ranks. Labour organisation has actually declined in the post-war period.

In all five large democracies labour organisation has stagnated or declined somewhat in the post-war period taken as a whole. This is the most discouraging result found in this study. If examination of the Swedish case has cast an optimistic light on the possibility of a parliamentary transition to socialism, the situation in the large democracies casts an equally negative picture of the probability of such a transition in the West as a whole. And given the international character of the capitalist system, this obviously has repercussions for the possibilities of the small democracies. Our initial finding, that labour organisation is indirectly related to country size was discouraging enough for socialism's future, but the stagnation of labour organising in the large countries raises the further question of whether the economic structure of large countries does result in some strong structural restraint to labour organising.

However, the connection of the level of labour organisation to market structure and ethnic and linguistic diversity should not be reified. The strength of the labour movement is not totally fixed by these factors. After all, they explain 44 per cent of the variation in labour organisation in 1930, which means these structural factors *do not* explain 56 per cent of the variation in labour organisation. Furthermore, very little of the change in the level of labour organisation since 1930 is accounted for by changes in these structural factors. Labour organisation can be increased through voluntary human action.

Given the great importance we have attached to the strength of the labour movement, it is incumbent on us to address the question of the possibilities for successful organising drives in the future. Examining the historical development of labour organisation, we can identify a number of factors which have aided sudden organising drives as well as slower long-term growth. Dramatic changes have occurred in two situations. During and immediately after the two world wars trade union membership increased rapidly, particu-

larly in the defeated powers. The disastrous consequences of nuclear world war rule out this factor for the future. The second
situation in which dramatic changes have occurred is the *combination* of severe economic crisis and the accession of leftist parties to
power. (Crisis alone causes membership to deteriorate.) This has
occurred only once (in the depression) so it might have been an
idiosyncratic unrepeatable event.

Consistent gradual long-term change has occurred in a number of
situations. Aside from the special conditions associated with crisis,
organising efforts have been more successful when unemployment
was low. High unemployment makes workers more insecure about
losing their jobs and increases ethnic conflict in competition for
jobs. This hurts the left at the polls as well. So, contrary to the
opinions of many radical leftists, the current economic stagnation of
the West should not be welcomed by socialists. Changes in the
structure of the labour force aided unions until recently when the
growth of the non-manual ranks began to exceed the decline in
employment in the rural sector and self-employment. White-collar
workers can be organised, of course, and, in fact, the level of
white-collar organisation is the single most important source of
variation in labour organisation. This, in turn, points to the most
important cause of variations in the growth of organisation in the
post-war period, incumbency of socialist parties (see Chapter 4).
An examination of year-by-year changes in union membership for a
number of countries shows that membership figures follow shifts in
government with incredible regularity. Thus, the decline in union
membership in the large democracies is primarily due to the exclusion of the socialists from government. This seems to put these
labour movements in a vicious cycle of declining organisational
density and declining political influence. But this apparent crisis is
only acute in the United States. In the United Kingdom, substantial
periods of Labour rule have resulted in an increase in union
strength. The recent Social Democratic government in Germany
has reversed a downward trend in organisational density in that
country. And the end of the political exclusion of the Communist
Parties in Italy and France may lead to similar effects in those
countries.

In the United States, the immediate task is the creation of a social
democratic movement. Two factors hold the key to the future. The
first is that trade union organising must be stepped up substantially

in order to reverse the trend in membership, which declined in 1977 in *absolute* terms. The US labour movement is at a critical turning point in its history. Capital centralisation has proceeded to the point where many unions are losing their effectiveness. Conglomeration in many sectors of the economy has strengthened capital's bargaining position so much that workers are increasingly in the position of attempting to limit roll-backs of benefits previously won, as the mineworkers' strike of 1977 – 8 shows. Not only do these conglomerates have unorganised subsidiaries in the south and west, they also have subsidiaries in a number of different industries which increases their ability to break a strike in any one given industry at a given point in time. According to our argument in Chapter 2, this situation can lead either to vigorous counter-organising or to a crushing of the effective power of the labour movement. While current conditions are not favourable for a strong organising drive, the surge of Italian organising since 1968 suggests that great membership growth can occur even under the worst objective conditions. Second, the labour movement, in coalition with minorities and like-minded groups, must adopt a political strategy which entails the development of a disciplined caucus within the Democratic Party as was suggested in Chapter 5.

The most significant event for the future of socialism in Italy and France is the development of 'Eurocommunism'. As a result of the decline of cold war tensions and religious divisions as well as the internal reorientation of the Communist Parties (at least, of the Italian party), the possibility of a renewal of the popular front type coalitions has changed the political picture in these countries considerably. From some quarters, particularly the French Socialist Party, there is talk of skipping the social democratic stage of development and proceeding to building democratic socialism.

Our analysis leads us to have very serious reservations about this possibility. In both France and Italy, the large petty bourgeoisie poses a serious obstacle to putting socialism on the agenda. In France, the left has chosen to put forth a socialist programme calling for substantial expansion of workers' control and significant nationalisation. Even if the divisions on the left are mended before 1983, the election of the Union of the Left is likely to be by a very narrow majority given that the programme excludes any possibility of increased petty bourgeois support. In the face of the capital flight and investment stop that the election of the left with such a radical programme is bound to set off, it is quite likely that the marginal supporters of the left would defect quickly. The return of the right in the next election would result in the reversal of the reform process. An additional *big* problem for the French left is the weakness of the French trade unions. Though membership figures may be an inadequate measure of the hegemony of the French labour movement, since French trade unions rely heavily on rank-and-file mobilisation rather than formal organisation, the membership figures are so low that it is obvious that the ability of the French unions to influence opinion outside of the core of the working class is very limited. Thus, to draw a comparison with Sweden, the core of the French working class – male industrial workers in the medium and larger plants – is more radical than the core of the Swedish working class. But in the periphery of the working class, the Swedes are much more leftist as they are very likely to have direct contact with LO through their own or their spouses' union membership. The success of the French left in the government will depend on support from these peripheral elements. The decentralised nature of French labour organisation also may present a leftist government with some problems. The communist-led CGT may be able to substitute ideological discipline for organisational centralisation and deliver consistent support to the government. The independent socialist CFDT, on the other hand, has refused formally to pledge support for the left and is certainly incapable of delivering it on unpopular issues, such as wage restraint, which may be necessary at some points.

The Italian unions have introduced more formalised organisation – such as dues check-offs – since the late 1960s, and consequently have been able to make significant and permanent gains in organising since 1968. In this respect, the Italian left is in a much better position than the French. Influenced by the Chilean events, the Italian Communist Party has rejected the strategy of a narrow-based coalition with the socialists and opted for a 'historic compromise' with the Christian Democrats. As Korpi (1978b: 321) points out, this compromise is similar to the one contracted by the Swedes in the 1930s. If our analysis is correct, this compromise will result in the Communists following the same sort of policy followed by the northwest European social democratic parties in an earlier period. The Christian Democrats depend politically on support from the petty bourgeoisie, thus the historic compromise is bound to involve a suppression of the socialisation issue. The Communists will have two big domestic problems if the historic compromise is consummated. To get the Italian economy back on its feet, considerable wage restraint will be necessary to pay for capital accumulation. It is questionable whether the decentralised Italian unions can deliver this. The second problem the Communist Party faces is that in its years of opposition it has built up an opinion among a large minority of the working class calling for rapid and radical change in the system. Some of these people are bound to be disillusioned with the results the party delivers once in the government.

The Swedish example would seem to be a natural model for the German and UK labour movements. A comparison to the Swedish case reveals that the biggest problem that the Germans face in going beyond the welfare state is the low level of white-collar union organisation. Though it is fashionable on the left now to characterise German Social Democracy as a hopelessly compromised movement, a closer inspection will reveal that German Social Democracy, particularly the trade unions, have come up with some fairly radical proposals which were so heavily compromised in the coalition with the Liberals that they bore little resemblance to the original proposal. For instance, the DGB did support a plan for the development of collectively-owned funds similar to the LO plan. Though the upturn in labour organisation is a favourable development, the continued impact of the cold war and the increasingly reactionary opposition (particularly Strauss and the CSU) impede the process of ideological reorientation.

Oddly enough, we would argue that the UK labour movement has the best possibility of any labour movement in the large democracies of moving beyond the welfare state toward socialism. The logic behind this reasoning is that immediate UK problems require a socialist solution. The United Kingdom faces an urgent need for modernisation of its physical capital. This can only be achieved by very substantial increases in investment, which as always must ultimately come from wage restraint. But given that the UK working class would probably have to suffer a *decline* in its standard of living, the UK trade unions are unlikely to accept such a formula. However, if the capital growth that results from wage restraint went to the workers rather than the capitalists, the TUC and the working class might look at the situation in an entirely different light. This would be a daring course for the Labour Party to embark on, but its only other choice is to carry out a principally capitalist policy.

This brings up the whole question of capital formation and the growth of various supracorporate sources of investment and economic control raised in our discussion of pensions and employee investment funds in the last chapter. It seems clear that one of the most significant developments in the near future will be the growth of various supracorporate funds, either in a corporate collectivist or democratic socialist form. On this account some speculations can be ventured which brighten our dreary picture of the future of socialism in the larger democracies. The Swedish employee investment fund model, which essentially calls for the socialisation of capital growth, is almost certain to replace nationalisation as the primary path to gradual socialisation of the economy in the programmes of most socialist parties attempting to move beyond the welfare state toward socialism. The brilliance of the policy is that it not only results in socialisation of the economy with no financial layout from the government, but it also provides for new sources of capital formation, which is likely to be a serious problem in all capitalist countries, when and if the current recession is over. Thus the policy is a practical solution to an immediate problem. In fact, it may be the only solution for countries like the United Kingdom and Italy where a high reinvestment rate is necessary and where strong organisation among blue-collar workers makes it impractical to impose a wage stop for capital accumulation which accrues to the bourgeoisie. The immediate practical aspects of the policy might make it possible to put it on the political agenda much earlier than one would predict by the distribution of social and political forces alone.

The capitalist answer to this policy is likely to be similar to US pension funds – collective ownership with corporate control. From a Marxist viewpoint, this development, which the United States is headed for, represents a further increase in the centralisation of capital and reveals capitalism in its most contradictory form. Marx believed that the corporation revealed the contradictory nature of capitalism by separating ownership and management and centralising control to a small élite of shareholders, thereby revealing among other things that the dividends of owners were obviously not payment for productive labour. But the contradictions involved in the development of corporate capitalism pall besides those involved

in pension fund capitalism, which entail the socialisation of ownership but a further centralisation of control in private hands. Pension
fund capitalism, not the corporation as Marx (1894: 438) thought,
'is the abolition of the capitalist mode of production within the
capitalist mode of production itself ... It is private production
without the control of private property.' But this development may
not be without its dangers for the capitalists. Marx thought that the
centralisation of capital would pave the way for socialism and
certainly, from a technical point of view, what is easier than giving
workers' representatives the voting rights to stock they already
own. And while it is unimaginable that the US left could raise
support for the socialisation of a quarter of US business, it is
imaginable that they could raise support for the immanently capitalist demand that people be allowed to control their own private
property. Obviously this is speculative, but our point here is to raise
the question of what impact the development of collective fund
capitalism might have on socialist strategy rather than provide an
answer to that question.

Up to this point, we have primarily considered the question of
whether the left was sufficiently strong to put socialism on the
agenda and only touched on what the reaction of capitalist forces,
both domestic and international, would be. Any prediction on this
account is highly speculative since the reaction of capital depends
not just on rational economic calculations, such as the rate of return
on capital after the introduction of employee investment funds, but
also on rational political considerations and on subjective feelings
of capitalists which may be entirely irrational. For instance, the
reaction of French capital to the Popular Front reforms was partly
irrational from a purely economic point of view. Irrational reactions
are characteristic of small paternalistic employers and thus are
likely to be of less importance in the developed industrial world of
today than in France in the 1930s or Chile in the 1970s. But this
factor still cannot be discounted.

In the Swedish case, the rational economic behaviour of an
investor upon introduction of employee investment funds is to do
nothing in the short run. The funds are unlikely to change the rate of
return on capital. They will socialise capital growth and not present
capital. And since they are a new investment source and will make
wage restraint more acceptable, they may even increase profitability of a firm. To precipitate massive capital exit is the stupidest thing

an investor could do because this would create a drastic drop on the Swedish stock market. The Swedish government could partially counteract an investment slowdown by releasing the counter-cyclical investment funds. And since the supplementary pension funds, which are now invested primarily in the housing and credit markets, are large enough to buy all the stocks on the Swedish stock market at current market prices, it would be an easy matter for the fund to buy all stocks on the market were the stock prices to drop drastically. The result would be an immediate socialisation of the entire Swedish economy. It also should be noted that it is illegal to take large amounts of Swedish money out of the country without permission. Such laws are notoriously hard to enforce but they do provide some barrier to capital flight.

In the long run, the activity of investors from a rational economic point of view will be determined by the performance of Swedish business. Few investors own enough capital to sit on corporate boards, so control relations in the enterprise are of little concern to them as long as their rate of return is adequate. If capital exit does not occur before a given firm goes over the 50 per cent mark in terms of collective ownership, it is unlikely to occur then. And by that point the combined collective ownership in the economy through the employee investment funds and pension funds would be so high that private capital exit and investment stops would not be a serious threat.

From a political point of view, action by Swedish capital makes more sense. If the employee investment funds were passed by a Social Democratic government over the vocal opposition of all the bourgeois parties and without the support of TCO, limited economic sabotage designed to increase unemployment to, say, 4 per cent – which is politically intolerable in Sweden – might be enough to ensure the victory of a bourgeois government at the next election. For this very reason, the Social Democrats certainly will not pass this legislation without the support of TCO. And with TCO on their side, a compromise with the bourgeois left is probable leaving the Conservatives and SAF politically isolated. The com-promise might entail limiting the collective ownership in any firm to, say, 49 per cent. This is of little consequence because it can be changed later anyway. More important is the structure of control of the fund. As long as the fund is controlled by the elected representa-tives of the people and invested in Swedish enterprises, it will represent a progressive socialisation of Swedish capital and a protection against future capital flight.

The possibility of compromise with the bourgeois left on this issue again highlights the importance of the change in the distribution of power caused by the growth of TCO. And this also points out the great difference between Sweden and a country like the United Kingdom. Though it seems quite possible that the Labour Party could go through an ideological reorientation that would include a proposal for collective funds, it would face much stiffer political opposition. Conservative opposition to the plan would make economic sabotage against the Labour government politically desirable since it might bring the Conservatives back to power who then would repeal the legislation. Much more than in the case of welfare statist legislation, the hegemonic social block required for a successful attack on capital must be much broader than organised blue-collar workers.

In the Swedish case, retaliation by international capital directly or via its influence on the US government is not probable. Most multinationals in Sweden are Swedish based and it is such a small country that a socialist Sweden poses little threat to international capital. And since Sweden is not in NATO and the left is dominated by the Social Democrats and not the Communists, Sweden will probably not be the object of censure from the United States for political reasons.

All of these factors pose problems for the large European democracies. International capital would almost certainly react strongly to any government which proposed to put through legislation of the sort the Swedes have proposed. In the cases of Italy and France, the election of a government with Communist participation would have the same result whatever its programme. And, given that the US government had to be dissuaded by German Social Democratic leaders from co-ordinating economic sanctions against Soares' Socialist government in Portugal, they are very likely to carry out such a policy against a French or Italian government containing Communists. For these countries, a change in US policy is very important. And in all four countries, greater democratic control over US capitalism would be beneficial, which is to say the development of a social democratic United States would be an important contribution to the development of a socialist Europe. If Europe did move in a socialist direction without supportive developments in the

United States, it is possible that the reacion of international capital might force the government in question to choose between rapid transition to socialism or retreat from its socialist policies. Thus the revolutionary scenario we pointed out in Chapter 3 could occur. But this is not to be hoped for because defeat is more likely than victory especially if the army has any influence on events. To weather this economic and political crisis with substantial political support, a socialist movement would have to have established an even greater hegemonic presence in civil society than would be necessary to push through a gradualist programme along Swedish lines. Thus, in every case, the immediate task of the socialist movement is to build the hegemony of the movement; to organise and to educate. This takes time. Gramsci was very right when he said that the socialist movement had to fight a war of position rather than a war of manoeuvre. Like the First World War, the struggle for civil society has required and will require great efforts to gain just a few yards of social terrain.

List of Abbreviations

Austria

ÖGB Österreichischer Gewerkschaftsbund – Austrian Trade Union Federation.

France

CFDT Confédération Française et Démocratique du Travail – French Democratic Workers' Confederation.
CFTC Confédération Française des Travailleurs Chrétiens – French Confederation of Christian Workers.
CGT Confédération Générale du Travail – General Confederation of Labour.
MRP Mouvement Républicain Populaire – Popular Republican Movement.

Germany

CSU Christlich-Soziale Union – Christian Social Union.
DGB Deutscher Gewerkschaftsbund – German Trade Union Federation.

Sweden

LO Landsorganisationen – Swedish Federation of Trade Unions.
SAF Svenska Arbetsgivareföreningen – Swedish Employers' Association.
TCO Tjänstemännens Centralorganisation – Central Organisation of Salaried Employees.

United Kingdom

TUC Trades Union Congress.

United States

AFL American Federation of Labor.
CIO Committee for Industrial Organisation (later Congress of Industrial Organisations).
UAW United Automobile, Aerospace and Agricultural Implement Workers of America.

Notes

Chapter 1

1. It might be argued that science is the new productive force in socialism. However, the parallel to previous transitions cannot be taken very far. The proletariat does not 'own' science and does not derive its power from science. Furthermore, science is used in conjunction with machines, not independently of them. For an attempt to treat science (or technical knowledge) as a force of production and the basis for a new system of domination, see Touraine (1971).

2. No social order is 'purely capitalist' since all capitalist societies contain some simple commodity production. Furthermore, in most historical cases, labour organisation began before feudal production disappeared.

3. We will not attempt to mediate this debate on what Marx meant. Our own position on the role of contradictions and crises in the transition will be stated in subsequent chapters.

Chapter 2

1. The author owes a great debt to John Low-Beer for comments on earlier drafts and extensive discussions of the theoretical ideas in this chapter. A version of the sections on control relations and distribution relations was co-authored with Low-Beer (Low-Beer and Stephens 1976).

2. The next few pages of the text draw heavily on Stephens and Stephens (1978).

3. It could be argued that the apparent relationship between control rights and the buyer/seller relationship is entirely due to the differences in the physical characteristics of land and capital. This would not seriously damage our overall argument here and it would have no effect at all on our theory of the transition to socialism.

4. This was not the only way in which producers were separated from the means of production. Coercion, usually politically supported, was probably more important. It obviously was in the transition to capitalist agriculture in England. The enclosure movement is a very good example of the interaction of political power with the development of the market mentioned earlier.

5. Carchedi has four criteria for the economic identification of classes. We are interested only in developing a theory of control relations here, so we chose not to discuss Carchedi's work in detail. Both his and Wright's works will be addressed at length in a manuscript on class formation and class consciousness now under way. It should be pointed out here that empirically the identification of classes by Wright's or Carchedi's method will be very similar.

6. The relationship is not a one-to-one relationship. Since the distribution of power in civil society does not completely determine the action of the state but rather sets limits on it, it makes a difference whether the incumbent in the government is the representative of labour or capital.

7. We find Carchedi's introduction of 'political and ideological' criteria unconvincing. While it is clear that wage and salary differentiation can be used to divide the working class, market conditions certainly explain more than Carchedi admits. See especially his example of the systems engineer (Carchedi 1975a: 81, note 67).

8. Again, really renting not buying. Unfortunately, the distinction between buying and selling cannot be captured with the English word 'rent' so we must use 'buy' and 'sell'.

9. Occupational prestige is measured according to Blau and Duncan's method in both Wright and Perrone's and Robinson and Kelly's studies. This variable should not be used as an independent variable in the analysis of income distribution since the occupational prestige score of an occupation is partly a product of the income of the occupation. Since Robinson and Kelly do not present a regression using their refined definition of authority without occupational prestige, the figures from Wright and Perrone represent the best approximation of our model.

10. The fact that measured IQ explains only 5 per cent of the variation in income (Jencks 1972) and that the measurement error involved in using IQ as an indicator of innate ability is correlated with the dependent variable (income) indicates that substantial exploitation is characteristic of contemporary capitalist societies.

11. There are differences in the rural population based on the size of holdings, propertyless or propertied states, etc., which are of particular importance at early stages of capitalist development. But to analyse these differences would take us far from the subject of this book.

12. Of course, women dominate non-manual working-class occupations. It has been argued that the consequences of the growth of this class for politics is not great, since the long-term life chances of most families in a sexist society (which all existing capitalist societies are) are determined more by the husband's occupation than the wife's. But even if married women are classified by their husbands' occupations, the non-manual working class is of substantial size in the more advanced capitalist societies. In Sweden, for example, a breakdown of classes in 1974 reveals that the non-manual working class defined by the most restrictive criteria possible is at least 17 per cent of the population.

13. Most writers discussing the difficulties of developing socialism in underdeveloped countries have emphasised the problem of scarcity. See Harrington (1972) and Anderson (1965). For Marx on scarcity, see Marx (1846: 49). For underdeveloped countries attempting a gradual transition to socialism, the lack of centralisation is also a problem. The independent truckers' 'strike' in Chile is a case in point. This could not have happened in a country with a centralised transportation system. The failure of the Peruvian government's participation scheme was also partly due to the small average size of enterprises in that country (see E. H. Stephens 1977).

14. Late relative to other capitalist democracies. This term will be used repeatedly in this book always with this qualification.

15. The tendency for the state to reflect the distribution of power in civil society is probably greater in the industrial democracies we are interested in analysing than in any societies except those where civil society and the state are actually fused, e.g. feudalism. In societies where the military plays an important role in politics the Marxian model is less adequate. The military derives its political power from the use of force rather than its relation to the productive process. It is beyond the scope of this work to consider the problems of Marxian theory other than those related to the problem immediately at hand. See Mann (1977) on the state in pre-capitalist societies.

16. Both of these countries are characterised by low industrial centralisation (thus low employer solidarity) and strong blue-collar labour organisation. There may be a link between this situation and the acquisition of control in the enterprise.

17. Thus one cannot argue that the US government owns 50 per cent of the income rights in US corporations due to the 50 per cent profits tax. Pryor (1973) makes this point.

18. This discussion assumes that democratic socialism is a viable system.

Chapter 3

1. Where the old middle class is a substantial minority (for example France and Italy) they do reduce the strength of the socialist movement.

2. The syndicalism of the Tranmael wing of the Norwegian Labour Party was not really compatible with the centralism advocated by the Comintern. Had the syndicalists remained dominant, the party would have left the Comintern anyway.

3. The United Kingdom, Sweden, Norway, New Zealand, Australia.

4. Public opinion is not the only constraint on reform. See the discussion on other constraints (for example, the danger of capital flight) below.

5. Some very recent Marxist works have presented a point of view more similar to ours. Esping-Andersen *et al.* (1976), Hicks *et al.* (1978) and Reich and Edwards (1978) argue that the state is an arena for class struggle and that state policy can be influenced by working-class organisation. Korpi's (1978b) theory of state policy formation is virtually identical to ours.

6. This does not mean that all such policies were not in the long term interests of capital. For instance, the initiation of Keynesian economic policy in the New Deal was opposed by most businessmen. But once the policy was applied successfully, they slowly came to accept and then support it. Thus the maintenance of Keynesian policies can be explained, at least in part, by the fact that they are functional for capital. But the origin of such policies cannot be explained by the political action of businessmen. Of course, the origin of any policy or structure cannot be explained by the functional need for it. This is a sore point not only in structural functional analysis *à la* Parsons but also in Marxist 'functional' analysis.

7. Anderson (1965) presents a view close to ours though he later (1977) amends it attributing greater importance to the resistance of the state. His position is now closer to Trotsky.

8. Craft unions in racially divided societies are a possible example of this.

9. Interestingly, Gorz's theory has a lot in common with Guild Socialism.

10. See Low-Beer (1978) for a discussion and analysis of class consciousness and militancy in the Italian new working class. Low-Beer shows that Gorz's inference was partly incorrect. He (p. 237) concludes that, though not *revolutionary* in the traditional sense, 'the new working class may contribute cadres, objectives, and ideology to a socialist movement'.

Chapter 4

1. Japan does fit the Western model to the extent that it is characterised by a low level of labour organisation, no leftist rule and thus low welfare spending. Likewise, control over social development has remained entirely in the hands of the business élite.

2. Pryor probably underestimates the increase in enterprise and establishment size because he excludes small business from his analysis.

3. Some countries have extremely complex bargaining systems where regional agreements play an important role (e.g., Germany and Australia) or where collective agreements become part of the legal code and thus violation is subject to criminal sanction (e.g., Australia). This index is obviously insensitive to these variations.

4. We use this term with such reservation since its historical connotations range from fascist (at worst) to co-optation of the working class by capitalist interests. Wilensky claims to be building on Schmitter's (1974) concept of 'societal corporatism', which clearly has the latter connotation. But Wilensky's definition is based on the policy-making process whereas Schmitter's emphasises the structural characteristics of the system (which is why they disagree on the classification of Switzerland). The co-optative connotation Schmitter gives to the concept is very misleading as we shall show subsequently.

5. The Swedish Level of Living Survey is the first extensive effort in this area. See Johansson (1971).

6. For a discussion of these problems see Titmuss (1963) on the United Kingdom and Kolko (1962) on the United States.

7. This has been contested by some of the liberal defenders of capitalism. These critics of collective ownership schemes include only dividends and realised capital gains in their calculations.

8. Sawyer's study also contains a very good discussion of the deficiencies of much of the income distribution data.

9. It might be claimed that the strength of association between federalism and socialist rule is partly an artefact of our (incorrect) decision to code Switzerland as 0 on the socialist rule index. Since the Swiss Social Democrats always have had two members in the Bundesrat, the seven member executive, one might argue that Switzerland should be coded as 7 not 0. However, membership in the Bundesrat does not give one effective power over policy-making. It is not a coalition government, operating on the basis of parliamentary support, making policy, etc., at all. The effective policy-making mechanism is the referendum which impedes coalition formation and isolates the Social Democrats from any effective influence over policy-making. Thus, since the party has no direct power over state policy, Switzerland should be coded 0 on the socialist rule index.

10. Wilensky errs in his measurement of political ideology. He lumps democratic countries together with totalitarian and authoritarian regimes. All communist countries are considered to have the most leftist governments in his index of ideology. This overlooks the fact that Eastern European Communist Parties do not have to deliver on their promises in the way that socialist parties in democracies do. Wilensky's errors are not limited to his measurement of the political variable. For instance, he argues that the age of the system is caused by the aged percentage of the population (see any of the path analyses in Wilensky 1975). Obviously, this cannot be the case since the institution of the social security system is temporally prior to the *present* proportion of the population over sixty-five by as much as eighty years.

11. Earlier versions of our analysis can be found in Stephens (1971, 1976).

12. We use male suffrage as an indicator here as it was the more crucial breakthrough for class relations. In the sexist division of labour of Western industrial societies, women have been assigned a role as guardians of religion and traditionalism. This, along with their partial isolation from production, has impeded the development of class consciousness among women. Thus female suffrage has often strengthened the right initially.

13. Swiss democracy can be dated from the secret ballot reform of 1872. White male democracy was achieved in the United States in the 1840s, Blacks were enfranchised with the passage of the Fifteenth Amendment after the Civil War. We have dated US democracy from this date. But this ignores *de facto* exclusion of

Blacks in the South. A good case can be made for dating US democracy from the 1965 Voting Rights Act.

14. These events are obviously not exogenous to the development of Western capitalism and could be integrated theoretically into our model of the development of the labour movement and the transition to socialism. But this would be a huge task involving a complete shift of focus from nation state to the world system as the unit of analysis and to a detailed historical examination of the last century and a half. This is beyond the scope of this book. Thus in the discussion in the following two chapters these international events will appear largely as exogenous factors.

15. The Italian pattern is slightly different. There the Catholic Church bears a major responsibility for preventing the earlier development of a Catholic party committed to democracy and thus legitimating the republic among Catholics.

Chapter 5

1. This section on Sweden and the next chapter is a summary of our earlier work (Stephens 1976:165–328). Unfortunately, most discussions of Sweden in English have de-emphasised class conflict and presented a highly idealised 'spirit of compromise' and 'end of ideology' point of view. Some recently published works by Andrew Martin (1973, 1975, 1977) and Walter Korpi (1978b) argue along lines similar to ours. Both Korpi's and Martin's work are highly recommended to the reader who wishes to examine the Swedish case in more detail.

2. The coalition of the Social Democrats and the Agrarian (Centre) Party on the issue of education extended beyond 1957 up to the university reforms of the early 1970s.

3. The only generally unpopular programme is cash benefits to the chronically unemployed. Ordinarily this is a very small percentage of total public expenditure so it affords little opportunity for economising by conservative governments. It is, however, a convenient whipping boy for conservative election propaganda. This is not to say that the level of taxation has not been an effective issue for the right. It has. But the right has *generally* not been able to deliver on its promises to cut the overall level of taxation because it has also usually promised to maintain social services.

4. It is important to point out that the Social Democrats in Scandinavia have been responsible for the introduction of value-added taxes in the 1960s and 1970s. The crucial difference is that they have done this in order to expand social services rather than to finance existing social services in a different way. For the reasons for the shift to indirect taxation, see Chapter 6.

5. Lindhagen (1974) emphasises the importance of this change, but points to slightly different antecedents than we have.

6. Stephens (forthcoming). A preliminary report on this research can be found in Stephens (1979).

7. It could be argued that this was in part due to the structure of the electoral system and the possibilities for coalition governments. Labour outpolled the Conservatives in 1951 48·8 per cent to 48·0 per cent, yet the Conservatives received an absolute majority in the House of Commons. The socialist block received 50·4 per cent of the vote in the 1952 election resulting in a 115–115 deadlock in the lower house. Thus it seems that the coalition with the Agrarian Party was decisive in keeping the Social Democrats in government. However, no other party could have governed given the Social Democratic majority in the upper house. Furthermore, there is good reason to believe that the British Liberals would have fared much better cutting into Labour's support if Britain had had a proportional representation system (see Butler *et al.* 1968).

8. Germany in the late 1940s and early 1950s is the only exception that comes to mind. See p. 127.

9. Officially the AFL–CIO is party neutral, but it rarely supports Republican candidates and has never supported the Republican candidate for President.

10. The Catholic unions did not re-emerge from the fascist period in either Austria or Germany.

11. The main sources are Reynolds and Smolensky (1977), Schnitzer (1974), Westergaard and Resler (1975), Bentzel (1961), Nicholson (1974), Atkinson (1975) and research we did in 1969 on the United States.

12. With the exception of Reynolds' and Smolensky's work, virtually all studies which attempt to estimate the redistribution effected by the welfare state refer to this data, and, interestingly enough, the various authors come to very different conclusions. Compare Westergaard and Resler (1975), Wilensky (1975), Schnitzer (1974) and Nicholson (1974). This data is much more comprehensive than that available for other countries but it is *not* by any means complete. For instance, there is no attempt to measure the use of roads, public transport, national parks, to mention a few things.

Chapter 6

1. The true figure was between 20 and 25 per cent (Rifkin and Barber 1978: 10). Though Drucker's work is filled with inaccuracies (Henry 1977), he did perform the important service of drawing attention to the importance of pension fund capital in the United States.

2. For an account of the pension struggle in Sweden see Molin (1966) and Heclo (1974). Esping-Anderson (1978) presents an interesting comparison of the Swedish and Danish cases. The Danish Social Democrats suggested a plan similar to the one adopted in Sweden but were forced to compromise on the issue, eliminating the fund, because of their position as a coalition partner with a centre party based in the petty bourgeoisie.

3. Given that increased corporate control results from the growth of American pension funds, a better name for Drucker's book would be 'The Obscene Revolution' rather than *The Unseen Revolution*.

4. Whether the white-collar/blue-collar coalition has resulted in a moderation of the Social Democrats' efforts to equalise income is not clear. The introduction of the value-added tax to finance new state services has been taken as an indication of this change. But the fact that the Danish Social Democrats who were still in coalition with a petty bourgeois-based centre party did the same thing indicates that the shift to indirect taxation was probably a result of the Social Democratic leadership's opinion that the public would not accept yet higher direct taxes. The fact that the Swedish Social Democrats developed their entire programme in the late 1960s around the issue of 'increased equality' argues that they have not moderated their stand on equalisation.

5. This is not very surprising since we were influenced by their arguments. See J. D. Stephens (1976: 288–302) for a fuller description of these interviews.

6. See Martin (1977) for a more complete discussion of this issue.

7. See SIFO (1976) and Korpi (1978a) for analyses of the election. Undoubtedly, the most important cause of the defeat was a series of scandals, the most important of which were Astrid Lindgren's and Ingmar Bergman's confrontation with the tax authorities in the spring of 1976. It was in this period that the Social Democrats' position in the opinion polls fell sharply from 44 per cent of those questioned on party preference in February to 38·5 per cent in April. The second big factor was the atomic energy question which became the completely dominant issue in the last

weeks of the election campaign. The Centre Party, which favoured a halt to the expansion of nuclear energy, apparently gained voters at the Social Democrats' expense. Most of the differences are within the margin of error but a comparison of the last poll and the election result supports the argument that a last-minute move to the Centre Party provided the critical margin that led to a bourgeois victory.

8. Already in 1977, the Liberals were reassessing their position on the question of collective funds. In a report the following year, the party seemed to be moving toward acceptance of the concept. Meidner (1978:7) believes that 'though very circuitously formulated, the [Liberals'] report seems compatible with the main principles of the TCO report'.

Chapter 7

1. The absence of this opportunity for compromise with a centrist petty bourgeois party can be seen in the cases of New Zealand and Australia. There, despite strong labour organisation, the Labour Parties were held out of the government for most of the post-war period, the result being modest welfare state development. Were it not for its peculiar class structure, it is likely that the United Kingdom would have followed the same path.

2. Stephens (1976, 1979) and a forthcoming manuscript on class formation and class consciousness in Britain and Sweden. Also see Goldthorpe *et al.* (1969), Hamilton (1967, 1972), Korpi (1978b) and Low-Beer (1978).

Bibliography

ADLER-KARLSSON, GUNNAR (1967), *Functional Socialism* (Stockholm: Prisma).

ALTVATER, ELMAR (1972), 'Notes on Some Problems of State Interventionism', *Kapitalistate*, 2, 3.

ANDERSON, PERRY (1965), 'Problems of Socialist Strategy', in Perry Anderson and Robin Blackburn (eds), *Towards Socialism* (London: Fontana).

—— (1977), 'The Antinomies of Antonio Gramsci', *New Left Review*, 100.

ATKINSON, A. B. (1975), *The Economics of Inequality* (Oxford University Press).

AVINERI, SCHLOMO (1968), *The Social and Political Thought of Karl Marx* (Cambridge University Press).

BENTZEL, RAGNAR (1961), *Inkomstfördelning i Sverige* (Uppsala: Almqvist and Wiksell).

BERLE, A. A., and MEANS, GARDINER (1937), *The Modern Corporation and Private Property* (New York: Macmillan).

BERNSTEIN, EDWARD (1909), *Evolutionary Socialism* (New York: Huebsch).

BJÖRN, LARS (1976), 'Labor Parties and the Redistribution of Income in Capitalist Democracies' (Ph.D. dissertation, University of North Carolina).

—— (1979), 'Labor Parties, Economic Growth and the Redistribution of Income in Five Capitalist Democracies', in Richard Tomasson (ed), *Comparative Studies in Sociology II* (Greenwich: JAI Press).

BURNHAM, JAMES (1941), *The Managerial Revolution* (New York: John Day).

BUTLER, DAVID, and STOKES, DONALD (1976), *Political Change in Britain* (New York: St Martin's Press).

BUTLER, DAVID, *et al.* (1968), 'The Strength of the Liberals under Different Electoral Systems', *Parliamentary Affairs*, 22.

CAMERON, DAVID (1976), 'Inequality and the State' (paper delivered at the Meetings of the American Political Science Association, Washington, DC).

CARCHEDI, G. (1975a), 'On the Economic Identification of the New Middle Class', *Economy and Society*, 4.

—— (1975b), 'Reproduction of Social Classes at the Level of Production Relations', *Economy and Society*, 4.

COLE, G. D. H. (1956), *A History of Socialist Thought III: The Second International* (London: Macmillan).

—— (1958), *A History of Socialist Thought IV: Communism and Social Democracy* (London: Macmillan).

—— (1960), *A History of Socialist Thought V: Socialism and Fascism* (London: Macmillan).

CROSLAND, C. A. R. (1967), *The Future of Socialism* (New York: Schocken Books).

CROZIER, MICHEL (1965), *The World of the Office Worker*, tr. D. Landau (Chicago University Press).

DAHRENDORF, RALF (1959), *Class and Class Conflict in Industrial Society* (Stanford University Press).

DAVIS, KINGSLEY, and MOORE, WILBERT (1945), 'Some Principles of Stratification', *American Sociological Review*, 10.

DRUCKER, PETER F. (1976), *The Unseen Revolution* (New York: Harper and Row).

ERIKSON, ROBERT (1976), 'Patterns of Social Mobility', in Richard Scase (ed), *Readings in Swedish Class Structure* (New York: Pergamon Press).

ESPING-ANDERSEN, GØSTA (1978), 'Social Class, Social Democracy, and State Policy: A Comparison of Denmark and Sweden' (Ph.D. dissertation, University of Wisconsin).

ESPING-ANDERSEN, GØSTA, *et al.* (1976), 'Modes of Class Struggle and the Capitalist State', *Kapitalistate*, 4–5.

FLAES, R. M. B. (1972), 'Yugoslavia: An Experience of Workers' Self-Management', *First International Conference on Participation and Self-Management* (Zagreb) 6.

FRIEDLAND, ROGER (1977), 'Class Power and the City' (Ph.D. dissertation, University of Wisconsin).

GALBRAITH, JOHN KENNETH (1973), *Economics and the Public Purpose* (Boston: Houghton-Mifflin).

GIDDENS, ANTHONY (1971), *Capitalism and Modern Social Theory* (Cambridge University Press).

—— (1973), *The Class Structure of Advanced Societies* (New York: Harper and Row).

GOLD, DAVID A., *et al.* (1975), 'Recent Developments in Marxist Theories of the Capitalist State', *Monthly Review*, 27.

GOLDTHORPE, JOHN H., LOCKWOOD, DAVID, *et al.* (1969), *The Affluent Worker in the Class Structure* (Cambridge University Press).

GORDON, MILTON M. (1964), *Assimilation in American Life* (New York: Oxford University Press).

GORZ, ANDRE (1964), *Strategy for Labor*, tr. Martin Nicolaus and Victoria Ortiz (Boston: Beacon Press).

GRAMSCI, ANTONIO (1971), *Selections from the Prison Notebooks* (New York: International Publishers).

GREENSTONE, J. DAVID (1969), *Labor in American Politics* (New York: Vintage Books).

HAMILTON, RICHARD F. (1967), *Affluence and the French Worker in the Fourth Republic* (Princeton University Press).

—— (1972), *Class and Politics in the United States* (New York: Wiley).

HARRINGTON, MICHAEL (1972), *Socialism* (New York: Saturday Review Press).

—— (1976), *The Twilight of Capitalism* (New York: Simon and Schuster).

HEADEY, BRUCE (1970), 'Trade Unions and National Wages Policy', *The Journal of Politics*, 32.

HECLO, HUGH (1974), *Modern Social Politics in Britain and Sweden* (New Haven: Yale University Press).

HEIDENHEIMER, ARNOLD J., *et al.* (1975), *Comparative Public Policy* (New York: St Martin's).

HENRY, JAMES (1977), 'How Pension Fund Socialism Didn't Come to America', *Working Papers for a New Society*, 4.

HEWITT, CHRISTOPHER (1977), 'The Effect of Political Democracy and Social Democracy on Equality in Industrial Societies', *American Sociological Review*, 42.

HIBBS, DOUGLAS A. (1976), 'Industrial Conflict in Advanced Industrial Societies', *American Political Science Review*, 70.

—— (1977), 'Political Parties and Macroeconomic Policy', *American Political Science Review*, 71.

HICKS, ALEXANDER, *et al.* (1978), 'Class Power and State Policy', *American Sociological Review*, 43.

HOLLOWAY, JOHN and PICCIOTTO, SOL (1977), 'Capital, Crisis and the State', *Capital and Class*, 2.

INGHAM, GEOFFREY K. (1974), *Strikes and Industrial Conflict* (London: Macmillan).

JACKMAN, ROBERT W. (1975), *Politics and Social Equality* (New York: Wiley).

JENCKS, CHRISTOPHER, *et al.* (1972), *Inequality* (New York: Basic Books).

JOHANSSON, STEN (1971), *Om Levnadsnivåundersökningen* (Stockholm: Allmänna Förlaget).

KARLSSON, LARS ERIK (1973), 'Experiences in Employee Participation in Sweden: 1969–1972' (Cornell University: Program on Participation and Labor-Managed Systems; Program on Comparative Economic Development).

KAUTSKY, KARL (1902), *Social Revolution* (Chicago: Kerr).

—— (1909), *Road to Power* (Chicago: Bloch).

—— (1971), *The Class Struggle* (New York: Norton & Co).

KOLKO, GABRIEL (1962), *Wealth and Power in America* (New York: Praeger).

KORPI, WALTER (1978a), 'Social Democracy in Welfare Capitalism' (Institute for Poverty Research Discussion Papers. University of Wisconsin–Madison).

—— (1978b), *The Working Class in Welfare Capitalism* (London: Routledge and Kegan Paul).

KUZNETS, SIMON (1966), *Modern Economic Growth* (New Haven: Yale).

LAFFERTY, WILLIAM (1971), *Economic Development and the Response of Labor in Scandinavia* (Oslo: Universitetsförlaget).

LENIN, VLADIMIR ILYICH (1934), *The Proletarian Revolution and Renegade Kautsky* (New York: International Publishers).

—— (1966), *Essential Works of Lenin* (New York: Bantam Books).

LICHTHEIM, GEORGE (1961), *Marxism* (New York: Praeger).

LIJPHART, AREND (1968), *The Politics of Accommodation* (Berkeley: University of California Press).

LINDHAGEN, JAN (1974), *Bolsjevikstriden: Socialdemokratins Program* (Karlskrona: Tiden).

LIPSET, S. M. (1967), *First New Nation* (Garden City: Anchor Books).

LIPSET, S. M. and ROKKAN, STEIN (eds) (1967), *Party Systems and Voter Alignments* (New York: Free Press).

LOW-BEER, JOHN R. (1978), *Protest and Participation* (New York: Cambridge University Press).

LOW-BEER, JOHN R., and STEPHENS, JOHN D. (1976), 'Occupation and Property Ownership as Dimensions of Class' (unpublished paper, Yale University).

LUXEMBURG, ROSA (1961), *The Russian Revolution* (Ann Arbor: University of Michigan Press).

LYKKETOFT, MOGENS (1977), 'Toward Economic Democracy: Wage Earners' Funds', *Scandinavian Review*, 2.

MANN, MICHAEL (1973), *Consciousness and Action among the Western Working Class* (London: Macmillan).

—— (1977), 'States: Ancient and Modern', *European Journal of Sociology*.

MARTIN, ANDREW (1973), 'The Politics of Economic Policy in the United States', *Sage Professional Paper*, 01–040 (Beverly Hills: Sage Publications).

—— (1975), 'Is Democratic Control of Capitalist Economies Possible?', in Leon Lindberg *et al.* (eds), *Stress and Contradiction in Modern Capitalism* (Lexington, Mass.: Lexington Books).

—— (1977), 'Sweden: Industrial Democracy and Social Democratic Strategy', in G. David Garson (ed), *Worker Self-Management in Industry* (New York: Praeger).

MARX, KARL (1852), 'The Chartists', in T. B. Bottomore and Maximilian Rubel (eds) *Selected Writings in Sociology and Social Philosophy*, (New York: McGraw-Hill).

—— (1857), *The Grundrisse*, ed David McLellan (New York: Harper and Row, 1971).

—— (1865), *Value, Price and Profit* (New York: International Publishers, 1969).

—— (1867), *Capital I* (New York: International Publishers, 1967).

—— (1875), 'Critique of the Gotha Program', in Lewis A. Feuer (ed), *Basic Writings on Politics and Philosophy* (Garden City: Anchor Books).

—— (1894), *Capital III* (New York: International Publishers, 1967).

MARX, KARL, and ENGELS, FRIEDRICH (1846), *The German Ideology*, in *Collected Works V* (New York: International Publishers, 1976).

—— (1848), *Manifesto of the Communist Party*, in *Collected Works VI* (New York: International Publishers, 1976).

—— (1882), 'Preface to the Russian Edition', in *The Communist Manifesto* (Baltimore: Penguin Books).

McLELLAN, DAVID (1973), *Karl Marx, His Life and Thought* (New York: Harper and Row).

MEIDNER, RUDOLF (1974), *Co-ordination and Solidarity: An Approach to Wage Policy* (Stockholm: Prisma/LO).

—— (1978), 'Employee Investment Funds and Capital Formation', *Working Life in Sweden* (New York: Swedish Information Service).

MILIBAND, RALPH (1969), *The State in Capitalist Society* (London: Weidenfeld and Nicholson).

MILLER, HERMAN (1964), *Rich Man, Poor Man* (New York: New American Library).

MILLER, S.M. (1960), 'Comparative Social Mobility', *Current Sociology*, 9.

MILLS, C. WRIGHT (1951), *White Collar* (New York: Oxford University Press).

MOLIN, BJÖRN (1966), 'Swedish Party Politics: A Case Study', *Scandinavian Political Science Studies*, 1.

MOORE, BARRINGTON (1966), *Social Origins of Dictatorship and Democracy* (Boston: Beacon Press).

NICHOLSON, J. L. (1974), 'The Distribution and Redistribution of Income in the United Kingdom', in Dorothy Wedderburn (ed), *Poverty, Inequality, and Class Structure* (Cambridge University Press).

O'CONNOR, JAMES (1973), *The Fiscal Crisis of the State* (New York: St Martin's Press).

OECD (1971), *Group Disparities in Educational Participation* (Paris: OECD).

OFFE, CLAUS (1972a), 'Advanced Capitalism and the Welfare State', *Politics and Society*, 2.

—— (1972b), 'Political Authority and Class Structures', *International Journal of Sociology*.

—— (1973a), 'The Abolition of Market Control and the Problem of Legitimacy', *Kapitalistate* 2 and 3.

—— (1973b), 'Structural Problems of the Capitalist State' (mimeo).

—— (1975), 'The Theory of the Capitalist State and the Problem of Policy Formation', in Leon Lindberg *et al.* (eds), *Stress and Contradiction in Modern Capitalism* (Lexington, Mass.: Lexington Books).

PARETO, VILFREDO (1971), *Manual of Political Economy*, tr. Ann Schweir (New York: Kelly).

PARKIN, FRANK (1971), *Class Inequality and Political Order* (New York: Praeger).

—— (1974), 'Strategies of Social Closure in Class Formation', in Frank Parkin (ed), *The Social Analysis of Class Structure* (London: Tavistock Publications).

PIVEN, FRANCES FOX, and CLOWARD, RICHARD A. (1972), *Regulating the Poor* (New York: Vintage Books).

POULANTZAS, NICOS (1973), 'On Social Classes', *New Left Review*, 78.

—— (1975), *Classes in Contemporary Capitalism* (London: New Left Books).

—— (1978), 'The State and the Transition to Socialism', *Socialist Review*, 38.

PRICE, ROBERT, and SAYERS BAIN, GEORGE (1976), 'Union Growth Revisited', *British Journal of Industrial Relations*, 14.

PRYOR, FREDERIC (1973), *Property and Industrial Organization in Communist and Capitalist Countries* (Bloomington: Indiana University Press).

RATNER, RONNIE STEINBERG (1977), 'To Them That Hath Shall Be Given' (paper delivered at the Meetings of the Eastern Sociological Society in New York).

REICH, MICHAEL, and EDWARDS, RICHARD (1978), 'Political Parties and Class Conflict in the United States', *Socialist Review*, 39.

REICHEL, HANS (1971), 'Recent Trends in Collective Bargaining in the Federal Republic of Germany', *International Labor Review*, 104.

REYNOLDS, MORGAN, and SMOLENSKY, EUGENE (1977), *Public Expenditures, Taxes, and the Distribution of Income* (New York: Academic Press).

RIFKIN, JEREMY, and BARBER, RANDY (1978), *Pensions, Politics and Power in the 1980s* (Boston: Beacon Press).

ROBERTI, PAOLO (1974), 'Income Distribution: A Time Series and a Cross Section Study', *The Economic Journal*, 84.

ROBERTS, BEN C. (ed) (1968), *Industrial Relations* (London: Methuen).

ROBINSON, ROBERT V., and KELLEY, JONATHAN (1977), 'Marx and Dahrendorf on Income Inequality, Class Consciousness and Class Conflict' (paper delivered at the Meetings of the American Sociological Association in Chicago).

ROKKAN, STEIN (1973), 'Cities, States, and Nations', in S. N, Eisenstadt and Stein Rokkan (eds), *Building States and Nations: Models and Data Resources* (Beverly Hills: Sage Publications).

ROSS, ARTHUR M., and HARTMAN, PAUL T. (1960), *Changing Patterns of Industrial Conflict* (New York: Wiley).

ROTH, GUENTHER (1963), *The Social Democrats in Imperial Germany* (Totowa: Bedminster Press).

SÄRLVIK, BO (1974), 'Sweden: The Social Bases of the Parties in a Development Perspective', in Richard Rose (ed), *Electoral Behavior* (New York: Free Press).

SAWYER, MALCOLM (1976), 'Income Distribution in OECD Countries', *Occasional Studies* (Paris: OECD).

SCASE, RICHARD (1977), *Social Democracy in Capitalist Society* (London: Rowman and Littlefield).

SCHMITTER, PHILIPPE C. (1974), 'Still the Century of Corporatism?', in Frederick B. Pike and Thomas Stritch (eds), *The New Corporatism* (Notre Dame: University of Notre Dame Press).

SCHNITZER, MARTIN (1974), *Income Distribution* (New York: Praeger Publishers).

SHORTER, EDWARD and TILLY, CHARLES (1974), *Strikes in France 1830–1968* (Cambridge University Press).

SIFO (Svenska Institutet för Opinionsundersökningar) (1976), *Indikator*, November.

SPÅNT, ROLAND (1973), 'Förmögenhetsfördelningen i Sverige', Stockholm (mimeo).

STATISTISKA CENTRALBYRÅN (1974), *Inkomst och Förmögenhet 1972* (Stockholm: Statistiska Centralbyrån).

STEPHENS, EVELYNE HUBER (1977), 'The Politics of Workers' Participation: The Peruvian Approach in Comparative Perspective' (Ph.D. dissertation, Yale University).

STEPHENS, EVELYNE HUBER, and STEPHENS, JOHN D. (1978), 'The Politics of Workers' Control' (paper delivered at the Meetings of the International Sociological Association in Uppsala, Sweden).

STEPHENS, JOHN D. (1971), 'The Causes of Inequality' (unpublished paper, Yale University).

—— (1976), 'The Consequences of Social Structural Change for the Development of Socialism in Sweden' (Ph.D. dissertation, Yale University).

—— (1979), 'Religion and Politics in Three Northwest European Democracies', in Richard Tomasson (ed), *Comparative Studies in Sociology* (Greenwich: JAI Press).

SWEEZY, PAUL M. (1942), *The Theory of Capitalist Development* (New York: Monthly Review Press).

TAYLOR, CHARLES LEWIS, and HUDSON, MICHAEL C. (1972), *World Handbook of Political and Social Indicators* (New Haven: Yale University Press).

THERBORN, GÖRAN (1977), 'The Rule of Capital and the Rise of Democracy', *New Left Review*, 103.

TINGSTEN, HERBERT (1973), *The Swedish Social Democrats: Their Ideological Development*, tr. Greta Frankel and Patricia Howard-Rosen (Totowa: Bedminster Press).

TITMUSS, RICHARD M. (1963), *Income Distribution and Social Change* (London: Allen and Unwin).

TOMASSON, RICHARD F. (1970), *Sweden: Prototype of Modern Society* (New York: Random House).

TOURAINE, ALAIN (1971), *The Post Industrial Society*, tr. Leonard F. X. Mayhew (New York: Random House).

TROTSKY, LEON (1961), *Terrorism and Communism* (Ann Arbor: University of Michigan Press).

WEBER, MAX (1922), *Economy and Society* (New York: Bedminster Press, 1968).

WEISS, JOSEPH W., and WILLIAMSON, JOHN B. (1977), 'The Convergence Theory Reconsidered' (paper delivered at the Annual Meeting of the American Sociological Association in Chicago).

WESTERGAARD, JOHN, and RESLER, HENRIETTA (1975), *Class in a Capitalist Society* (New York: Basic Books).

WILENSKY, HAROLD L. (1975), *The Welfare State and Equality* (Berkeley: University of California Press).

—— (1976), 'The "New Corporatism", Centralization, and the Welfare State', *Sage Professional Paper*, 06–020 (Beverly Hills: Sage Publications).

WRIGHT, ERIK O. (1976), 'Class Boundaries in Advanced Capitalist Societies', *New Left Review*, 98.

WRIGHT, ERIK O., and PERRONE, LUCA (1977), 'Marxist Class Categories and Income Inequality', *American Sociological Review*, 42.

YERBURY, DIANE, and ISAAC, J. E. (1971), 'Recent Trends in Collective Bargaining in Australia', *International Labor Review*, 103.

ZETTERBERG, HANS (1976), 'Opinionen och makten över företagen', in Carl-Johan Westholm (ed), *Vi kan ännu välja* (Stockholm: Askild & Kärnekull).

Index

Other Titles of Interest

Women and American Socialism, 1870-1920
MARI JO BUHLE

The Symbolic Uses of Politics
With a New Afterword
MURRAY EDELMAN

Workingmen's Democracy
The Knights of Labor and American Politics
LEON FINK

Power and Powerlessness
Quiescence and Rebellion in an Appalachian Valley
JOHN GAVENTA

Law in the Soviet Society
Edited by WAYNE R. LAFAVE

The ABCs of Soviet Socialism
The Soviet Economic Experiment, 1917-80
JAMES R. MILLAR

The Political Integration of Women
Roles, Socialization, and Politics
VIRGINIA SAPIRO

For more information please write or call the University of Illinois Press, 54 E. Gregory Drive, Champaign, IL 61820, 217/244-0626.